RS
Workbook

All the questions on all the topics, immaculately presented and dangerously close to being funny.

Contents

Section One — Perspectives
Spirituality 1
The Nature of Truth 2
Believing in God 3
Religious Experiences 4
The Nature of God 5
Christian and Jewish Teaching on God 6
Muslim Teaching on God 7
Evil and Suffering 8
Judaism and Islam — Evil & Suffering 9
The Origin of the World 10
Life After Death 11
Jewish Beliefs about Life After Death 12
Muslim Beliefs about Life After Death 13
Life & Death and the Christian View 14
Life & Death in Judaism 15
Life & Death in Islam 16
Fertility Treatment 17
Marriage in Christianity 18
The Christian Church and Divorce 19
Marriage in Judaism 20
Marriage in Islam 21
Religious Attitudes to Sex 22
Children and Religion 23
Prejudice and Equality 24
Race and Religion 25
Injustice and Protest 26
Jewish Attitudes towards Equality 27
Muslim Attitudes towards Equality 28
Christianity and Other Religions 29
Judaism, Islam and Other Religions 30
Christianity and Poverty 31
Judaism, Islam and Poverty 32
Religion and the Environment 33
Religion and Animals 34
Religion and Crime 35
Christianity and War 36
Judaism, Islam and War 37
Religion and Drugs 38
Religion and the Media 39

Section Two — Christianity
Basic Christian Beliefs 40
The Bible 41
Christian Values 42
Love and Forgiveness 43
The Sermon on the Mount 44
Spreading the Gospel 45
Living the Christian Life 46
The Church 47
Traditions and Denominations 48
Members of the Church 49
A Christian Church 50
Religious Symbolism 51
Sunday Worship 52
Christian Festivals 53
Private Prayer and the Sacraments 54
Baptism 55
Funerals, Burial and Cremation 56
Jesus and Mark's Gospel 57
The Kingdom of God 58
Jesus and Miracles 59
Miracles, Faith and Conflict 60
Discipleship 61
Jesus' Trial and Death 62

Section Three — Judaism
The Beginnings of Judaism 63
Basic Jewish Beliefs 64
Sources of Guidance 65
The Holocaust 66
Different Jewish Traditions 67
Judaism and Day-to-Day Life 68
The Synagogue 69
Signs and Symbols 70
Judaism and Children 71
Jewish Beliefs about Death 72
Jewish Prayer and the Sabbath 73
Pilgrimage, Food and Fasting 74
Jewish Festivals 75

Section Four — Islam
Basic Islamic Beliefs 76
Prophets and Angels 77
The Qur'an 78
The Prophet Muhammad 79
Different Islamic Traditions 80
Sufism 81
Islam and the Shari'ah 82
Islamic Living and Jihad 83
The Mosque 84
Worship and Prayer 85
Birth and Death Ceremonies 86

Answers 87

Published by Coordination Group Publications

Contributors:
Paul Cashman, Mark Chambers, Charley Darbishire,
Julie Green, Gemma Hallam, Kevin Jones, Andy Park,
Stephen Radford, Alice Shepperson, Moira Siara,
Paul D. Smith, Nicola Thomas and David Walmsley

With thanks to Glenn Rogers, Dominic Hall,
Katherine Reed and Glennis Atkinson for the proofreading

ISBN: 978 1 84146 286 8
Groovy website: www.cgpbooks.co.uk
Jolly bits of clipart from CorelDRAW®
Printed by Elanders Hindson Ltd, Newcastle upon Tyne.
Text, design, layout and original illustrations
© Coordination Group Publications Ltd. 2003
All rights reserved.

Section One — Perspectives

Spirituality

General

Q1 Which of these are spiritual questions?
  a) What's for lunch?
  b) Why are we here on this planet?
  c) Why is it hot in summer?
  d) Why should we try to be nice to other people?

Very nice.

Q2 Can non-religious people have spirituality?

Q3 A person of which religion might use a fish symbol to display their faith?

Q4 Give an example of how a Muslim woman might publicly show her spirituality.

Q5 *Douglas listens to a piece of music by Bach. He thinks the music is beautiful, and gets a strong sense of being on a "higher plane" when he hears it. Douglas is not a religious person, and the music is not religious music.*

Can Douglas' experience be considered spiritual?

Q6 Chaim is Jewish. He shows his spirituality by following the rules of the Torah. Give examples of two other ways that he might demonstrate his Jewish spirituality.

EXAM-STYLE QUESTION Q7 Explain two ways in which religious believers make external displays of their spirituality. *(4 marks)*

EXAM-STYLE QUESTION Q8 Give a brief explanation of how each of these terms can help to explain spirituality. *(6 marks)*
  a) Meaning of life
  b) Awe
  c) Self-awareness

EXAM-STYLE QUESTION Q9 Describe how spirituality can be displayed through membership of a voluntary organisation. *(6 marks)*

Spirituality is like a butterfly — it's hard to pin down...

These probably seem like slightly weird questions — they're certainly not the sort of thing you'd get asked in a Science exam, that's for sure. Thing is, it's on the syllabus, so you have to know about it.

Section One — Perspectives

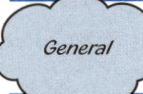

The Nature Of Truth

Q1 *There are different kinds of truth. Write down the type of truth referred to in each of the following sentences.*

    a) "Scientists do experiments to test a theory."

    b) "It's wrong to hurt other people's feelings."

    c) "God created the world in exactly six days."

The nature of lies.

Q2 *Historical truth describes what happened in the past, using accounts from the past, and other sources (e.g. archaeology).*

Give two problems with using evidence to find out what happened in the past.

Q3 Can religious truth be proved to be true?

Q4 *Read this description of a scene and answer the questions below.*
The front room window of Mrs Smith's house is broken. There is a football in the middle of the room, surrounded by bits of broken glass. A child wearing football boots is standing in the garden, looking sheepish.

Evidence isn't the same as proof.

    a) Is there evidence to suggest that the child broke the window?

    b) *The child in Mrs Smith's garden says "We were playing football and my brother kicked the ball through your window. We're really sorry. Can we have our ball back".*
Does this mean that the brother definitely broke the window?

    c) Is there any proof that either the child or his brother broke the window?

Q5 *People read holy books to look for spiritual truth.*

    a) Give examples of books used to find spiritual truth.

    b) Do all the people who find spiritual truth in the same book believe the same things?

Q6 *People use the advice of spiritual leaders and the Church to find truth.*

Why can this be an unreliable way of finding spiritual truth?

Q7 "Holy Scripture is the only source of religious truth."
Do you agree? Give reasons for your answer. Show that you have thought about more than one point of view. Refer to at least two religious traditions. (8 marks)

Q8 Discuss the importance of sacred books in Judaism, Islam and Christianity. (6 marks)

Section One — Perspectives

Believing in God

General

Q1   Are people brought up by religious parents more likely to be religious than people brought up by atheists?

Q2   *People turn to religion because they want answers to questions like, "Why are we here?". Give two other reasons why people become religious.*

Q3   *"Arguments from design" are sometimes used to justify belief in God. Which of the following are arguments from design?*

   a) "The world is so complicated and intricate. It couldn't have got that way by chance."

   b) "Mathematical truths are simple and beautiful. They must be meant to be that way."

   c) "There is so much love in the world, and that love is proof of God's love."

Q4   Is everyone convinced by arguments from design?

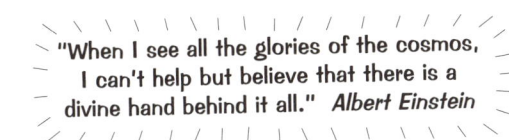

> "When I see all the glories of the cosmos, I can't help but believe that there is a divine hand behind it all." *Albert Einstein*

Q5   How do scientific atheists and agnostics explain the following?

   a) Miracles.

   b) The range of living things in the world, all suited exactly to their habitat.

EXAM-STYLE QUESTION Q6   How might a belief in divine creation affect how a person thinks about life?   (5 marks)

EXAM-STYLE QUESTION Q7   "We would not exist if we had not been created." Do you agree? Give reasons for your answer and show that you have thought about more than one point of view.   (6 marks)

EXAM-STYLE QUESTION Q8   Explain why a person might convert to a religion.   (6 marks)

Section One — Perspectives

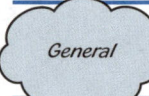

Religious Experiences

General

Q1 What is a numinous experience?

Q2 What is a miracle?

Q3 Describe in a short paragraph how praying can help people to believe in God and to experience God.

Q4 Some Christians have "charismatic experiences". Give three examples of charismatic experiences that may take place during worship.

Q5 Who or what, according to many Christians, causes charismatic phenomena?

Q6 Some people focus their minds on God in order to have a close experience of the Divine. What is this process called?

Q7 *General revelation is something everyone can see.*
Special revelation is something that only an individual or select group can see.
For each of the following, write down whether it is a general revelation or a special revelation.

a) Reading the Qur'an.

b) Having a vivid dream of the prophet Elijah, in which he gives a specific message.

c) Meditating and having a vision of a saint.

Q8 *[EXAM-STYLE QUESTION]* Give a brief outline of a charismatic act of worship. (5 marks)

Q9 *[EXAM-STYLE QUESTION]* Explain how religious experiences may influence a person's faith. (7 marks)

Numinous — has nothing at all to do with numbers *(thankfully)*
There are different kinds of religious experience. Lots of religious people pray to God and read sacred books. Not everyone has visions or "speaks in tongues" — that's pretty rare, like a good Bruce Willis film.

Section One — Perspectives

The Nature Of God

General

Q1 Do all religious thinkers agree that God is present within the Universe?

Q2 *Christians believe in a 'personal' God. Answer these questions about belief in a 'personal' God.*

   a) Can someone pray to a 'personal' God?

   b) Does a 'personal' God feel emotions like love and sadness?

   c) What is the problem with the idea of a God who is personal, but also omnipresent (present everywhere in the Universe)?

Q3 What is meant by an **immanent** God?

Q4 What is meant by a **transcendent** God?

Q5 In Christianity and Islam, is God seen as outside the world, inside the world, or both at once?

Q6 Which of the following religions are polytheistic?

   a) Islam   d) Sikhism

   b) Hinduism   e) Judaism

   c) Christianity   f) Old Norse and Ancient Greek religions

EXAM-STYLE QUESTION Q7 *"To experience God, a person must have a personal relationship with Him."* Do you agree? Give reasons for your answer. Show that you have considered more than one point of view, and include views from at least one world religion. (5 marks)

EXAM-STYLE QUESTION Q8 Explain how an immanent God can appear weak in the face of suffering within the world. (4 marks)

EXAM-STYLE QUESTION Q9 *"God is immanent and transcendent, personal and impersonal."* Do you agree? Give reasons for your answer. Show that you have considered more than one point of view. (8 marks)

Section One — Perspectives

Christian and Jewish Teaching On God

Christianity & Judaism

Q1 Match each of the three descriptions of God below to the correct definition:

> **Omniscient**   All-powerful.
>
> **Omnipresent** All-knowing. Knows everything you do and everything you think.
>
> **Omnipotent**   Everywhere in the Universe at the same time.

Q2 *There's a big difference between Jewish and Christian ideas of God. What is the difference?*

Q3 What does the Shema prayer say about the Jewish idea of God?

Q4 Answer these questions about the Trinity.

   a) Who died on the Cross to save people from sin?

   b) Which part of the Trinity is the Creator?

   c) Which part of the Trinity is immanent, but impersonal?

Q5 *Many Christians believe in the Devil. What does the Devil do to humankind?*

Q6 Is there a Devil in modern Judaism?

EXAM-STYLE QUESTION Q7 Explain what the Nicene Creed says about the Trinity?   (7 marks)

EXAM-STYLE QUESTION Q8 Describe Christian beliefs about the Devil.   (7 marks)

So there's one God... but there's also three...

Don't get your knickers in a twist... Christians definitely believe in just the one God — the Trinity just describes three different aspects. Make sure you know the differences between Christianity and Judaism.

Section One — Perspectives

Muslim Teaching On God

Islam

Q1 Is Islam a monotheistic religion or a polytheistic religion?

Q2 What's the literal translation of "Allah"?

Q3 *Muslims have many names for Allah.*
   a) How many names does Allah have in the Qur'an?
   b) Give four names for Allah that tell you something about Him.

Q4 *God can be seen as immanent or transcendent.*
    Do Muslims see Allah as immanent, transcendent, or both?

Q5 According to Islamic teaching, has Allah intervened in human history?

Q6 Do Muslims believe that the Qur'an is the direct word of God?

Come back... you're not on till page 77.

Q7 How many prophets are mentioned in the Qur'an?

Q8 Who is the last of the prophets of Allah?

EXAM-STYLE QUESTION Q9 *"There is no way of knowing for certain what Allah is like."*
    Do you agree? Give reasons for your answer and show
    that you have thought about different points of view.   (5 marks)

EXAM-STYLE QUESTION Q10 Describe Muslim beliefs about Allah.   (5 marks)

EXAM-STYLE QUESTION Q11 In what ways do Muslims seek to know Allah?   (5 marks)

Section One — Perspectives

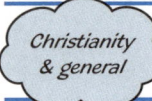

Evil and Suffering

Christianity & general

Q1   Give an example of natural evil.

Q2   What kind of evil is murder?

Q3   *The division between human-made evil and natural evil isn't always clear cut. Give an example of a disaster that is caused by human interference in the world.*

Q4   *The existence of evil makes some people question their faith in God.*
    a) How does evil damage the idea of an all-powerful God?
    b) How does evil damage the idea of a God who answers prayers?

Q5   Explain how suffering can be a test of faith. Say how a person would pass the test.

Q6   Do Christians and Jews believe that evil was in the world from the start?

Q7   *After Adam and Eve ate the fruit of knowledge in the Garden of Eden, people were born imperfect and flawed.*
    a) What is the idea of this flawed nature called?
    b) What's this big change from perfect to imperfect called?
    c) Was it up to Adam and Eve whether to eat the fruit of knowledge or not?

Q8   Who is Satan?

EXAM-STYLE QUESTION Q9   "When people suffer, they deserve it for their own wrongdoing."
Do you agree? Give reasons for your answer showing that you have thought of different points of view. Refer to Christianity in your answer. (5 marks)

EXAM-STYLE QUESTION Q10   Explain how and why, according to Christianity, humans cause evil. Give examples in your answer. (4 marks)

EXAM-STYLE QUESTION Q11   How do Christians explain the origin and existence of suffering? (5 marks)

Section One — Perspectives

Judaism and Islam — Evil & Suffering

Q1 Does Judaism say we have the free will to choose what to do, good or bad?

Q2 *The Book of Job demonstrates Jewish ideas about suffering.*
   a) How does Job respond to his suffering?
   b) Why does Job end up accepting his suffering?

Q3 *Judaism says that good can come out of suffering.*
Give two ways that this can happen.

Q4 *Some Muslims say that Shaytan (Iblis) tempts us.*
   a) Why does Allah allow this?
   b) According to Islam, do people have free will to give in to Shaytan or resist him?

Q5 Surah 2:214 of the Qur'an says, *"Do you expect to enter Paradise without being tested like those before you?"*
   a) How does Allah test people?
   b) What does the Qur'an say is the right response to Allah's test?

Q6 If a Muslim prays to Allah for forgiveness, will they be forgiven?

Q7 *"Good always comes from suffering in this world."*
Do you agree? Give reasons for your answer showing that you have thought of different points of view. Refer to Judaism in your answer. (5 marks)

Q8 *"Even the greatest suffering is part of God's plan for the world."*
Do you agree? Give reasons for your answer showing that you have thought of different points of view. Refer to Islam in your answer. (5 marks)

Q9 How do Muslims explain the origin and purpose of suffering? (6 marks)

A rare picture of Satan — caught taking a break between diabolical deeds.

"Surely We Shall Test You" (Brian Smith, Chief Examiner. 2003)
I know this book is causing you great suffering, but in the end, it will have positive results... trust me. It might not bring you closer to God, but it will help you pass your Exams. So that's evil done and dusted.

Section One — Perspectives

The Origin of the World

Christianity, Judaism, Islam & general

Q1   What is the main scientific argument for how the world began?

Q2   What is the main scientific argument for how living things came to be as they are today?

Q3   *The Bible says God created the world, the plants and animals, and Adam and Eve.*
   a) Taken literally, does this idea agree with science?
   b) Some people believe in both the religious and scientific explanations. How do they reconcile the two ideas?
   c) In what order do these things appear in Genesis: Space, people, the Earth, the atmosphere, plants, animals?
   d) In what order does science say that these things appeared?

Q4   Do Orthodox Jews see the creation story in the book of Genesis as literally true?

Q5   Do Liberal Jews see the creation story in the book of Genesis as literally true?

Q6   Which holy book's creation story is the easiest to square with science — the Bible's story or the story in the Qur'an?

EXAM-STYLE QUESTION Q7   "Science has already proved that God does not exist." Do you agree? Give reasons for your answer showing that you have thought of different points of view.   (5 marks)

EXAM-STYLE QUESTION Q8   What do Christians believe about the origin of the world?   (6 marks)

EXAM-STYLE QUESTION Q9   Explain why some religious believers have more trouble than others in believing scientific theories about creation.   (7 marks)

PLANET CONSTRUCTION TIP NO 112: **Shorten the trees — Don't stretch the animals**
Opinion is divided on how the world came into being. But I know how the world will end —
I saw the film about the big asteroid with that famous bloke in. I'm pretty sure that was fact.

Section One — Perspectives

Life After Death

Christianity & general

Q1 What part of a person is believed to live on after death?

Q2 Does everyone believe in life after death?

Q3 Some people who have been close to death (e.g. if their heart stops and is restarted) say that they have had near-death experiences.
  a) In a couple of sentences, describe a typical near-death experience.
  b) Does everyone agree that near-death experiences are proof of life after death?
  c) Give a non-spiritual explanation for near-death experiences.

Q4 Give another example of evidence for life after death, other than near-death experiences.

Q5 Christians believe in Heaven.
  a) According to Christian teaching, what two things must a person do in order to go to Heaven?
  b) What is the Communion of Saints?

Q6 Some Christians see hell as a real place full of fire and torment. Others see Heaven and Hell as states of mind. Briefly describe the "state of mind" version of Hell.

Q7 What is Purgatory? Which Christians believe in Purgatory?

Q8 Can people who have led sinful lives still be saved and go to Heaven?

EXAM-STYLE QUESTION Q9 Describe the Christian belief about what happens to people after they die. (7 marks)

EXAM-STYLE QUESTION Q10 "Dead people's spirits can contact the living. This is proof of life after death." Do you agree? Give reasons for your answer. Show that you have thought of different points of view. You must refer to Christianity in your answer. (5 marks)

EXAM-STYLE QUESTION Q11 Describe what Roman Catholics believe about what happens to the soul of a sinful person after death. (7 marks)

Section One — Perspectives

Jewish Beliefs about Life After Death

Judaism

Q1 What is Sheol? What is it like in Sheol?

Q2 Briefly describe modern Jewish beliefs about Heaven and Hell.

Q3 Do Jews believe that non-Jews can go to Heaven and Hell?

Q4 *Many Christians say that only the soul goes to Heaven, not the body.*
What do Jews believe about what happens to the soul and the body after death?

Q5 *Thousands of years ago, in the time of the Bible, Jews believed that the sins of the fathers could be "visited upon the sons".*
What does this mean?

Q6 *Orthodox Jews believe that a person will still need their body after death.*
a) When will the dead person need their body?
b) Do Orthodox Jews cremate the dead?
c) Some liberal Jews cremate the dead. What do they believe about the body and the soul?

EXAM-STYLE QUESTION Q7 Describe what Orthodox Jews believe about what happens to good people after they die.   (7 marks)

EXAM-STYLE QUESTION Q8 "Jews are more concerned with this life than the afterlife."
Do you agree? Give reasons for your answer. You must show that you have thought of different points of view. You must refer to Judaism in your answer.   (5 marks)

Section One — Perspectives

Muslim Beliefs about Life After Death

Islam

Q1 What is Akhirah in Islam?

Q2 What is yawm-ud-din (yawmuddin) in Islam?

Q3 What, according to Islam, are people judged on?

Q4 Briefly describe the Muslim Paradise.

Q5 Give the name for the Muslim Hell, and briefly describe it.

Q6 According to Islam, do we have free will?

Q7 How should a Muslim respond when bad things happen in his or her life?

Q8 *According to Islamic teaching, there's something that we humans know about our destiny that animals don't know.*
    What is it?

EXAM-STYLE QUESTION Q9 Describe what Muslims believe happens to the soul after death. (8 marks)

EXAM-STYLE QUESTION Q10 Explain how Muslim beliefs about the afterlife affect the way Muslims live their lives. (7 marks)

EXAM-STYLE QUESTION Q11 Describe how Muslims believe a bad person can end up in Paradise. (4 marks)

I sentence you to 50,000 years community service...

Jews, Christians and Muslims all believe that people are judged after they die on how well they lived their life. Doing the wrong thing could have consequences that last for eternity — i.e. for ever and ever. Scary.

Section One — Perspectives

Life & Death and the Christian View

Christianity & general

Q1 Up until what week of pregnancy is abortion legal in England, Scotland and Wales?

Q2 *Doctors consider the quality of life of the pregnant woman when deciding whether she can have an abortion.*
Whose quality of life must they also take into account?

Q3 What does the Roman Catholic Church say about whether abortion is acceptable or not? Why does the Catholic Church say this?

Q4 Give two examples of situations where liberal Christians might say that abortion would be OK, even if they were against it on general principle.

Q5 What is the opinion of the Roman Catholic Church on contraception?

Q6 What is meant by the "sanctity of life" argument?

"Your body is a temple of the Holy Spirit."

Q7 What's it called when an ill person asks for help to die?

Q8 Why might a Christian think that euthanasia could be the Christian thing to do in some circumstances?

Q9 Give one benefit and one danger to society of legalising euthanasia.

EXAM-STYLE QUESTION Q10 How might the teachings of Christianity influence a Christian when deciding what to do about an unwanted pregnancy? (6 marks)

EXAM-STYLE QUESTION Q11 *"What a woman does with her body is up to her. Abortion is her choice alone."*
How might a Roman Catholic argue against this point of view? (5 marks)

EXAM-STYLE QUESTION Q12 Explain some of the arguments against the legalisation of euthanasia. You must refer to Christianity in your answer. (9 marks)

Section One — Perspectives

Life & Death in Judaism

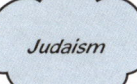

Q1 For each of the following things, write down if Judaism generally views it as good or bad:

a) Abortion

b) Euthanasia

> "Be fruitful and increase in number... fill the earth." Genesis 1:28

Q2 Contraception is often used by married couples for planning how many children to have and when to have them.

Is using contraception in this way acceptable to most Jews?

I told you lot to wait till page 77.

Q3 Do all Jewish rabbis agree on abortion?

Q4 Is suicide a sin in Judaism?

Q5 A doctor gives a lethal injection to speed the death of a terminally ill patient who is suffering a great deal.

Is this considered wrong from a Jewish perspective?

> "There is no God besides me. I put to death and I bring to life." Deuteronomy 32:39

Q6 In Judaism, is it acceptable for a doctor to switch off a life-support machine or withhold life-extending treatment or food in order to speed the death of a terminally ill patient who is suffering a great deal?

EXAM-STYLE QUESTION Q7 Describe Jewish attitudes towards suicide.   (6 marks)

EXAM-STYLE QUESTION Q8 A married Jewish couple are told by a doctor that any children they have are at a high risk of being severely disabled. Explain how Jewish teachings might influence their decisions about what to do.   (6 marks)

EXAM-STYLE QUESTION Q9 *"Contraception and abortion are morally the same."*
Do you agree? Give reasons for your answer showing that you have thought of different points of view. Refer to Judaism in your answer.   (5 marks)

Section One — Perspectives

Life & Death in Islam

Q1 Write down True or False for each of the following statements.

a) Islam teaches that life is a gift from Allah.

b) Islam teaches that we can decide when to end our lives.

c) Euthanasia is seen as wrong in Islam.

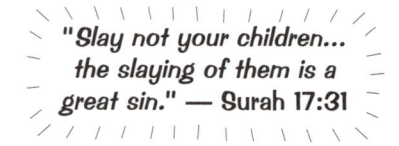

> "Slay not your children... the slaying of them is a great sin." — Surah 17:31

Q2 In Islamic teaching, when would abortion be seen as lawful and permissible?

Q3 Faiza has four children. She and her husband don't think that they could afford to bring up another one without their family sinking into poverty.

a) Would it be OK under Islamic law for the couple to use the Pill or condoms as a method of contraception? Explain your answer.

b) Would it be OK under Islamic law for Faiza's husband to get a vasectomy? Explain your answer.

Q4 A Muslim couple have genetic testing done, and find that they have a greater than average chance of having children with cystic fibrosis (a genetic disease).

Would it be acceptable under Islamic law for the couple to use contraception?

Q5 Is it acceptable in Islam to end someone's suffering by euthanasia?

Q6 How should suffering Muslims respond to their suffering?

EXAM-STYLE QUESTION Q7 Describe Muslim teachings about contraception. (8 marks)

EXAM-STYLE QUESTION Q8 Explain how a Muslim might respond to a suffering person who wanted to die quickly in order to end their suffering. (6 marks)

There's always two sides to an argument...
It's easy to learn how these religions view contraception, abortion and euthanasia — they're all bad. But they're badder in some circumstances than in others — you need to know all the stuff and all the biz.

Section One — Perspectives

Fertility Treatment

Christianity, Judaism, Islam & general

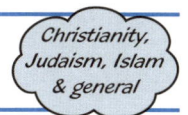

Q1 What is AIH?

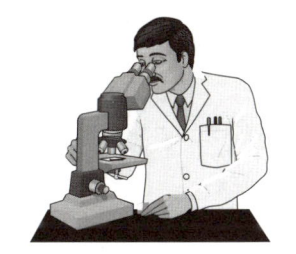

Q2 What is AID?

Q3 Explain why Christians, Muslims and Jews prefer AIH to AID.

Q4 In Britain, what happens to spare embryos from IVF (in vitro fertilisation) treatment?

Q5 Briefly explain why the Roman Catholic Church opposes IVF.

Q6 *Merav, who is Jewish, can't get pregnant. She asks her rabbi for advice on infertility treatment. The rabbi says infertility treatment would be a good thing.*
   a) Why does Merav's rabbi says it's good for her to get treatment for her infertility?
   b) What conditions might the rabbi place on egg donation, if it turned out that Merav and her husband needed it?

EXAM-STYLE QUESTION Q7 Describe how religious beliefs and teachings might influence a childless couple, when deciding what kind of treatment they will seek to help them conceive. (7 marks)

EXAM-STYLE QUESTION Q8 Explain why Jews and Muslims see artificial insemination by donor as an unacceptable method of treating infertility. (5 marks)

EXAM-STYLE QUESTION Q9 Describe the Roman Catholic approach to infertility and infertility treatment. (5 marks)

Section One — Perspectives

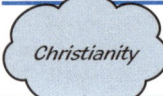

Marriage in Christianity

Christianity

Q1 Compared to 20 years ago, are more or less people in Britain getting married?

Q2 Compared to 20 years ago, are more or less unmarried couples in Britain living together?

Q3 According to Christianity, what are two purposes of marriage?

Q4 Which of the following are genuine Bible teachings on marriage?

   a) Husbands and wives must be faithful to one another.

   b) Husbands and wives must share everything, including all the chores.

   c) Marriage needs a lot of work, and husbands and wives must forgive each other.

   d) The relationship between a husband and a wife is supposed to be like the relationship between Jesus and his followers.

Cheer up — you're getting married.

Q5 What is the Christian view on sex before marriage?

Q6 What happens during each of these parts of a wedding ceremony?

   a) The declaration.

   b) The proclamation.

   c) The priest or minister's opening statement.

EXAM-STYLE QUESTION Q7 Describe what happens in a Christian wedding service.   (8 marks)

EXAM-STYLE QUESTION Q8 Explain how religious beliefs and teachings might influence the sexual activity of a Christian throughout his or her life.   (7 marks)

EXAM-STYLE QUESTION Q9 *"Sex is a sin outside of marriage."*
Do you agree? Give reasons to support your answer and show that you have thought about more than one point of view.
You should refer to Christianity in your answer.   (5 marks)

Section One — Perspectives

The Christian Church and Divorce

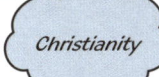

Q1 What is a nuclear family?

Q2 What is a reconstituted family?

Q3 In Britain, roughly how many marriages end in divorce? Choose from one of the options below.

> one in three   one in ten   one in thirty

Q4 *Christians don't all agree on divorce.*
   a) Which branch of Christianity considers divorce to be impossible?
   b) Why does this denomination believe that divorce is impossible?

Q5 What is an annulment?

Q6 *Claude and Iris are Catholics. They get married. However, Claude refuses to have sex with Iris on the wedding night (or indeed at all).*
   Can Iris get an annulment? Explain your answer.

Q7 What did Jesus say about remarrying after divorce?

Q8 Which of the following statements is true?
   a) If you've been divorced, you can get married in any Protestant church.
   b) If you've been divorced, you can't have a church wedding at all.
   c) Some Protestant churches will let divorced people remarry, it depends on the minister.

EXAM-STYLE QUESTION Q9 Describe Christian beliefs about marrying again after a divorce. (8 marks)

EXAM-STYLE QUESTION Q10 *"People shouldn't divorce, but should work at the problems in their marriage."* Do you agree? Give reasons to support your answer. Show that you have thought about different points of view. Refer to Christianity in your answer. (5 marks)

Well, Elizabeth Taylor sure isn't Catholic...

You might have to discuss the <u>pros and cons</u> of divorce in the Exam, so be prepared. It depends on two things — Christian ideas about marriage, and Christian <u>compassion</u> for people having a hard time.

Section One — Perspectives

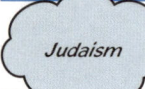

Marriage in Judaism

Q1　Which of the following statements is true?

　　i) Judaism sees sex as natural, God-given and holy.

　　ii) Judaism sees sex as dirty and tinged with sin.

Q2　How do Jews view the union between man and wife?

Q3　*Many Jews in Britain marry people who aren't Jewish.*
　　Why does this worry religious Jews?

Q4　What is a shadchan?

Q5　What is a ketubah?

Q6　*A Jewish wedding ceremony takes place under a cloth canopy.*
　　What is this canopy called?

"Ah, look how happy they are. I give it 3 years — tops."

Q7　Why does the bridegroom smash a glass under his foot?

Q8　What is a get?

Q9　*There are no agunot in Reform synagogues.*
　　Why is this?

Q10　Describe a Jewish marriage ceremony.　(8 marks)

Q11　Explain how a Jewish woman can go about getting a religious divorce.　(5 marks)

Q12　"Marrying out is a threat to the Jewish people."
　　Do you agree? Give reasons to support your answer.
　　Show that you have thought about different points of view.　(5 marks)

Section One — Perspectives

Marriage in Islam

Q1 Was Muhammad a married man?

Q2 What does Islam teach about the sexual instinct?

Q3 Give two reasons why Muslims are advised to marry, other than to channel their sexuality appropriately.

Q4 Why is dating discouraged in Islam?

Q5 Match each of the four features of a Muslim wedding below to the correct descriptions:

Nikah	A speech given after the marriage vows.
Mahr	The marriage contract.
Khutbah	A saying of Muhammad, read out after the marriage vows.
Hadith	Dowry — money paid by the groom to the bride.

Q6 Describe the quick way that a man can divorce his wife under Shari'ah law.

Q7 Answer the following questions about quick divorces under Shari'ah law.
   a) Normally, how long is the "cooling off period" after the first declaration?
   b) What's the Arabic name for this kind of divorce?
   c) Can a British man divorce his wife in this way?

EXAM-STYLE QUESTION Q8 Describe Muslim teaching on divorce. (7 marks)

EXAM-STYLE QUESTION Q9 Explain how and why Muslim parents often choose marriage partners for their children. (7 marks)

EXAM-STYLE QUESTION Q10 *"The purpose of marriage is to provide companionship."* Do you agree? Give reasons to support your answer and show that you have thought about different points of view. You must refer to Islam in your answer. (5 marks)

Section One — Perspectives

> Christianity, Judaism, Islam & general

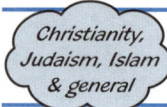

Religious Attitudes to Sex

Q1   What is the traditional religious view of sex outside marriage?

Q2   What is promiscuity?

> Christianity, Islam and Judaism have a lot in common when it comes to attitudes towards sex — but they're not identical.

Q3   Is polygamy permitted in Judaism and Christianity?

Q4   How many wives may a Muslim man have?

Q5   Read the following paragraph, and answer the questions below:

Karim has one wife. He would like to marry a second wife. Financially, he and his first wife are finding it hard to make ends meet.

a) Would it be OK by Islamic teaching for Karim to marry a second wife? Explain your answer.

b) If Karim did marry again, would it be OK for him to have a favourite wife and take her out on more dates than his other wife? Explain your answer.

Q6   What is the legal age of consent for homosexual acts between males in the UK?

Q7   Which of the following statements best describes the general Christian view of homosexuality?

a) "Homosexuality is a very bad sin, and should be condemned."

b) "There are no gay marriages, so all homosexual sex is outside marriage. For that reason, gay men and lesbians should be celibate."

c) "Homosexuality is the same, morally, as heterosexuality."

EXAM-STYLE QUESTION Q8   Describe Muslim teaching on polygamy.   (6 marks)

EXAM-STYLE QUESTION Q9   Explain how Christian teaching might influence a gay Christian man's decision whether to have a sexual relationship with another man or not.   (7 marks)

EXAM-STYLE QUESTION Q10   "Religious beliefs about sex are out of touch with the modern world." Do you agree? Give reasons to support your answer and show that you have thought about different points of view.   (8 marks)

Section One — Perspectives

Children and Religion

Christianity, Judaism & Islam

Q1 Which of the following statements best sum up the Christian and Jewish ideas about how children should treat their parents?

a) Respect and honour your parents.

b) Get as much money and stuff from them as possible — you'll be looking after them one day.

Q2 Briefly write down what Islam says about how parents should treat their children.

Q3 According to Christian, Jewish and Muslim teaching, do grown up children have to look after aged parents?

Q4 Who is born a Muslim, according to Islam? Pick the right answer from the following options:

a) Everyone is born a Muslim, in submission to Allah.

b) No one is born a Muslim, you have to make the decision yourself.

c) Only the children of Muslims are born Muslim.

Q5 According to Christianity, can children be born Christian?

Q6 What conditions does a baby have to meet to be born Jewish?

EXAM-STYLE QUESTION Q7 Describe in a paragraph what Christians believe about the relationship between parents and children. (8 marks)

EXAM-STYLE QUESTION Q8 *"It is difficult to bring up children to be religious believers."* Do you agree? Give reasons to support your answer and show that you have thought about different points of view. (5 marks)

Children — they're the future of any religion...

I believe that children are our future. Teach them well and let them lead the way. Show them all the beauty they possess inside. Give them a sense of pride to make it easier. And so on.

Section One — Perspectives

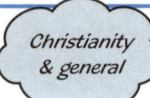

Prejudice and Equality

Christianity & general

Q1 What is the legal principle of fairness called?

Q2 What is prejudice?

Q3 How can whole societies discriminate against groups of people?

Q4 Which of these is the most usual cause of someone's prejudice?

a) Direct experience of the group that the person's prejudiced about.

b) Ignorance and wrong beliefs about another group.

Q5 What is sometimes referred to as the "Golden Rule" in Christian teaching?

Q6 Why do Christians try to treat people equally?

Q7 Write down a brief outline of the story of the Good Samaritan.

Q8 Colossians 3:11 says, "There is no Greek or Jew ...barbarian, Scythian, slave or free, but Christ is all, and is in all."

What does this say about the Christian view of race?

EXAM-STYLE QUESTION

Q9 a) Explain how Christian teachings might influence people's views on discrimination and prejudice in the world today. (5 marks)

b) Say how Christians could put those beliefs into use on a day-to-day basis. (4 marks)

EXAM-STYLE QUESTION

Q10 Explain what the parable of the Good Samaritan says about how Christians should treat people. (5 marks)

Section One — Perspectives

Race and Religion

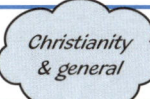

Christianity & general

Q1 What are stereotypes?

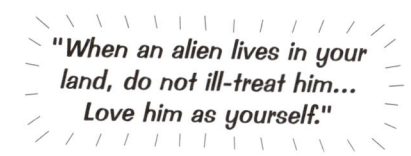

"When an alien lives in your land, do not ill-treat him... Love him as yourself."

Q2 What is segregation?

Q3 In the UK, is it legal to draw up a shortlist of candidates for a job based on their race?

Q4 Briefly describe the view of today's Anglican Church on racism.

Q5 Which Church was partly responsible for the racist apartheid system in South Africa?

Q6 What is the name of the English bishop who fought apartheid, arguing that it was against God's will?

EXAM-STYLE QUESTION Q7 To what extent does British society today conform to Christian teachings about race relations? Give examples of racial prejudice and racial tolerance in today's society.   (8 marks)

EXAM-STYLE QUESTION Q8 Explain how a Christian might use Christian teachings to argue against someone who had racist beliefs.   (7 marks)

EXAM-STYLE QUESTION Q9 In what ways has the Christian church worked to combat racial prejudice?   (5 marks)

Prejudice — It's nothing to be proud of...

As well as asking about how each religion sees racism and equality, you might be asked a general question about prejudice and equality in modern society. Don't get caught out — make sure you read the question.

Section One — Perspectives

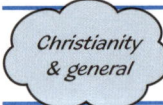

Injustice and Protest

Christianity & general

Q1 In the UK, is it legal to discriminate on the basis of sex — e.g. by paying a man more than a woman for doing exactly the same job?

Q2 What was unusual about the fact that Jesus had female friends?

Q3 What does St Paul say about the position of women?

Q4 Why did the Nazis put a Christian called Dietrich Bonhoeffer in a concentration camp?

Q5 *Archbishop Oscar Romero spoke out against the government of El Salvador.* What happened to him?

Q6 Name a Christian organisation that works against racism and injustice.

Q7 What are "prisoners of conscience"?

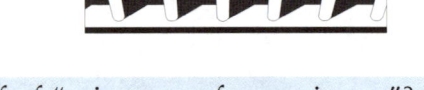

Q8 What is the name of the main charity that campaigns on behalf of "prisoners of conscience"?

EXAM-STYLE QUESTION Q9 Describe Christian teachings about the role of women in society. Are these reflected in British society today?   (8 marks)

EXAM-STYLE QUESTION Q10 Describe the ways in which Christians have campaigned for human rights.   (7 marks)

EXAM-STYLE QUESTION Q11 *"There's no use in pretending that people are equal."* Do you agree? Give reasons to support your answer and show that you have thought about different points of view.   (5 marks)

Section One — Perspectives

Jewish Attitudes towards Equality

Judaism

Q1 In the Bible, the Jewish people are called "the Lord's people". Does this mean they're better than everyone else.

> For the last time... Not till page 77.

Q2 Ruth was a great hero of the Jewish people. Was she Jewish herself?

Q3 What is the traditional role of women in Judaism?

Q4 Which of the following statements describes an Orthodox synagogue?

　a) Men pray downstairs. Women pray upstairs. The two sexes don't mix at the synagogue.

　b) Men and women sit together. Women can read from the Torah.

Q5 Which branch of Judaism is least strict about the roles of men and women?

Q6 For Jewish services, a minimum number of people is required.

　a) What is this minimum number called?

　b) Can women make up this minimum number of people in a Reform synagogue?

EXAM-STYLE QUESTION Q7 Describe what Jews believe about the relationship between men and women.　(8 marks)

EXAM-STYLE QUESTION Q8 Explain how a Jew might use Jewish teaching to argue against someone who had racist beliefs.　(7 marks)

EXAM-STYLE QUESTION Q9 "Jews shouldn't mix with non-Jews."
Do you agree? Give reasons to support your answer and show that you have thought about different points of view.　(4 marks)

Section One — Perspectives

Muslim Attitudes towards Equality

Islam

Q1 Can people of any race be Muslims?

> "All people are equal...as the teeth of a comb. No Arab can claim merit over a non-Arab, nor a white over a black person, nor male over female." **Hadith**

Q2 What is the international community of Muslims called?

Q3 What is the Muslim view of racial discrimination?

Q4 How does the Hajj demonstrate equality between Muslims?

> In a mosque, women and men must pray separately.

Q5 Does Islam say that men are created better than women?

> A family that prays separately, stays together.

Q6 What is the traditional role of women in Islam?

Q7 Were all of Muhammad's wives stay-at-home mums and housewives?

Q8 Explain why many Muslim women see wearing a veil (or hijab) and dressing modestly as liberating, rather than oppressing.

EXAM-STYLE QUESTION Q9 Describe Muslim beliefs about equality and unity.   (7 marks)

EXAM-STYLE QUESTION Q10 Explain how a Muslim might use Islamic traditions and teaching to argue against someone who said that not all races are equal.   (7 marks)

EXAM-STYLE QUESTION Q11 "In a Muslim home, the husband must be the main earner." Do you agree? Give reasons to support your answer and show that you have thought about different points of view.   (5 marks)

Section One — Perspectives

Christianity and Other Religions

Q1 Is Christianity today tolerant of other religions?

Q2 During which periods in history did Christians fight wars against Muslims for control of the Holy Land?

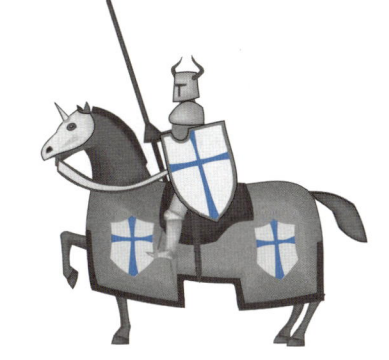

Q3 Which of the following statements best sums up the view of most Christians about other faiths?

   a) All other faiths are untrue.

   b) All faiths are equally valid — people should follow the faith that feels best to them.

   c) Other faiths have some truth to them, but only Christianity has the whole truth about God.

Q4 What does evangelising mean?

Q5 Name a branch of Christianity which says it can and should try to convert everyone in the world.

Q6 Describe briefly what missionaries do.

Q7 What is the name for the idea that there's room for all religions, and that religions should show tolerance and understanding towards each other?

Q8 What does *The Inter-Faith Network for the UK* do?

Q9 Explain what is meant by the following terms, giving examples for each:
   a) Religious exclusivity. (4 marks)
   b) Religious pluralism. (4 marks)

Q10 Explain the attitudes of Christians to other world faiths. (7 marks)

Q11 "Children must learn about other religions in school to combat prejudice." Do you agree? Give reasons to support your answer and show that you have thought about different points of view. You must discuss Christianity. (5 marks)

Section One — Perspectives

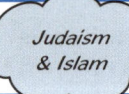

Judaism, Islam and Other Religions

Judaism & Islam

Q1   In Judaism, is it considered OK for a person born Jewish to convert to another religion?

Q2   Do religious Jews try to convert non-Jews to Judaism?

Q3   What religious laws should non-Jews follow to be considered decent and righteous by Jews?

Q4   What does Islam say about Jews and Christians who believe in God and do the right thing in their lives?

Q5   Do Muslims try to convert non-Muslims to Islam?

Q6   What does Islam say about Jesus?

"Those who believe in the Qur'an, and those who are Jews, and Christians — whoever believes in God and the Last Day and does right — surely their reward is with their Lord." Surah 2:62

Q7   Name four prophets of Allah, other than Muhammad.

EXAM-STYLE QUESTION   Q8   Describe Jewish views on other religions.   (8 marks)

EXAM-STYLE QUESTION   Q9   "Jews, Muslims and Christians have so much in common that pluralism is the only sensible standpoint." Do you agree? Show that you have considered more than one point of view.   (7 marks)

Bill and Ted got it right — we should all be excellent to each other*

Basically, all three religions think roughly the same — we should all be tolerant of other religions and try to live together. But there are always those who take a more hard-line view. Make sure you learn the details.

Section One — Perspectives   *(and party on...)

Christianity and Poverty

Christianity & general

Q1 Give two examples of things that cause poverty in the Third World.

Q2 Give two examples of things that could make a family in the UK a lot poorer than the majority of families.

Q3 Is it considered OK for a Christian to make lots and lots of money?

Snap.

Q4 Which industries does Christianity specifically frown upon?

Q5 If money belongs to God, should Christians try to redistribute wealth from rich to poor?

Q6 Give an example of a Christian agency which helps poor people.

Q7 Jesus said, "Whenever you did this for the least important brothers of mine, you did it for me." How does this inspire Christians to do good works for charity?

EXAM-STYLE QUESTION Q8 Explain why some Christians disapprove of the National Lottery. (4 marks)

EXAM-STYLE QUESTION Q9 Explain why Christians might give money to charities. (5 marks)

EXAM-STYLE QUESTION Q10 "Charity begins at home. Christians should help the poor in their own towns instead of sending money overseas." Do you agree? Give reasons to support your answer, showing that you have thought about different points of view. (5 marks)

Section One — Perspectives

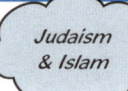

Judaism, Islam and Poverty

Q1 Judaism expects people to give money to charity to help the poor.
According to Jewish teaching, what is the best way to help a poor person?

Q2 What are pushkes?

Q3 What is tzedaka?

Q4 What's the minimum percentage of wealth that a Jew should give to charity?

Q5 Is gemilut hasadim a good thing or a bad thing?

Q6 Which industries and lines of work should Muslims not work or invest in?

Q7 Why is it problematic for a Muslim to get a loan, when banks charge interest?

Q8 What is the 2.5% Islamic tax given to the poor and needy called?

Q9 What is sadaqah?

Q10 Explain the problems facing Muslims in a capitalist society.   (8 marks)

Q11 "It is wrong to be poor; it makes you a burden on society."
Do you agree? Give reasons to support your answer, showing that you have thought about different points of view. Refer to Judaism in your answer.   (5 marks)

Q12 How important is charitable work to Jews and Muslims, as part of living a righteous life?   (5 marks)

Section One — Perspectives

Religion and the Environment

Christianity, Judaism, Islam & general

Q1   Give three examples of environmental problems in the world.

Q2   Give a reason why a business might choose a polluting way of doing something instead of a clean, green, non-polluting method.

Q3   Whose job is it to look after the Earth, in the opinion of Christianity?

Q4   Why is extinction of species worrying, from a Christian and Jewish point of view?

Q5   What do Jews believe about the position of humankind in creation?

Q6   According to Islam, when will we be called to explain how we treated the environment?

Q7   What is interdependence?

EXAM-STYLE QUESTION Q8   *"We are stewards of God's World."*
Describe Christian attitudes towards the natural world.   (5 marks)

EXAM-STYLE QUESTION Q9   Explain how Jewish teachings might encourage someone to use "green" products, recycle waste and conserve energy.   (5 marks)

EXAM-STYLE QUESTION Q10   *"God created the world, so it's God's job to look after it."*
Do you agree? Give reasons for your answer, and show that you have thought about different points of view.   (6 marks)

Pollution is naughty — well, we can all agree with that...

With broad questions like, "Should we look after the environment?" you still have to know what different religions believe, and say <u>why</u> they support opinions either way. A load of <u>waffle</u> won't cut it.

Section One — Perspectives

Religion and Animals

Christianity, Judaism, Islam & general

Q1 Are humans and animals equal in Christianity?

Q2 What is the relationship between humans and animals in Judaism?

Q3 What does Christianity teach about cruelty to animals?

Q4 Can a Christian be vegetarian?

Q5 Name a Christian denomination which is particularly opposed to hunting and animal circuses.

Q6 Name a Christian denomination which is generally more accepting of animal experiments than other denominations.

Q7 What is the Jewish view of medical experiments on animals?

Q8 How must animals for meat be slaughtered according to Jewish law?

Q9 What is the Islamic view of cruelty to animals?

EXAM-STYLE QUESTION Q10 Explain and compare Christian and Muslim attitudes towards animals. (5 marks)

EXAM-STYLE QUESTION Q11 Explain how religious beliefs might influence a woman's decision whether or not to wear makeup that had been tested on animals. (5 marks)

EXAM-STYLE QUESTION Q12 "Religious believers should be concerned about people instead of animals." Do you agree? Give reasons for your answer, and show that you have thought about different points of view. (5 marks)

Section One — Perspectives

Religion and Crime

Q1 Who enforces the laws of the land?

Q2 What is the difference between a sin and a crime, according to Christianity?

Q3 What is shari'ah?

Q4 What is a Bet Din?

Q5 Which of the following statements are true of Judaism?

a) "Jews must obey the 613 Torah laws first and foremost. The laws of the land are of secondary importance and can be broken."

b) "Jews must obey the laws of the land as well as the Torah laws in order to be considered righteous."

Q6 "Many people think that punishing criminals deters people from committing crime."

Give three other things that people think that punishment should achieve.

Q7 Can punishment deter people from committing crimes that aren't premeditated? Give a reason for your answer.

Q8 For what crimes does Judaism permit the death penalty?

Q9 a) Explain why some religious believers support capital punishment for some crimes. (5 marks)

b) Give a religious argument against capital punishment. (5 marks)

Q10 "The main purpose of punishment must be to reform criminals." Do you agree? Give reasons to support your answer, showing that you have thought about different points of view. (8 marks)

I say string them all up — not revising is a terrible crime...

Make sure you know the differences between a sin and a crime. In most countries, sins like adultery are not punishable by law — but in some Islamic countries, religious and state law are almost the same.

Section One — Perspectives

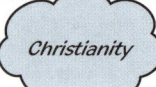

Christianity and War

Q1 What is the Christian view of war in general?

Q2 "War must be declared by a proper authority."
What is a proper authority?

Q3 Give an example of something that Christianity would consider a just cause for war.

Q4 "Wars must be fought with discrimination."
What does this mean?

Q5 What is a pacifist?

Q6 What is a martyr?

Q7 Give two examples of non-conventional warfare.

Q8 Why do Christian churches oppose nuclear weapons?

Q9 What is unilateral disarmament?

Q10 *(Exam-style question)* Describe what Christians believe about war. (4 marks)

Q11 *(Exam-style question)* "Christians have the duty to end all wars and disarm all governments."
Do you agree? Give reasons to support your answer, showing that you have thought about different points of view. (8 marks)

Holy war, Batman — they've deployed God...

You might think that all war is wrong, but Christianity accepts that sometimes they have to be fought. This is why over the centuries the Church has laid down certain rules.

Section One — Perspectives

Judaism, Islam and War

Judaism & Islam

Q1 What does "shalom" mean?

Q2 What does "milchemet mitzvah" mean?

Q3 Which of the following are obligatory wars, according to Judaism?

> a) A war to take over another country.
>
> b) A war fought against a country that has invaded your own country.
>
> c) A war fought against a country that you think is going to attack your country very soon.
>
> d) A war fought against an enemy after negotiations have broken down.

Q4 Why are Muslims advised to "Hate your enemy mildly"?

Q5 What is Greater Jihad?

Q6 Which of the following are just wars, according to Islam?

a) A war to make people free from oppression.

b) A war to conquer a country and force the people there to become Muslims.

Q7 Who can declare a military Jihad?

Q8 What happens to someone who dies in a Jihad?

EXAM-STYLE QUESTION Q9 Describe what Muslims mean by 'Jihad'. (8 marks)

EXAM-STYLE QUESTION Q10 Explain how a Jewish government might respond to another country threatening to invade. Include Jewish teaching in your answer. (4 marks)

EXAM-STYLE QUESTION Q11 "Sometimes, war is the only way of restoring peace."
Do you agree? Give reasons to support your answer, showing that you have thought about more than one point of view.
You should refer to religious ideas in your answer. (5 marks)

Section One — Perspectives

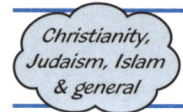

Religion and Drugs

Christianity, Judaism, Islam & general

Q1 Give two examples of hard drugs.

Q2 Give an example of a soft drug.

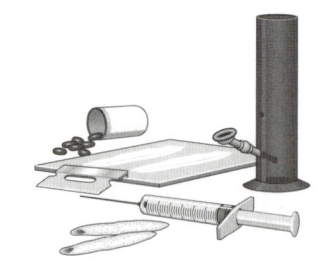

Q3 Give an example of a social drug widely used in British society.

Q4 *Christianity, Judaism and Islam all completely disapprove of illegal hard drugs.*
Give three reasons why all three religions disapprove of drug use.

Q5 For each of these religions, say whether alcohol is permitted in general, or forbidden.
   a) Judaism
   b) Christianity
   c) Islam

Q6 What's the religious view of performance enhancing drugs in sport?

EXAM-STYLE QUESTION Q7 Explain why one main world religion forbids the drinking of alcohol, and why other world religions allow it. *(8 marks)*

EXAM-STYLE QUESTION Q8 The New Testament says, *"Your body is a temple of the Holy Spirit."* How does this affect the Christian view of drug abuse? *(5 marks)*

EXAM-STYLE QUESTION Q9 "Cannabis and alcohol are both soft drugs. The Government should either legalise cannabis or make alcohol illegal."
Do you agree? Give reasons to support your answer, showing that you have thought about more than one point of view.
Use religious arguments in your answer. *(5 marks)*

Oh no, not another lecture...

Don't say, "Drugs are bad, okay," and leave it at that — you have to put religious arguments in your answer too (it's a Religious Studies exam, duh). The faiths have pretty similar ideas, so it's not too hard.

Section One — Perspectives

Religion and the Media

General

Q1 How has the number of people going to church changed over the last 50 years?

Q2 How have TV viewing figures changed over the last 50 years?

Q3 What does it mean to say that most broadcasting is secular?

Q4 Give two reasons why Jewish communities might be frustrated about the British media.

Q5 Give an example of a TV series that covers Muslim issues.

Q6 Give a reason why a religious person might be offended by soap opera characters and comedy characters.

Q7 What is the danger of relying on one newspaper for all your news and opinions?

Q8 Give an example of a book considered blasphemous by Muslims.

Q9 Why are some people concerned about allowing children to access the Internet freely? Give two reasons.

EXAM-STYLE QUESTION Q10 Explain why some religious believers dislike the religious programmes available on television. (4 marks)

EXAM-STYLE QUESTION Q11 *"There's no point in having a television. Television is immoral, and degrades people who watch it."* Do you agree? Give reasons to support your answer, showing that you have thought about more than one point of view. (5 marks)

EXAM-STYLE QUESTION Q12 Explain why some religious believers support censorship of the media. (6 marks)

Section One — Perspectives

Basic Christian Beliefs

Q1 What is the basic summary of Christian belief called?

    a) Apostles' Screed   b) Apostles' Creed   c) Saints' Creed   d) Apollo Creed

Not all Christians believe exactly the same things, but most accept certain basic doctrines.

Q2 *Christians say Jesus is "The Christ". What does this mean?*

Q3 Which of the following statements best summarises Christian beliefs about whether Jesus was human or God?

    a) Jesus was all God. He was not human.

    b) Jesus was a human. He was no more God than anyone else is.

    c) Jesus was 100% human and 100% God at the same time.

    d) Jesus was half human and half God.

Q4 How do Christians say that Mary, the mother of Jesus, got pregnant?

Q5 What is meant by "the Resurrection"?

Q6 Give two examples of how Christians symbolise the Holy Spirit.

Q7 How were humankind's sins atoned (paid) for, according to Christianity?

Q8 What do Christians believe will happen at the Last Judgement?

EXAM-STYLE QUESTION Q9 Describe Christian teachings about Christ's incarnation on Earth.   (6 marks)

EXAM-STYLE QUESTION Q10 Explain why many Christians believe that Christ's death was the most important part of his ministry.   (7 marks)

The Bible

Q1 For each of the following questions, answer either "Old Testament" or "New Testament".

> a) Which part of the Bible is sacred to Jews?
>
> b) Which part of the Bible contains the Gospels?
>
> c) Which part of the Bible contains the Revelation of St John?
>
> d) Which part of the Bible contains the Ten Commandments?

Q2 Whose example do Christians believe everyone should follow?

Q3 Give an example of a sacrament which appears both in the Bible and in modern worship.

Q4 Which branch of Christianity claims its authority from its teachings and traditions, as well as from the Bible?

Q5 What is: a) literalism?
b) fundamentalism?

Q6 *Brian says that the Bible was inspired by God, but it wasn't directly dictated by God.*

a) What is the name for this view of the Bible?

b) Is Brian's view of the Bible rare in Christianity?

Pastor Fred's "Sundaes on Sunday" Bible Study and dessert session went down a storm with the flock.

Q7 Give two reasons why a Christian would read the Bible.

EXAM-STYLE QUESTION Q8 Explain why the books of the New Testament (other than the Gospels) are important to Christians. (5 marks)

EXAM-STYLE QUESTION Q9 *"To be a good Christian, you must follow the teaching of the Bible."*
Do you agree with this? Give reasons for your answer.
Show that you have thought about other points of view. (5 marks)

Jesus and the Bible — you really HAVE to know this stuff...

This is all fundamental stuff — the kind of knowledge you can't get very far without. I mean, how can you answer questions about Christianity if you don't know what Christianity actually is... learn it all.

Section Two — Christianity

Christian Values

Q1 *Judaism teaches that 613 commandments from the Old Testament should be obeyed. Which of these Old Testament commandments are most important to Christians?*

Q2 Why did Jesus get into trouble for healing a man on the Sabbath.

Q3 Which were more important to Jesus — your actions or your intentions?

Q4 What did Jesus say was the most important commandment?

(Give yourself a pat on the back if you remember the exact wording without looking it up.)

Q5 Match the type of love to the description.

Eros	Christian love, like God's love.
Philia	Friendship, with give and take involved.
Storge	Sexual love.
Agape	Family affection.

Q6 Does Christian love involve keeping score, and making sure you take as much as you give?

Q7 What do Christians believe is the source of all love?

Q8 According to Saint Paul in his first letter to the Corinthians, which is most important?

a) Faith   b) Hope   c) Love

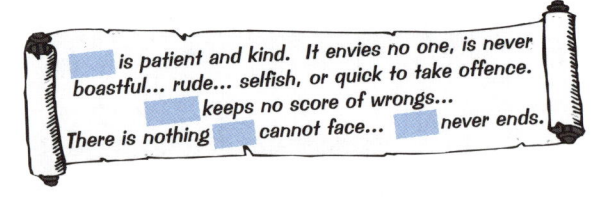

____ is patient and kind. It envies no one, is never boastful... rude... selfish, or quick to take offence. ____ keeps no score of wrongs... There is nothing ____ cannot face... ____ never ends.

EXAM-STYLE QUESTION

Q9 According to the teachings of Christianity, what should people do in order to be considered righteous at the Last Judgement? Refer to ideas about love in your answer.

(7 marks)

EXAM-STYLE QUESTION

Q10 *"The spirit of the Law is more important than the letter of the Law"*
Do you agree with this? Give reasons for your answer, showing that you have thought about other points of view.
You must consider Christianity and the Gospels in your answer.

(5 marks)

Section Two — Christianity

Love and Forgiveness

Q1 What must we do to get God's forgiveness, according to Christianity?

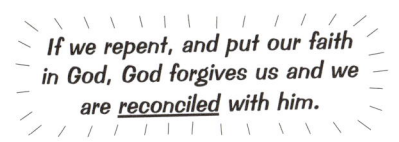

If we repent, and put our faith in God, God forgives us and we are reconciled with him.

Q2 What does reconciliation mean?

Q3 What disadvantage do some people see to giving the poor lots of help?

Q4 Which of these is the most appropriate response for a Christian who has been hurt or wronged by someone?

> a) Do nothing, and let the person hurt you again.
>
> b) Sort out the problem, then forgive the person and move on.
>
> c) Get revenge. Make the person sorry they ever thought about ticking you off.

Q5 Give three examples of things that Christians base moral decisions on other than Christian love.

"God forgives us our sins."

Q6 Is it necessary in Christianity to forgive each other, or is that only for God to do?

Q7 *Punishing criminals brings up plenty of dilemmas for Christians.*

a) Give a possible reason why a Christian might want to 'punish a criminal lightly'.

b) Give a possible reason why a Christian might want to 'punish a criminal harshly'.

EXAM-STYLE QUESTION Q8 Describe what Christianity teaches about the forgiveness of sins. (8 marks)

EXAM-STYLE QUESTION Q9 Explain why repentance is so important in Christianity. (7 marks)

Love is all around, it's everywhere I go — discuss...

Forgiveness is vital in Christianity, but even Jesus might have had trouble forgiving the British record-buying public for some of the shockers that have been Number 1 on his birthday. Take Cliff Richard... Mistletoe and Wine AND Saviour's Day. Then the Spice Girls... Christmas Number 1 for 3 years running (2 become 1, Too Much, and Goodbye). But at least we then had Bob the Builder... sanity clearly prevailed that year.

Section Two — Christianity

The Sermon on the Mount

Q1   What kind of people did Jesus say would "inherit the earth"?

Q2   What was the opinion of Jesus on doing good deeds in order to make people think you're a nice person?

Q3   Describe briefly Jesus' message about judging people.

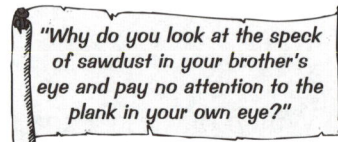

"Why do you look at the speck of sawdust in your brother's eye and pay no attention to the plank in your own eye?"

Q4   What is the Golden Rule that Jesus said summed up all the Law?

Q5   *Jesus said that people should be "the salt of the earth" and "the light of the earth". Describe briefly what he meant.*

Q6   Give an example of a Christian vocation.

Q7   What did Reverend Dr Martin Luther King try to achieve?

Q8   What did Mother Teresa of Calcutta try to do?

EXAM-STYLE QUESTION Q9   Describe what Jesus said about 'displaying religion' in the Sermon on the Mount.   (4 marks)

EXAM-STYLE QUESTION Q10   Explain why Christianity teaches it's so important to serve other people. Give some examples of how Christians might choose to serve others.   (6 marks)

Blessed is the Brian — for he shall act and shout a lot...

The Sermon on the Mount is probably THE most important sermon that Jesus gave. It's all there — the Golden Rule, judgement, sincerity, the Law of Moses, the Lord's Prayer and so on and so on.

Section Two — Christianity

Spreading the Gospel

Q1 What does "spreading the gospel" mean?

> Jesus told his followers to 'spread the gospel' (Matthew 28:19-20).

Q2 Write down two ways in which Christians can seek to challenge the society around them.

Q3 What is meant by "Christian apologetics"?

> I want to spread Jesus' message of love and forgiveness. So I'm off on a crusade.

Q4 Why are Evangelical Christians so keen to convert people to Christianity?

Q5 What is absolute morality?

> "If any of you is without sin... let him be the first to throw a stone at her."

Q6 What is relative morality?

Q7 Why do some Christians get involved with politics, and campaign about things like abortion and euthanasia?

Q8 Why are some Christians happy to stand back and let people make up their own minds on tricky moral issues?

EXAM-STYLE QUESTION Q9 Describe the importance in Christianity of spreading the Gospel. (5 marks)

EXAM-STYLE QUESTION Q10 Explain how Christianity might have an effect on politics in this country. (7 marks)

Section Two — Christianity

Living the Christian Life

Q1 *"Witnessing for Christ" is said to be the duty of every Christian. In what way do Evangelical Christians witness for Christ?*

Practising Christians witness for Christ in different ways, depending on their <u>denomination</u>, <u>culture</u>, <u>background</u>, <u>personal taste</u> or <u>talents</u>.

Q2 What are "Alpha Courses"?

Q3 Suggest one reason why some Christians might find it difficult to explain their faith to other people.

Q4 *Christians can witness for Christ through their lifestyle. Suggest an area of their life where they might do this.*

Q5 Give another way that Christians can 'witness for Christ' (apart from through talking to others, and through their lifestyle).

'Sound of Music' jokes get on my wick.

Q6 *Nuns and monks are members of religious orders. Some members of religious orders take three vows. Name and describe each vow.*

Q7 There are different kinds of congregation.

a) What are "contemplative congregations"? Give an example of one.
b) What are "apostolic congregations"? Give an example of one.

EXAM-STYLE QUESTION Q8 Describe how members of a particular religious community live their lives. Why do this community's members live this way? (12 marks)

EXAM-STYLE QUESTION Q9 *"Spending your life shut away as a monk or a nun is a waste."* Explain whether you agree with this, giving reasons. Show that you have also thought about other points of view. Refer to and explain any relevant Christian beliefs in your answer. (8 marks)

Section Two — Christianity

The Church

Q1   *St Paul said that the Church was the body of Christ.*

> a) What is the aim or mission of the Church?
> b) Who called the Church into being?
> c) If the Church is the body, who is the head?

Q2   What is the name of the group consisting of all Christians who have died?

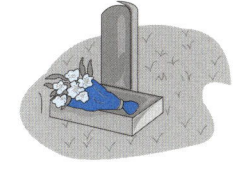

Q3   What is the name for work aimed at unifying all the different churches?

Q4   Whose teaching do Catholics follow on modern moral issues like abortion and contraception?

Q5   Who are the lay ministry and what do they do?

Q6   *Christians follow the teachings of the Church on ethical issues. Give examples of two other ways that the Church influences society.*

Q7   Give three examples of ways that the Church puts Christian faith into action.

EXAM-STYLE QUESTION Q8   Explain how the Church influences and guides Christian believers. Make particular reference to the role of religious leaders.   (7 marks)

EXAM-STYLE QUESTION Q9   Describe the role and function of a local Christian church.   (7 marks)

Here's the church, here's the steeple...

It's pretty likely that you'll get some Exam questions about what the Church does and how Christians view the Church. It's pretty central as far as Christianity goes, so learn this stuff, plus the rest of the above rhyme.

Section Two — Christianity

Traditions and Denominations

Q1 Whose authority is most important to Protestants? Choose an answer from the options below.

> The Church's   The Bible's   The Sacraments'

Q2 When did the Greek and Russian Orthodox Churches split from Roman Catholicism? What name is given to this split?

Q3 Which branches of the Church believe in the Seven Sacraments?

Q4 Which denomination holds worship services in silence until someone is "moved to speak"?

Q5 Which denomination has worship services with lots of singing, inspired by the Holy Spirit?

Q6 Explain the following terms: Magisterium   Dogma

Q7 What is special about pronouncements on morals that the Pope makes when he is sitting on his Papal throne?

Q8 *Catholics believe that Mary was born without any original sin (the sin that the rest of us are born with). What is the name for this doctrine?*

Q9 What is the doctrine of transubstantiation?

Q10 What is the aim of Liberation Theology?

Q11 Describe the main differences between Catholicism and Protestantism.   (7 marks)

Q12 *"The similarities between different Christian traditions are more important than the differences"*
Do you agree with this? Give reasons for your answer, showing that you have thought about other points of view.   (5 marks)

Q13 Explain why many Catholics try to follow the example of Mary.   (6 marks)

Section Two — Christianity

Members of the Church

Q1 Who was the first Pope?

Q2 In the Roman Catholic Church, what's the next rank down from Pope?

Q3 Who appoints Catholic bishops? Choose an answer from the options below.

> a) A group of cardinals.
> b) All the priests in the diocese.
> c) The Pope.

Q4 What can priests do that deacons can't?

Q5 Who are the laity?

Q6 Where is a bishop's throne?

Q7 Who is the clergyman at the head of the Anglican Church?

Q8 Say whether priests in each of these denominations can marry.
a) Anglicans   b) Catholics   c) Greek Orthodox

Q9 Who appoints Presbyterian elders?

Q10 Who are patriarchs?

EXAM-STYLE QUESTION Q11 Describe the hierarchy of the Roman Catholic Church.   (8 marks)

EXAM-STYLE QUESTION Q12 *"It is an important principle that Roman Catholic priests should remain celibate."*
Do you agree with this? Give reasons for your answer, showing that you have considered different points of view. In your answer, you must refer to the teachings of the Roman Catholic Church.   (5 marks)

Section Two — Christianity

A Christian Church

Q1 Why were churches traditionally built in a cross shape?

Q2 Why do churches traditionally face east?

Q3 Look at this diagram and answer questions a)-c).

   a) What is the purpose of this part of the church?

   b) What are the two side wings called?

   c) What is special about the ground surrounding a church?

Q4 Match the door or gate to the correct description of its use.

Porch	Large door used only for ceremonial occasions, e.g. when a bishop visits the church.
West Door	Where coffins are placed until the minister arrives to conduct the funeral service.
Lych-gate	Day to day entrance used by everyone.

Q5 What's the name for the part of the church where the congregation sits?

Q6 *Many Christian churches contain an altar.*

   a) At what end of the church is the altar?
   b) Name two denominations which don't have an altar.
   c) Why don't those two denominations have an altar?

Q7 Describe the important external features of a church, and explain the function of each one. (8 marks)

Q8 Describe the important internal features of a church, and explain the function of each one. (8 marks)

Section Two — Christianity

Religious Symbolism

Q1   Why are cathedrals built so big?

Symbols are used to represent what's believed. Think of the cross — it's used to represent the sacrificial death of Jesus Christ.

Q2   *Orthodox churches have a dome on top. Describe the symbolism of the dome.*

Q3   Why is the pulpit the focus of attention in a Baptist church?

Q4   Answer these questions about a particular branch of Christianity.

   a) Which denomination has icons in its churches?

   b) What do worshippers do to the icons when they enter the church?

   c) What is the purpose of icons?

Q5   In what kind of church would you be likely to see dancing?

Q6   Why is music used in Christian worship services?

EXAM-STYLE QUESTION   Q7   Describe the religious symbolism in Orthodox churches.   (8 marks)

EXAM-STYLE QUESTION   Q8   Explain the ways in which a sense of awe and wonder might be inspired in a cathedral.   (6 marks)

I got a sense of awe in a cathedral — it cost a fortune to get in...

There's all kinds of symbolism in Church buildings and services of worship. Rather interesting if you're into that sort of thing. And even if not, you might still have to answer a question on it in the Exam.

Section Two — Christianity

Sunday Worship

Q1   On what day of the week would Jesus, as a Jew, have celebrated the Sabbath?

Q2   Give two reasons why Christians observe the Sabbath on a Sunday.

Q3   What does it mean to say that a service is "liturgical"?

   Q4   What did Jesus say about the bread and wine at the Last Supper?

Not all of Jesus' utterances at the Last Supper are equally famous.

(Speech bubble: "Pass that bread — I'm starving...")

   Q5   What do Roman Catholics believe about the bread and wine of Communion?

Q6   What happens to leftover consecrated bread and wine?

   Q7   Put these parts of the Mass in the right order.

   | **Penitential Rite** | **Readings** |
   | **Rite of Communion** | **Eucharistic Prayers** |

   Q8   What happens during each of these parts of the Mass?
      a) Penitential Rite
      b) Eucharistic Prayers

EXAM-STYLE QUESTION   Q9   Describe what happens at a Catholic Mass.   (8 marks)

EXAM-STYLE QUESTION   Q10   "Holy Communion is the most important way for Christians to worship."
Do you agree with this? Give reasons for your answer.
Show that you have thought about other points of view.   (5 marks)

Section Two — Christianity

Christian Festivals

Q1 When does Advent begin?

Q2 Which of the following is the first day of Lent?

   a) Shrove Tuesday   b) Ash Wednesday   c) Maundy Thursday

Q3 What do each of the following festivals commemorate?
   a) Epiphany
   b) Palm Sunday
   c) Pentecost

Q4 What is the transfiguration?

Q5 Why do people put ash on their foreheads on Ash Wednesday?

Q6 What is the name of the feast that marks Jesus going to Heaven?

Q7 Mary is a central figure in some branches of Christianity.
   a) What do Catholic and Orthodox Christians believe happened to Mary, mother of Jesus, at the end of her earthly life?
   b) What day of the year is the feast day dedicated to Mary?

Q8 Describe what Christians might do to get ready spiritually for Easter.   (8 marks)

Q9 "There's no point in having Advent when shops start Christmas in September."
Do you agree with this? Refer to Christianity in your answer, giving reasons.
Show that you have thought about other points of view.   (5 marks)

Pancake Day — a fine tradition worth upholding...

Hard though it may be to believe, Christmas has something to do with religion. Easter too. Well, it must be true what they say — you learn something new every day. But anyway... just remember the famous parable about Jesus and the Easter Bunny going to the North Pole to get their toys from Santa, and you'll be okay.

Section Two — Christianity

Private Prayer and the Sacraments

Q1   What is a contemplative prayer?

Q2   a)   What is the rosary?

   b)   Name two prayers said using the rosary.

Q3   Which of the following are Sacraments in the Catholic Church?

   a)   Birth
   b)   Marriage
   c)   Ordination
   d)   Tea and biscuits
   e)   Redemption
   f)   Reconciliation

Q4   a)   Give another name for the anointing of the sick.

   b)   What are the sick anointed with?

Q5   In the sacrament of reconciliation, what must follow after the person confesses their sin to the priest?

Q6   Which sacraments are accepted by mainstream Protestants?

Q7   Which of the following statements best sums up the Catholic and Anglican view of Sacraments?

   a)   "Sacraments are only special because they're special times in a Christian's life."
   b)   "Sacraments are so special because the grace of God enters into a person through the Sacrament."

EXAM-STYLE QUESTION Q8   Describe the Christian sacraments and how they are viewed by different branches of the Church.   (8 marks)

EXAM-STYLE QUESTION Q9   Describe two different kinds of private prayer.   (4 marks)

Section Two — Christianity

Baptism

Q1 Who baptised Jesus?

Q2 When did Jesus tell his disciples that they should baptise people?

> "Go and make disciples of all nations, *baptising* them in the name of the Father, Son and Holy Spirit."

Q3 Baptism is an important rite in Christianity.

a) Why do Baptists and Pentecostal Christians only baptise Christian believers (who will be young teens and upwards) rather than babies?
b) Why do Catholics, Orthodox and Anglicans think it's good to baptise babies?

Q4 Who makes promises to be a good Christian on behalf of a baby being baptised?

Q5 What's the name of the water container over which the baby is baptised?

Q6 Why do parents and godparents hold a candle?

Q7 When do Catholic children have their first Communion?

Q8 Describe what happens at the baptism of an adult believer.

EXAM-STYLE QUESTION Q9 Explain the significance of baptism in Christianity. (7 marks)

EXAM-STYLE QUESTION Q10 Describe what happens at the baptism of a baby. (5 marks)

EXAM-STYLE QUESTION Q11 "Babies must be baptised."
Do you agree with this? Give reasons for your answer.
Show that you have thought about other points of view. (5 marks)

Baptism — go on, dive straight into the topic...

Baptism is one of just two sacraments (direct grantings of God's grace) accepted by both Protestants and Catholics, so it must be important. And prayer — what do you reckon... important or not...

Section Two — Christianity

Funerals, Burials and Cremation

Q1 Who do Christians believe can be resurrected after they die?

Q2 What does the Christian Church believe about sin, God's standards of behaviour, and going to Heaven?

Q3 What does the Christian Church believe Jesus did to the link between sin and death?

Q4 Give an example of a New Testament verse that is commonly read at funeral services.

Q5 Why doesn't it matter if the body is cremated?

Q6 What is a Requiem Mass for?

Q7 What is the name of the white cloth that covers the coffin during a Requiem Mass?

Q8 How can the funeral service sometimes help the bereaved person?

Q9 What can priests and vicars do to try and comfort the bereaved?

EXAM-STYLE QUESTION Q10 Describe a Christian burial service. (8 marks)

EXAM-STYLE QUESTION Q11 Explain how Christians might comfort someone whose close friend has recently died. (4 marks)

Christianity tries to view death in a positive way...

Death is usually a very upsetting time for those left behind, but Christians try to take comfort from the fact that the person who died has gone to Heaven (hopefully). It can make an upsetting time easier to cope with.

Section Two — Christianity

Jesus and Mark's Gospel

Q1   Which 3 Gospels are the Synoptic Gospels?

Christians consider the Gospels to be Scripture (holy writings inspired by God).

Q2   When do people think that Mark's Gospel was written?

Q3   Do people think that Mark knew Jesus himself?

Q4   Give three times from Mark's Gospel where Jesus is called the Son of God.

Q5   Which Old Testament prophet wrote about a Son of Man who would have authority from God?

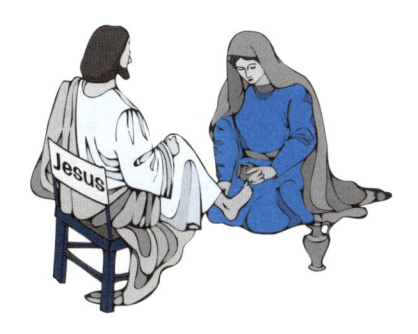

Q6   Give another title that means the same as Messiah.

Q7   What is the significance of the woman at Bethany pouring perfume on Jesus' feet?

Q8   Who is the first person to call Jesus Son of David in public, without being criticised or shouted down.

Q9   When in Mark's Gospel does Jesus save a Gentile (a non-Jew)?

EXAM-STYLE QUESTION Q10   Give two titles used for Jesus from Mark's Gospel, and explain the significance of each.   (4 marks)

EXAM-STYLE QUESTION Q11   Explain what is meant by 'Messiah'. Describe the different attitudes that are shown in Mark's Gospel regarding Jesus as the Messiah.   (6 marks)

Section Two — Christianity

The Kingdom of God

Q1 *The Pharisees asked Jesus when he believed that the Kingdom of God would come. What was Jesus' answer?*

Q2 When did Jesus say, "The Kingdom of God is at hand."

Q3 What did Jesus mean when he said that people should approach the Kingdom of God "like a little child"?

Q4 What did Jesus say about being rich and going to Heaven?

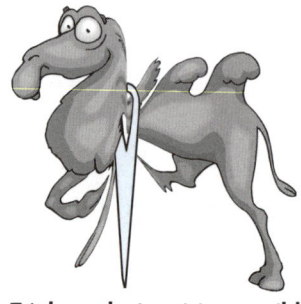

Tricky... but not impossible.

Q5 What do the parables of the *growing seed* and the *mustard seed* (4:26-32) say about the Kingdom of God?

Q6 In the parable of the vineyard:

    a) Who is represented by the vineyard owner?

    b) Who are the tenants of the vineyard supposed to be?

Q7 What does the parable of the lamp say about Jesus?

EXAM-STYLE QUESTION Q8 Give an outline of the parable of the vineyard, and explain its significance. (8 marks)

EXAM-STYLE QUESTION Q9 Explain Jesus' teachings about the Kingdom of God. (7 marks)

EXAM-STYLE QUESTION Q10 "Jesus confused people by talking in parables. He should have said what he meant." Do you agree with this? Give reasons for your answer. Show that you have thought about other points of view. (5 marks)

Before you go learning all this stuff, just pause for a moment...

There's a load of stuff that you <u>might</u> need to learn in Mark's Gospel — but it's not included on all syllabuses. So before you get too carried away with committing all this stuff to memory, it's probably a good idea to check that you actually need to know it. You might need the brain-space for other things.

Section Two — Christianity

Jesus and Miracles

Q1 Give an example of Jesus calming Nature.

Jesus' miracles involved controlling nature and curing mental and physical illness.
He performed miracles to show had God's power and to demonstrate the importance of faith.

Q2 What happened at the feeding of the 5000?

Q3 In the story of the man possessed by many evil spirits, where did Jesus send all the spirits?

Q4 Give four examples of the types of illness and disability that Jesus cured.

Q5 *Jesus asked some folk to keep quiet about the miracles, and asked others to spread the news.*
Give an example of a healing miracle that Jesus asked to be kept quiet.

Q6 Why was Jesus accused of blasphemy when he healed the paralysed man?
Choose the correct answer from the options below:

> a) Because God obviously meant the man to be paralysed.
>
> b) Because the crowd thought it was witchcraft.
>
> c) Because he also forgave the man his sins, and the crowd said that only God can forgive sins.

EXAM-STYLE QUESTION Q7 Describe one of Jesus' nature miracles, and explain its significance in Christianity. (6 marks)

EXAM-STYLE QUESTION Q8 *"Jesus' miracles were impossible. They never really happened."*
Do you agree with this? Give reasons for your answer.
Show that you have thought about other points of view. (5 marks)

Don't rely on miracles to pass your Exams...

Jesus performed many miracles — he believed nothing was impossible. Although to be fair, he never tried to get put through to a human operator on a Customer Helpline. Feeding the 5000 was probably relatively easy.

Section Two — Christianity

Miracles, Faith and Conflict

Q1 In the story of Jairus' daughter, how does Jairus show he has faith?

Q2 *In Mark 5:25-34, Jesus heals a woman who touches his cloak.*

  a) Does Jesus know which person in the crowd touched his cloak?
  b) How does Jesus explain the woman's healing?

Q3 Faith is an important part of any religion.

  a) According to Jesus' healing miracles in the Gospel of Mark, is it enough to sit back and trust God to 'sort it all out'?
  b) If not, what do people have to do as well?

Q4 Give an example of a time when the disciples failed to cure a sick person, and explain why they failed.

Q5 What did Jesus say to the Pharisees about paying tax?

Q6 What did Jesus say to the Pharisees about the ritual washing laws?

Q7 Give an example of a time when the disciples were accused of breaking Sabbath laws.

Q8 [EXAM-STYLE QUESTION] Explain the difference between Jesus' attitude towards religious rituals and those of the Pharisees. (7 marks)

Q9 [EXAM-STYLE QUESTION] What do healing miracles show about the relationship between Jesus and the people he healed? (5 marks)

Q10 [EXAM-STYLE QUESTION] "Christians have a duty to challenge authority." Do you agree with this? Give reasons for your answer. Show that you have thought about other points of view. (5 marks)

Section Two — Christianity

Discipleship

Q1 *Jesus gathered his disciples and sent them off on a mission.*

    a) Who or what did Jesus give the disciples authority over?

    b) Give two examples of things that the disciples were not allowed to take with them.

    c) What did Jesus say the disciples were to do when they were made unwelcome?

Q2 What did Jesus mean about his ministry when he said that healthy people didn't need a doctor?

> *"Whoever does God's will is my brother and sister and mother."*

Q3 *Peter said he'd tell people that Jesus is the Christ. What did Jesus tell Peter to do?*

Q4 Which of the following are qualities that a disciple should have?

    a) Must speak Greek

    b) Must love kids

    c) Must be faithful to husband or wife

    d) Must not eat meat

    e) Must make financial sacrifices

    f) Must preach the Gospel

Q5 *Which story gives the example of making financial sacrifices and digging deep in your pockets to make offerings?*

Q6 According to the Gospel of Mark, how much bigger are the rewards of discipleship than the costs?

Q7 *(EXAM-STYLE QUESTION)* Describe what Jesus taught his disciples about serving others. (4 marks)

Q8 *(EXAM-STYLE QUESTION)* *"You can't have a house and possessions if you're a disciple of Jesus."* Do you agree with this? Give reasons for your answer. Show that you have thought about other points of view. (5 marks)

Discipleship has its ups and its downs...

There's actually a version of the Bible written in Cockney rhyming slang. In fact, historians now believe that this is how Jesus spoke most of the time. "I've come to heal the Tom and Dick..." "Why do you look at the speck of sawdust in your brother's mince pie..." "Accept the Kingdom of God like a dustbin lid..." "Those who Adam and Eve in me will never be brown bread..." and I could go on. Make sure you learn them.

Section Two — Christianity

Jesus' Trial and Death

Q1 The Last Supper was a meal to celebrate which Jewish festival? Choose an answer from the options below.

  a) Shavuot   c) Purim
  b) Sukkot   d) Passover

Q2 a) At the Last Supper, what did Jesus foretell about betrayal?

  b) What did Jesus foretell about someone denying that they knew him?

Q3 *Jesus was tried by a religious court.*

  a) Where was the religious trial held?
  b) Did the prosecution witnesses agree with each other?

Q4 Why did the people of Jerusalem tell Pilate to release Barabbas (a murderer) instead of Jesus?

Q5 What did the sign on Jesus' cross say?

Q6 What were Jesus' last words?

Q7 Who gave the news of Jesus' resurrection to the disciples?

Q8 Describe what Jesus told the disciples when he appeared to them after his resurrection.

EXAM-STYLE QUESTION Q9 Explain why the crucifixion and resurrection are so important to Christians. (6 marks)

EXAM-STYLE QUESTION Q10 Give an outline of Mark's account of the Last Supper. (6 marks)

Kind of the whole point of Christianity, this...

There's a lot to learn and remember about the crucifixion and resurrection. You can be asked to retell the whole crucifixion story, or the whole Last Supper story, so get those details well and truly learned.

Section Two — Christianity

Section Three — Judaism

The Beginnings of Judaism

Q1 Describe how Abraham's beliefs about God were very different from those of the people of Ur.

Q2 Where did God tell Abraham to go and live?

Q3 Why did Abraham's descendants go to Egypt?

Q4 For how long were the descendants of Abraham (the Jews) slaves of the Egyptians?

Q5 *The Jews were led out of Egypt and back to freedom.*

   a) Who led the Jews out of Egypt?
   b) How long did it take the Jews to get from Egypt back to the Promised Land?

Q6 Where did Moses receive the 10 commandments?

Q7 Why did the Jewish tribes ask God to give them a king?

Q8 Who built the first permanent Temple in Jerusalem?

Q9 *Jewish beliefs are based around the idea of a covenant with God.*

   a) What did God promise Abraham in the covenant?
   b) What did Abraham have to promise in return?

Q10 When do Jews believe that the whole of Israel will be theirs to live in?

EXAM-STYLE QUESTION Q11 Describe the giving of the Covenant to Abraham and the renewing of the Covenant with Moses. (6 marks)

EXAM-STYLE QUESTION Q12 Describe Jewish beliefs about the Promised Land. (7 marks)

Whoa-oa — the Israelites...

You've heard of Moses... you know that there's 10 Commandments... the name David rings a bell — well that's not good enough come the Exam. You need to know all this stuff like the back of your hand.

Section Three — Judaism

Basic Jewish Beliefs

Q1 Which of the following are believed by most Jews?

> There is only one God.   God denies people free will.
> God is a 'force' — not a person.   God's energy keeps the Universe going.

Q2 What is the name of the prayer which starts, *"Hear O Israel: the Lord our God, the Lord is One"*?

Q3 Why do Jews refer to God as Hashem and Adonai?

Q4 Why do Jews believe that God chose them to be his special people?

Q5 What is Zionism?

Q6 *The Jewish people have been evicted from Israel at several points in history.*

a) When were the Jews exiled to Babylon?
b) Who destroyed Jerusalem in 70CE?
c) What is the name for the time when Jews couldn't live in Israel?

Q7 When was the modern state of Israel established?

Q8 Give a religious reason why some Jews disagreed with the establishment of the state of Israel.

EXAM-STYLE QUESTION Q9 Describe Jewish beliefs about the nature of God.   (8 marks)

EXAM-STYLE QUESTION Q10 Describe the special role that Jews believe they have in the world, and why.   (5 marks)

Section Three — Judaism

Sources of Guidance

Q1 What is the Tenakh?

Q2 Write down the Hebrew word for each of the following:

a) The books of the Prophets

b) The books of the Law

c) The books of psalms, proverbs and philosophy

Q3 Give the names of two prophets whose writings are found in the "Latter Prophets" part of the Tenakh.

Q4 *There are lots of teachings which help Jews to interpret the Torah. Many of these were originally passed on by word of mouth, and were written down later.*

a) Who wrote down the Mishnah?

b) What is the Gemara?

c) What is the name for the Mishnah and Gemara together?

Q5 What is Halakhah?

Q6 *Modern technology raises new and tricky questions for Jews. How do modern Jews decide how to use technology in a way that doesn't break any Torah laws?*

Q7 A Bet Din can play an important role in Jewish life.

a) What is a Bet Din?

b) Give examples of three kinds of dispute that a Bet Din might sort out.

EXAM-STYLE QUESTION Q8 Describe what is in the Tenakh. (6 marks)

EXAM-STYLE QUESTION Q9 Explain why the Talmud is so important. (7 marks)

EXAM-STYLE QUESTION Q10 "The Torah is so old it is impossible to apply it to modern life." Do you agree with this? Refer to Judaism in your answer, giving reasons. Show that you have thought about other points of view. (5 marks)

Torah — didn't she have a few hits in the early 80s...

The 'Jewish Bible' is pretty much the same as the Christian Old Testament. But that's not the only source of religious guidance in Judaism — there are a few other collections of teachings you need to know about too.

Section Three — Judaism

The Holocaust

Q1 What is anti-Semitism?

Q2 Who did the National Socialist Party of Germany (the Nazi party) blame for Germany's problems?

Q3 What did Hitler and the other Nazi leaders call the plan to kill all the Jews in Europe?

Q4 Roughly how many Jews were killed by the Nazis during the Holocaust?

Q5 Give two examples of tricky theological and philosophical questions raised by the events of the Holocaust.

Q6 Explain why the Holocaust has caused some Jews to become atheist (i.e. they have concluded that there cannot be a God).

Q7 Why do some people think it would be impossible for God to destroy all evil people and save all good people?

Q8 Why do some Jews think that since the Holocaust, it's more important than ever to keep practising Judaism?

EXAM-STYLE QUESTION Q9 Explain how the Holocaust has challenged Jewish beliefs, and explain responses to the challenges posed by the Holocaust. (8 marks)

EXAM-STYLE QUESTION Q10 *"All suffering, including the Holocaust, is a test of faith."* Do you agree with this? Give reasons for your answer. Show that you have thought about other points of view. (4 marks)

Section Three — Judaism

Different Jewish Traditions

Q1   What does it mean for someone to be a "secular Jew"?

Q2   There are many different Jewish cultures and traditions.

    a)   Where do Sephardic Jews come from?
    b)   Where do Ashkenazi Jews come from?

Q3   In Judaism, there are two main types of commandment — ritual and moral.

    a)   Which type of commandment do Progressive Jews see as binding and unchangeable?
    b)   Which type of commandment do Progressive Jews think can be changed and adapted?

Q4   The Torah is interpreted differently by Orthodox and Progressive Jews.

    a)   What is the Orthodox Jewish opinion of how people should view the Torah today?
    b)   What is the Progressive Jewish opinion of how people should view the Torah today?

Q5   What ultra-Orthodox Jewish movement was started by a rabbi called the Baal Shem Tov?

Q6   Which Jewish tradition prays for the physical rebuilding of the Temple in Jerusalem?

    a) Reform Judaism   b) Orthodox Judaism   c) Liberal Judaism

Q7   Name two traditions in which women can be rabbis.

Q8   Name one tradition that uses only Hebrew in synagogue services.

Q9   What does Liberal Judaism teach about personal choice in religion?

EXAM-STYLE QUESTION Q10   Describe the major differences between Orthodox Judaism and Reform Judaism.   (8 marks)

EXAM-STYLE QUESTION Q11   "The Torah is God's word. It's wrong to change or adapt it."
Do you agree with this? Give reasons for your answer.
Show that you have thought about other points of view.   (8 marks)

Section Three — Judaism

Judaism and Day-to-Day Life

Q1 How many commandments are there in the Torah?

Q2 What is the Hebrew word for commandment? What about more than one commandment?

Q3 There are different kinds of commandments in the Torah.

- a) What is meant by a 'moral commandment'?
- b) What is meant by a 'ritual commandment'?

Q4 *Jews believe that the commandments and laws given by God are the main way that God communicates with humans.*

What do Jews believe is the best way of responding to God?

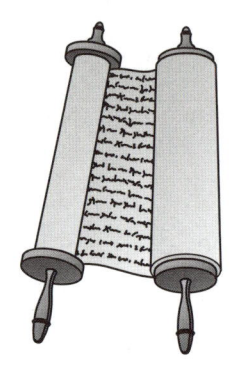

Q5 What two things do religious Jews believe that they should do in order to be considered good moral people?

Q6 When deciding what to do for the best, in what order do religious Jews consider the following Jewish teachings?

> The Talmud   The Torah
> Wider Jewish teaching (e.g. the *Mishneh Torah* commentaries of Maimonides).

Q7 Answer these questions about the mikveh.

- a) What is a mikveh?
- b) When do women go to the mikveh?
- c) When do men go to the mikveh?

EXAM-STYLE QUESTION Q8 Describe a mikveh and its uses.   (6 marks)

EXAM-STYLE QUESTION Q9 Explain how mitzvot are relevant to Jews in their everyday lives.   (8 marks)

Section Three — Judaism

The Synagogue

Q1 Give two other words for "synagogue".

Q2 Which symbols might you see on the outside of a synagogue? Choose from:

> Cross   Seven-branched candlestick
> Shield   Crescent moon
> Six-pointed star Mickey Mouse

Q3 Match each of the four features of a synagogue below to the correct descriptions:

> **Aron Hakodesh** — Raised platform with reading desk, normally in the centre of the hall.
>
> **Ner Tamid** — Large cupboard or alcove, with doors or a screen, set on the wall facing Jerusalem. This is the most important item of furniture in a synagogue.
>
> **Sefer Torah** — Parchment scrolls that must be handwritten by a sofer (scribe), and are usually decorated.
>
> **Bimah or Almemar** — A light which never goes out. It represents the menorah which was always kept alight in the Temple.

Q4 *The rabbi's role is similar in some ways to that of a minister in a Christian church — he leads prayers, conducts weddings and funerals, etc.*

Explain why rabbis are not considered to be priests.

Q5 *Many synagogues have a 'chazan' as well as a rabbi.*

a) Give another name for a chazan.
b) Describe the role of a chazan.

EXAM-STYLE QUESTION Q6 a) Describe the main features of a synagogue. (4 marks)

b) Explain the reasons for these features. (4 marks)

EXAM-STYLE QUESTION Q7 "The synagogue should be the centre of Jewish social life." Do you agree with this? Give reasons for your answer and refer to Jewish beliefs. Make sure you show you've thought about another point of view. (8 marks)

Section Three — Judaism

Signs and Symbols

Q1   Why are there no pictures of God in synagogues, or in Jewish homes?

Q2   The mezuzah is an important Jewish symbol.

   a)   What is a mezuzah?
   b)   Where are mezuzot found?
   c)   What are mezuzot for?
   d)   What Bible passages are contained in a mezuzah?

Q3   Why do many Jewish men and boys wear a yarmulka?

Q4   Tefillin are an important part of Jewish ritual dress.

   a)   What are tefillin?
   b)   Where are tefillin worn?
   c)   When are tefillin worn?
   d)   What Bible passages are contained in the tefillin?
   e)   What do the tefillin remind the wearer to do?

Q5   *Some Jewish men wear a special shawl during prayers.*

   a)   What is this prayer shawl called?
   b)   What are the fringes on the prayer shawl called?

Q6   Describe ritual dress sometimes worn by Jewish men.   (8 marks)

Q7   *"Being visibly different just makes people prejudiced against you."*
Do you agree with this? Refer to Judaism in your answer. Give reasons
for your answer, and show that you have thought about other points of view.   (7 marks)

In the Exam, they might give you some boxes Tefillin...

In the Exam, you can either be asked about a specific piece of ritual dress, or you can be asked to describe the whole lot. So there's only one thing for it... yep, learn everything about everything on this page.

Section Three — Judaism

Judaism and Children

Q1   The ceremony of circumcision is an important rite of passage in Judaism.

    a)   What is the Hebrew name for the ceremony of circumcision?

    b)   How old are Jewish baby boys when they are circumcised?

    c)   What is the Hebrew name for the man who carries out the circumcision?

Q2   How old are Jewish baby boys when they're ceremonially "bought back" from a life in the priesthood?

Q3   What is the Sephardic ceremony for naming a daughter called?

Q4   Give two examples of things that Jewish schools teach on top of the regular school curriculum.

Q5   *Some Jewish festivals have features that specifically involve children. Give two examples of these features.*

Q6   Judaism has different coming of age ceremonies for boys and girls.

    a)   At what age does a Jewish boy become Bar Mitzvah?

    b)   What can a boy wear once he is Bar Mitzvah?

    c)   What are the three parts of a Bar Mitzvah celebration?

    d)   What are Bat Mitzvah and Bat Chayil?

Look, just "no", OK?

EXAM-STYLE QUESTION Q7   Describe the ceremony of Brit Milah.   (5 marks)

EXAM-STYLE QUESTION Q8   Explain why Bar Mitzvah is so important to Jewish families and communities.   (4 marks)

Section Three — Judaism

Jewish Beliefs about Death

Q1   According to the Torah, where do the souls of the dead go?

Q2   What do religious Jews believe will happen to the dead when the Messiah comes?

Q3   According to Jewish tradition, what should a dying person do just before they die?

Q4   Why do bereaved family members make a little rip in their clothes?

Q5   What is done with the dead body immediately after is it washed?

Q6   When they die, Jewish people are often buried in a shroud and coffin.

   a)   What kind of shroud are Jews buried in?
   b)   What kind of coffin are Jews buried in?

Q7   What happens at the funeral service in the synagogue?

Q8   What is the name of the prayer Jewish men recite for the dead?

Q9   Judaism has various customs designed to help comfort the bereaved.

   a)   What is the first week after the funeral called?
   b)   What four things must the bereaved family avoid doing in the week after the funeral?
   c)   What happens in the month after the funeral?
   d)   For how long must someone mourn after the death of a parent?

EXAM-STYLE QUESTION Q10   Describe Jewish rituals and customs related to death, funerals and mourning.   (8 marks)

EXAM-STYLE QUESTION Q11   Explain how Jewish funeral and mourning rituals might help comfort the family of someone who has died.   (7 marks)

There are loads of Jewish teachings about death...
This is quite a heavy page, so to lighten the mood slightly, why not learn a bit of Hebrew... "Ani ohev otach." Which means "I love you," (so I'm told). Which makes for a lovely, warm and fluffy end to the page.

Section Three — Judaism

Jewish Prayer and the Sabbath

Q1   At what times of day are the three daily prayers?

Q2   What is the name for the minimum number of people required to have a service in the synagogue?

Q3   Why do Jews celebrate and rest on the Sabbath?

Q4   *The start and finish of Shabbat varies through the year.*
   a) When does Shabbat begin?
   b) When does Shabbat end?

Q5   *Friday evening services at the synagogue have singing.*
   a) Who leads the singing?
   b) Why is the singing not accompanied by musical instruments?

Q6   Describe the Saturday morning service at the synagogue.

Q7   Write down three things that Jewish families do to prepare for Shabbat at home.

Q8   Who lights the Shabbat candles?

Q9   What is the purifying ceremony at the start of Shabbat called?

Q10   Describe the havdalah ceremony at the end of Shabbat.

EXAM-STYLE QUESTION Q11   Explain why Sabbath observance is so important to religious Jews, and describe the synagogue services that take place over Shabbat.   (7 marks)

EXAM-STYLE QUESTION Q12   "Celebrating Shabbat at home is more important than celebrating at the synagogue."
Do you agree with this? Give reasons for your answer, and show that you have thought about other points of view.   (5 marks)

Section Three — Judaism

Pilgrimage, Food and Fasting

Q1 *In the days when the Temple was still standing in Jerusalem, Jews went to the Temple for three festivals.*

What were the names of these festivals?

Q2 *Three places are particularly important to Jewish pilgrims.*

  a) Where is the Wailing Wall?
  b) What happened at Masada?
  c) What is the Hebrew name for the Holocaust Memorial?

Q3 What is the opposite of kosher?

Q4 For each of these foods, write down if they are kosher or not. If they aren't kosher, write down why not.

  a) Beef   b) Pork   c) Lamb   d) Cod   e) Prawns   f) Eel

Q5 What's the important rule about meat and dairy?

Q6 How must animals be slaughtered to be considered kosher?

Q7 What does fasting symbolise in Judaism?

Q8 What is Rosh Hashanah?

Q9 On Rosh Hashanah, a *shofar* is blown — what does this symbolise?

Q10 Rosh Hashanah and Yom Kippur are known as the *Days of Awe*.

  a) What is Yom Kippur?
  b) What comes between Rosh Hashanah and Yom Kippur?
  c) For how long must Jews fast on Yom Kippur?

EXAM-STYLE QUESTION Q11 Explain Jewish beliefs concerning the significance of the Days of Awe. (8 marks)

EXAM-STYLE QUESTION Q12 Explain what is meant by the Kashrut, and the implications of Kashrut for a Jew's everyday life. (7 marks)

Section Three — Judaism

Jewish Festivals

Q1 *The Jewish festival of Purim is also known as Lots.*

  a) When is Purim?
  b) Whose story does it commemorate?

Q2 What does Shavuot commemorate?

Q3 *In early autumn, Jewish families camp out in shelters they build themselves.*

  a) What is the name of this festival?
  b) What is one of these shelters called?
  c) What does this festival commemorate?

Q4 Describe the events commemorated by Pesach.

Q5 *Before Pesach, Jewish households get rid of all ordinary bread (even the crumbs), all yeast and baking powder and some kinds of flour.*

  Why do they do this?

Q6 Give five components of the Seder meal.

Q7 Which festival celebrates the end of one round of Torah readings and the start of the next one?

Q8 Write down at which festival each of these things happens:

  a) Children play with spinning tops and doughnuts are eaten.
  b) People wear fancy dress costumes.
  c) Cheesecake is eaten.
  d) Men dance seven times around the synagogue.

EXAM-STYLE QUESTION Q9 a) Describe the Passover meal.   (4 marks)

  b) Explain the importance of Pesach to Jews.   (3 marks)

EXAM-STYLE QUESTION Q10 Give an outline of the celebration of Sukkot.   (6 marks)

A nice cheerful page to finish with...

This is a nice page to finish the section with — with its doughnuts and spinning tops and fancy dress costumes. But even though the subject matter's a bit more cheery, it still needs learning.

Section Three — Judaism

Basic Islamic Beliefs

Q1 What is tawhid?

Q2 What is shirk?

Q3 What is the Arabic name for the Muslim declaration of faith?

Q4 *The first part of the Muslim declaration of faith is, "There is no God but Allah."*
What is the second part of the declaration of faith?

Q5 How many times a day must Muslims pray?

Q6 *Muslims wash before prayers.*

   a) Name three parts of the body that a Muslim must wash before praying.
   b) What is the Arabic word for washing before prayers?

Q7 What is Zakah?

Q8 What is Sawm?

Q9 *The Fifth Pillar of Islam is Hajj — a pilgrimage.*

   a) Where do Muslims go on pilgrimage?
   b) What's special about the clothes Muslims wear on pilgrimage?

Q10 Briefly describe Muslim beliefs about Allah, and explain why Shirk is the very worst sin in Islam. (6 marks)

Q11 What are the five pillars of Islam? (5 marks)

Work, don't shirk...

There's more on Muslim beliefs about Allah on p7 and p9 of the CGP Revision Guide. Learn the Arabic names of the five pillars of Islam, as well as the English versions. The Exam paper will probably use the Arabic names.

Prophets and Angels

Q1 *According to Islam, Allah is so great that he doesn't communicate with humans directly — he uses prophets and messengers to carry his messages.*

    a) What is the Arabic word for the idea of having prophets and messengers?

    b) What is the Arabic word for prophet?

Q2 Which of the following statements best describes the way that Allah communicates with humankind?

    a) "Allah gives his message direct to a prophet, who passes it on to everyone else."

    b) "Allah speaks directly to everyone."

    c) "Allah gives his message to angels. Angels pass on Allah's word to prophets, and the prophets pass it on to everyone else."

Q3 Give three ways in which angels are different from human beings, according to Islam.

Q4 How many prophets are named in the Qur'an?

Q5 *There are five Mighty Prophets, according to Islam.*

    a) Who are the five Mighty Prophets?

    b) Who was the first prophet?

    c) Which prophet was asked by Allah to sacrifice his own son, as a test of faith?

    d) Which prophet was given the tablets of the law?

We are the Mighty Muslim Power Prophets.

Q6 Do Muslims believe that Allah gave humans free will to choose their own actions?

Q7 What's the Arabic name for the idea of taking responsibility for the world on God's behalf?

EXAM-STYLE QUESTION Q8 Explain Muslim teachings about khalifah. (8 marks)

EXAM-STYLE QUESTION Q9 Describe Muslim beliefs about risalah. (8 marks)

Section Four — Islam

The Qur'an

Q1   Do Muslims view the Qur'an as the literal word of God?

Q2   How did Muhammad and his followers make sure that none of the revelations of the Qur'an were forgotten or lost?

Q3   Who made sure that there was only one authoritative and 100% correct version of the Qur'an?

Q4   Why is it not really OK to read the Qur'an translated into English?

Q5   Describe three ways that many Muslims show special respect to the Qur'an.

Q6   During which month of the Islamic year is the Qur'an read from beginning to end during services at the mosque?

Q7   The Qur'an is divided up into various parts.
   a)   What is a surah?
   b)   What is an ayat?

Q8   What is the bismillah? Where in the Qur'an would you find the bismillah?

Q9   *There are other important Islamic texts as well as the Qur'an.*
   a)   What are the collected sayings of Muhammad called?
   b)   What is the biography of Muhammad's actions and way of life called?

EXAM-STYLE QUESTION Q10   Explain how the Qur'an and the Hadith affect the daily lives of ordinary modern Muslims.   (7 marks)

EXAM-STYLE QUESTION Q11   Describe Muslim beliefs about the Qur'an.   (8 marks)

EXAM-STYLE QUESTION Q12   "People need a holy book to tell them how to behave."
Do you agree with this? Give reasons for your answer and show you've thought about another point of view. Refer to Islam in your answer.   (5 marks)

Section Four — Islam

The Prophet Muhammad

Q1 When and where was Muhammad born?

Q2 How did Muhammad meet and get to know his first wife, Khadijah?

Q3 Where was Muhammad when Allah sent the angel Jibrail to him?

Q4 Which of the following were parts of the message that Jibrail told Muhammad to pass on to the people of Makkah?

> a) Be honest in business, and look after the poor in society.
> b) Take only one wife.
> c) Worship only one God, Allah.
> d) Prepare for a great flood.
> e) Listen to the words of Muhammad, prophet of Allah.
> f) Do God's will, or you'll end up in Hell.

Q5 Describe how the people of Makkah reacted to Muhammad's preaching.

Q6 Where did Muhammad go in 622?

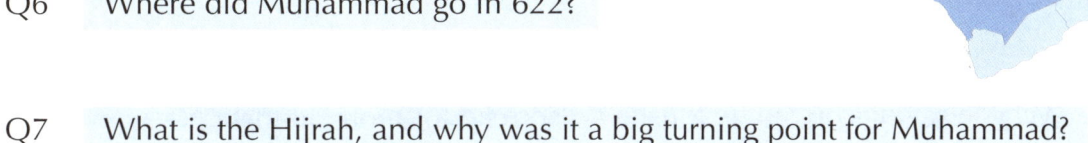

Q7 What is the Hijrah, and why was it a big turning point for Muhammad?

Q8 *Makkah and Madinah went to war.*

> a) What happened at the battle of Badr?
> b) What happened at the battle of Uhud?
> c) When did Muhammad and the Muslims of Madinah take over Makkah?

EXAM-STYLE QUESTION Q9 Describe how God called Muhammad to be his Prophet. (8 marks)

EXAM-STYLE QUESTION Q10 Give an account of what Muhammad achieved after the Hijrah. (6 marks)

You say Mecca, and I say Makkah...

There are some things you just can't afford to go into the Exam hall not knowing. And yep, when it comes to Islam, Muhammad and the Qur'an are two such topics. So buckle down and get the stuff learnt.

Section Four — Islam

Different Islamic Traditions

Q1 What are the two main strands of Islam?

Q2 What were the names of the first four Caliphs?

Q3 Which group accepted the appointment of the fifth Caliph?

Q4 What do Sunnis call the first four Caliphs?

Q5 According to Sunnis, does Allah give anyone after Muhammad special revelation?

Q6 Which Muslim tradition believes that imams are just prayer leaders in the mosque?

Q7 What do Shi'ites call the leaders of Islam who are given special knowledge by Allah?

Q8 *Muslims read the sayings of Muhammad for moral guidance.*
    Whose sayings do Shi'ite Muslims also read for moral guidance?

Q9 Whose martyrdom do Shi'ite Muslims commemorate?

Q10 What are ayatollahs?

EXAM-STYLE QUESTION Q11 Explain the differences between the Sunni idea of religious leaders and the Shi'a idea of religious leaders. (8 marks)

EXAM-STYLE QUESTION Q12 "Muslims should all agree about religion"
Do you agree with this? Give reasons for your answer, showing that you've thought about another point of view. (5 marks)

Ta-caliph out of my book and learn this...

Luckily, you don't need to know the finest details of the history and customs of both traditions, just the basics. The big difference between the two main traditions of Islam is their idea of religious leadership.

Section Four — Islam

Sufism

Q1   What are the aims of Sufism?

"It is not enough to observe the rituals of Islam... A humble soul may be religious even though ignorant of interpretations of the Qur'an. The core of religion is to repent of one's sins, purge the heart of all but God."

Q2   What do Sufis try and do to help them search for the mystical meaning of the Qur'an?

Q3   Which of the following are parts of the Sufi way of life?

> a) Sacred poetry and chanting   d) Meditation
>
> b) Worship of Muhammad   e) Self-denial
>
> c) Trying to live like Muhammad   f) Visits to the beach

Q4   *Most Muslims believe that obeying the rules of Islam is the heart of Islam.*
     What do Sufis believe is the heart of Islam?

Q5   Who are the Whirling Dervishes, and why do they whirl?

Q6   Which female Sufi mystic first described God as "the Beloved"?

Q7   Why do some Muslims disapprove of the Sufi idea of merging with God?

EXAM-STYLE QUESTION Q8   Describe the differences between the Sufi tradition and mainstream Islam.   (6 marks)

EXAM-STYLE QUESTION Q9   Explain how Sufis try to discover hidden mystical truths and become at one with God.   (8 marks)

EXAM-STYLE QUESTION Q10   *"Sufism is a deviation from the right path of Islam"*
Do you agree with this? Give reasons for your answer, showing that you've thought about another point of view.   (5 marks)

Section Four — Islam

Islam and the Shari'ah

Q1   How do Muslims please Allah?

Q2   What happens to Muslims who have failed to please Allah?

Q3   What is the literal meaning of the word Islam?

Q4   What is shari'ah?

Q5   *Shari'ah comes from several sources.*
   What are the three most important sources of shari'ah?

Q6   If Muslim scholars can't find the solution to a new problem by looking in the old books and traditions, what do they do?

Q7   How do scholars and lawyers trust that they'll make the right decision on a point of law?

Q8   Describe a situation where analogy is used to make a judgement on a moral question.

An analogy is when you find a similar situation and apply a rule for that situation to the original one too.

EXAM-STYLE QUESTION Q9   Explain how Islamic scholars and lawyers might decide whether something is right or wrong according to shari'ah.   (10 marks)

EXAM-STYLE QUESTION Q10   "People can only be good Muslims if they read the Islamic holy books." Do you agree with this? Give reasons for your answer, showing that you've thought about another point of view.   (5 marks)

The Shari-ah is a kind of rule book for Muslim life...
While on the subject of words for groups of things (ahem)... it's a little known fact that a group of ferrets is called a 'business', a number of rooks goes by the name of a 'parliament', and several elk gathered together are known as a 'gang'. And what's a 'drunkship'... that's right, a load of cobblers. All true.

Section Four — Islam

Islamic Living and Jihad

Q1   The Shari'ah says that things are either halal or haram.
   a)   What does halal mean?
   b)   What does haram mean?

Q2   What dress rule applies to both Muslim men and Muslim women?

Q3   What is a hijab?

Q4   How must animals be killed in order to be halal?

Q5   Which of the following fats are okay to cook with?
   a) Vegetable oil   b) Beef dripping   c) Bacon fat

Q6   *Muslims must not harm others.*
   Explain why this means that Muslims must not gamble.

Q7   Why are loans and mortgages from Western banks forbidden to Muslims?

Q8   What is the greater Jihad?

Q9   *War to defend Islam against its enemies is part of the lesser Jihad.*
   What else is part of the lesser Jihad?

EXAM-STYLE QUESTION   Q10   Describe what the Qur'an says about suitable clothes for Muslims.   (6 marks)

EXAM-STYLE QUESTION   Q11   Explain why Muslims might have problems dealing with investment and finance in a non-Muslim country.   (6 marks)

EXAM-STYLE QUESTION   Q12   *"You can't expect Muslims to follow the rules on halal food in a non-Muslim country."*
   Do you agree with this? Give reasons for your answer, showing that you've thought about another point of view.   (5 marks)

Section Four — Islam

The Mosque

Q1   Give another word for mosque.

Q2   *Mosques have at least one dome and one minaret.*

    a)   Why do mosques have a dome?
    b)   Why do mosques have a minaret?

Q3   What job does a muezzin do?

Q4   What is the purpose of a mihrab?

Q5   What is a minbar?

Q6   What is the name of the person who leads prayers in the mosque?

Q7   Are women allowed to lead prayers? Choose the right answer from the options below.

    a)   *Women are never allowed to lead prayers.*
    b)   *Women can lead all prayers in the mosque.*
    c)   *Women can only lead other women and children in prayer.*

Q8   Why is the mosque decorated with calligraphy instead of pictures of Muhammad?

Q9   Give two examples of things that Muslims learn at the Madrassah.

Q10   In which tradition of Islam are imams considered holy men?

EXAM-STYLE QUESTION

Q11   a)   Describe the main features of a mosque.   (4 marks)
      b)   What are the reasons for these features?   (8 marks)

EXAM-STYLE QUESTION

Q12   "Muslims can pray anywhere they like, so mosques aren't necessary to Muslim life."
Do you agree with this? Give reasons for your answer, showing that you've thought about another point of view.   (5 marks)

Worship and Prayer

Q1 What is the first pillar of Islam?

Q2 Why do Muslims wash before prayers?

Q3 What is qiblah and why is it important?

Q4 What's the special name for Friday prayers in the mosque?

Q5 Why can daily prayer be difficult for Muslims living and working in non-Muslim countries?

Q6 Between which two times of day must Muslims fast during Ramadan?

Q7 As well as food, which of the following are forbidden during fasting hours in Ramadan?

    a) *Drinking water*   d) *Smoking*
    b) *Drinking milk*   e) *Brushing the teeth with toothpaste*
    c) *Having sex*

Q8 Who can be excused from fasting during Ramadan?

Q9 Write down two things that Muslims believe fasting is for.

Q10 What is the name of the big festival that celebrates the end of Ramadan?

Q11 Whose story is commemorated by the repeated journeys between Safa and Marwa?

Q12 Describe the rituals surrounding salah.   (6 marks)

Q13 Describe and explain what Muslims do on the Hajj.   (12 marks)

What does the Imam sleep on — the five pillows of Islam...

If you've been praying for the end of the book then good news, it's only a couple of pages away.
Only a few more questions on the Five Pillars of Islam, Birth and Death to go.

Section Four — Islam

Birth and Death Ceremonies

Q1   According to Islam, what should be the first word a baby hears?

Q2   How old is a baby when it's named?

Q3   What is the Muslim naming ceremony called?

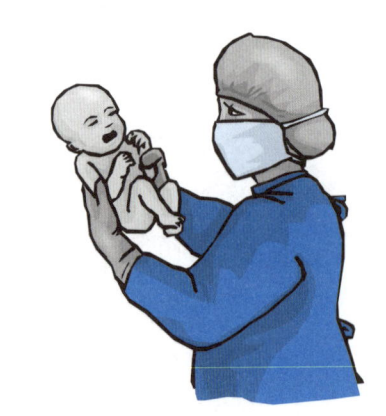

Q4   *Parents donate some gold or silver to charity when the baby is named.*
      How do they work out how much gold or silver to give?

Q5   Is circumcision required for Muslim boys?

Q6   What three things should friends and relatives do to help a dying Muslim?

Q7   How is the body of a Muslim prepared for the funeral?

Q8   *After someone's death, their body must be laid to rest in a certain way.*

   a)   Which side are the dead lying on when they're buried — right or left?
   b)   Where must the dead person's face be pointing?

Q9   How long is the "official" religious mourning period?

EXAM-STYLE QUESTION Q10   Describe a Muslim funeral.   (6 marks)

EXAM-STYLE QUESTION Q11   Describe the ceremony of aqiqa.   (8 marks)

So that's the bend of the book, then...
The final page of the final section is over... so you can relax, take a deep breath and have a nice cup of tea. Then just make sure you can answer any question in the whole book, and you can go do your Exam.

Section Four — Islam

Answers

The Answers

Mark Scheme for Answers to Exam-style Questions
- To get about a quarter of the marks you just need to write a couple of points, in note form.
- To get about half the marks, you need to write several points, in sentences.
- To get about three-quarters of the marks, you need to write a clear description of most of the points, using some specialist religious words (e.g. symbolism, beliefs, attitudes).
- To get all the marks for a question, you need to write a well-written answer, covering almost all the points, using specialist religious words well (e.g. symbolism, beliefs, attitudes, but this time knowing what they mean, not just sticking them in).

Section 1 — Perspectives

Page 1

Q1 b) Why are we here on this planet? and d) Why should we try to be nice to other people? are spiritual questions.
Q2 Non-religious people can have spirituality.
Q3 Christianity.
Q4 Accept any answer from: hijab or veil, modest dress, head covering, leading a virtuous life (chador or burqa are also acceptable).
Q5 This can be considered spiritual.
Q6 Accept any two from: Going to synagogue, wearing a kippah, belonging to local Jewish clubs, praying at home. (There are many other possible answers)
Q7 *Points that could be included:*
- Religious believers often express their spirituality through prayer either alone or with others.
- They may use religious objects like candles or religious pictures to help them to concentrate, or they may read a passage from their Holy Scriptures.
- Sometimes they use special gestures or physical movements to express themselves. Muslims have a special sequence of movements (called rak'ah) to express their prayer. Many Christians kneel or join their hands together.
- Religious believers may wear special religious clothes, for example the clothing worn by Christian priests or Buddhist monks. Others may wear symbols such as the Christian crucifix or the Five Ks worn by Sikhs.
- Some religious believers express themselves through music and singing or through religious art.
Conclusion: Although prayer is maybe the most common way for religious believers to express their spirituality, other ways might include physical movement, symbols, art or music.

Q8 *Points that could be included:*
a)
- People often want to know the purpose of their life, to discover why they are here or what they are meant to do with their life.
- They are often looking for something to believe in or a set of values that they can live by.
- Sometimes they feel that they want to make a difference to the world and to feel that their life has mattered in some way.

b)
- People often experience awe and wonder when they see a beautiful or amazing sight — like a powerful waterfall or a huge mountain.
- It makes them aware that there is something beyond themselves, perhaps a power or force much greater than they are. Religious believers might call this 'God'.
- People sometimes feel as though they are experiencing things on a deeper level. They become aware that there is something more to life than just their ordinary everyday existence.

c)
- A person who is self-aware has taken the time to discover their identity (to find out what kind of a person they really are).
- Self-awareness means knowing our own character, understanding our own feelings and the reasons why we do what we do.
Conclusion: All these things are about recognising that there is more to life than the material things we can see and touch, and that there may be a power or force greater than ourselves.

Q9 *Points that could be included:*
- Spirituality can involve recognising the value and worth of other people. Supporting voluntary organisations is a way of expressing concern for others.
- Christians might belong to or support organisations like Christian Aid or Cafod, which work to help people in developing countries.
- People might get involved by raising money, or they might give up some of their time (for example, to work in a charity shop or to answer telephone calls for groups like the Samaritans).
- Some people might work for organisations that are helping to improve the environment, doing conservation work or caring for wildlife.
- Helping a voluntary organisation may give people a sense of self-worth. It helps them to feel that they are doing something positive and worthwhile.
Conclusion: Many religions teach their followers to care for those in need, but you don't have to be religious to be spiritual or to support or belong to a voluntary organisation. For some people spirituality is about recognising the value of all human life and of the natural world and trying to improve the quality of life for everyone.

Page 2

Q1 a) Scientific truth
    b) Moral truth
    c) Religious truth/spiritual truth
Q2 Accept any two from: Evidence can be unreliable. Eyewitness accounts can be biased. Evidence is open to different interpretations. (or similar answers)
Q3 Religious truth cannot be proven.
Q4 a) Yes, there is evidence.
    b) No, you could argue that the child was lying.
    c) There is no definite proof either way in the description of the scene.
Q5 a) The Bible, the Qur'an, the Hadith, the Torah, the Tenakh (and any other sensible answers).
    b) No, people interpret scripture in different ways.
Q6 Humans aren't perfect, and it's not possible to be 100% sure that someone speaks on behalf of God.

The Answers

Q7 *Points that could be included:*
- All the major religions believe that their holy books have come to them directly or indirectly from God. For this reason, many religious believers would argue that the scriptures are the only reliable source of religious truth.
- For example, some fundamentalist Christians would accept every word in the Bible as being true and without error.
- Muslims would also see the Qur'an as the actual word of God and without error.
- However, some Christians believe that, although the Bible is the main source of authority, there are other ways of learning the truth about God. They might think that religious truth can be found in the teachings of their Church, or through their conscience or in their own experiences of prayer.
- Many Christians also believe that the Scripture needs to be interpreted. This means that you have to take into account the time and the circumstances in which the passages were written before trying to work out the message they are giving to people of today.
- Others would say that religious leaders and teachers often discover important truths and that they can help people to find new insights (new ways of seeing things).
- Muslims also use the Hadith as a guide, which is a collection of the sayings of the prophet Muhammad.
- Jews believe that the Tenakh is God's word but some might also argue that these scriptures need to be interpreted if people are going to be able to really discover the truth they contain. For example, Jews have a book called the Talmud, which is a collection of teachings interpreting the Jewish laws found in the Torah.
Conclusion: Although most religious believers consider their Holy Scripture to be the main source of religious truth, some believe that it is not the only source of truth.

Q8 *Points that could be included:*
- Holy books are used by all the world's major religions and are sometimes known as scriptures. Jews call their religious books the Tenakh, Muslims have the Qur'an and Christians use the Bible.
- Muslims believe that the words of the Qur'an were given by Allah to the prophet Muhammad and were recorded exactly as he heard them. They are so important that they cannot be altered, so Muslims always use the Qur'an in Arabic.
- The Qur'an is seen as having been revealed by God and as a complete guide to life. Some Muslims try to learn the whole Qur'an by heart because it is so important to them.
- The first five books of the Jewish Tenakh are called the Torah. They contain all the laws and teachings that help Jewish people to live as God wants.
- Jews believe that the word of God should be always close to their mind and heart. For this reason some Jewish men wear tefillin (little boxes containing sections of the Torah) strapped to their head and arm as they pray.
- The Christian Bible is divided into the Old Testament and the New Testament. Christians believe that it tells the story of the relationship or covenant between God and people.
- The Old Testament contains the same books as the Jewish Tenakh. The New Testament is particularly important to Christians because it contains the teachings of Jesus, whom they believe to be the Son of God.
Conclusion: All three religions believe that their sacred writings come from God, and so are one of the ways in which God communicates with people. The books are treated with great respect and seen as an important source of authority and guidance.

Page 3

Q1 Yes, they're more likely to be religious.

Q2 Two valid reasons, for example: some people are drawn to the good works done by religion; some people are drawn to the structure and security of religion; some people have religious experiences which strengthen or initiate their religious belief.

Q3 a) "The world is so complicated and intricate. It couldn't have got that way by chance." and b) "Mathematical truths are simple and beautiful. They must be meant to be that way." are arguments from design.

Q4 No, not everyone is convinced by arguments from design.

Q5 a) Atheists and agnostics have rational scientific explanations for miracles.
    b) Scientific atheists believe that Darwin's theory of evolution explains how living things are suited to their habitats.

Q6 *Points that could be included:*
- A divine creation may lead people to believe in the sanctity of life.
- Sanctity of life is the belief that all life is sacred and should be valued and preserved.
- If each person is a result of divine creation, then there must be some good in everybody.
- Everyone is connected and each person has value in the world.
- There is order and purpose in the world, even if we do not understand the purpose.
- If the earth was the result of divine creation, then people should treat it with respect and preserve the environment.
- If God created animals, then they should be treated with respect.
Conclusion: A belief in divine creation would make an individual value all forms of life and the world around them. This would have an effect on what they believed about many issues, such as war, poverty and capital punishment, abortion, as well as animal rights and treatment of the environment.

Q7 *Points that could be included:*
- Our bodies and minds are so complex, that they show evidence of an intelligent designer.
- The world around us, our bodies and minds are so complex that they could not have come about by chance.
- Most religions in the world believe that we are the result of a divine creation.
- Most sacred writings contain stories of creation.
- Each person has a soul. Some people see this as evidence of a creator.
- However, fossils and other evidence prove that creatures have evolved over millions of years.
- There is lots of evidence which suggests that humans have evolved, rather than been created.
- There is no scientific evidence that we have been created.
Conclusion: Scientific theories of the big bang and evolution remove the need for a creator, and can explain how life began. However, some people argue that human beings and the world around them are so complex that they must have been designed and created.

Q8 *Points that could be included:*
- People search for a sense of meaning, order or purpose in their lives and find it in a religion.
- A person may wish to marry someone religious and have to convert to his or her religion in order to do so.
- Many religions give a clear set of moral guidelines by which people can live their lives. Some people feel they need this kind of structure in their lives.
- Someone has a religious experience such as witnessing a miracle or hearing God through prayer and become religious.
- Somebody could study a religion and find themselves drawn to it.
- An inspirational person or family, friends, or a partner could influence somebody to convert to a religion.

The Answers

- An individual might experience a sense of awe and wonder, maybe inspired by the world around them or a religious building.
  <u>Conclusion:</u> There are many reasons why a person might convert to a religion. It could be as a result of something they have experienced that has convinced them, whether it be something amazing, such as a miracle or simply a feeling of closeness with God through prayer. It may be that the religion offers something they want, such as a sense of meaning in their lives or a clear structure of beliefs and morals.

Page 4

Q1   An experience of awe and wonder at the world.
Q2   A miracle is an event that can't be explained by the laws of nature.
Q3   Praying is a conversation with God. People can feel that God is more real when they talk to Him. People can feel that prayers are answered, which makes God seem more real. (or similar answers)
Q4   Any three from: singing, dancing, crying, having visions, talking or singing in unknown languages, making predictions of the future.
Q5   The Holy Spirit
Q6   Meditation
Q7   a)   General revelation
     b)   Special revelation
     c)   Special revelation
Q8   <u>Points that could be included:</u>
- Charismatic worship emphasises the gifts of the Holy Spirit, especially gifts like preaching, healing or speaking in tongues.
- This type of worship is often very informal. There will be readings from the Bible, but there will also be time for spontaneous prayer from any member of the group. People also believe that the Holy Spirit sometimes reveals special messages or prophecies which they share with the rest of the group.
- There is also an emphasis on praising God, particularly through singing hymns. People may raise their hands in the air as a symbol of praise or might even dance.
- Sometimes people pray in tongues. This sometimes happens when people get so caught up in praising God that they can no longer find the words to express their prayer, so it is as if the Holy Spirit gives them a new language to help them to pray. These prayers are sometimes interpreted or explained for others.
- Sometimes there is a time of healing during the service, when members of the group lay hands on and pray for those who come forward.
  <u>Conclusion:</u> This type of worship is most common in Pentecostal Churches, although some other Christian Churches also have charismatic prayer groups. Those taking part believe that it is important to remain open to the gifts of the Holy Spirit and to allow the Spirit to work through them as they pray.

Q9   <u>Points that could be included:</u>
- People might feel they have experienced God in different ways — e.g. through reading Scripture, through prayer, through meetings with other people or an experience of the natural world.
- Experiences of God may help to deepen a person's faith because they feel that they have a personal relationship with God, helping them to feel that they are loved and valuable.
- Sometimes people feel as though God is speaking directly to them when they are reading the Scriptures. They may feel that God is challenging them to put their faith into practice, for example by working for peace or trying to get rid of poverty.
- Powerful experiences of prayer and worship, or experiencing healing or prophecy, may also help to strengthen a person's faith, which may make them feel more open to God.
- An amazing sight in nature may remind people that there is a power greater than they are and make them more aware of their place within the universe.
- Sometimes when people are experiencing times of doubt, they say that meeting another person who shows great faith or goodness or courage helps them not to give up on their own faith.
- Occasionally people have other types of experiences of God. They may experience a sense of God's presence which gives them courage at a particularly difficult time. Some claim to have seen a vision, although this is quite rare.
  <u>Conclusion:</u> Religious experiences can help to strengthen a person's faith, as they come to know God better and develop a deeper relationship with Him.

Page 5

Q1   Not all religious thinkers agree.
Q2   a)   A person can pray to a personal God.
     b)   A personal God has emotions.
     c)   It's hard to imagine a person being everywhere in the Universe at the same time — an impersonal God who is more like a force can be imagined everywhere more easily. It's hard to imagine a God you can converse with, being everywhere, and talking to lots of other people at the same time as they're listening to your prayers.
Q3   An immanent God is present in the Universe.
Q4   A transcendent God is outside the Universe.
Q5   Both at once.
Q6   b) Hinduism and f) Old Norse and Ancient Greek religions are polytheistic.
Q7   <u>Points that could be included:</u>
- Some experiences of God may make more sense if someone already has a close personal relationship with God. For example, Jews, Christians and Muslims may feel that God is communicating with them when they read the Scriptures.
- Many Christians would say that prayer helps them to feel close to God and to develop their relationship with God. Prayer might feel more like a conversation with a friend.
- However, not all believers see God as someone with whom they can have a close personal relationship. This does not necessarily mean that they can't experience God. They may have a sense of a power or force greater than themselves, rather than a person they can relate to.
- It is possible that a person who does not have a personal relationship with God may not be open to experiences of God and may not recognise them if they happen. This may not always be true, though.
- However, sometimes people of no religious faith do have experiences of God and this is the beginning of their relationship with God. They come to know God as a result of their experience.
  <u>Conclusion:</u> Religious experiences may help a person's relationship with God to grow stronger. However, people sometimes experience God as a power or force rather than a person and may only start to believe in God because they have first had some sort of experience of God's presence.

Q8   <u>Points that could be included:</u>
- When people talk about an immanent God they usually mean a God who is present in the world and involved in it.
- Many believers also think of God as omnipotent (all-powerful) and omniscient (all-knowing). They therefore expect God to be able to get rid of all evil and suffering.
- The problem with this idea is that if God is in the world, then this limits God because God has to work within the limits of time and space.

The Answers

- Many people look at all the suffering in the world and wonder why God does not act to end it. They may decide that either God does not know or care about what is happening, or that God does not have the power to prevent it.
  Conclusion: Believers have many different ideas about God and sometimes these ideas seem to contradict each other. This is why some people might think that God is not able to overcome the suffering and evil in the world.
- Q9 *Points that could be included:*
  - When people describe God as immanent, they mean that God is near at hand, present in the world and involved in it.
  - Describing God as transcendent means that God is above and beyond all things. God exists outside time and space and is completely separate and uninvolved in the world.
  - When people say that God is personal this does not mean that God is like a human being, but it does mean that God is someone with whom they can have a relationship, like a person.
  - Sometimes God is described as impersonal, more like a power or force.
  - The difficulty is that some of these explanations of God seem to contradict each other. It does not seem possible for God to be both involved in the world (immanent) and completely beyond the world (transcendent). People might also wonder how God can be both personal and impersonal at the same time.
  - If God is completely transcendent, then no-one could ever get to know God, but religious believers speak of a God who communicates with them.
  - On the other hand it might seem impossible that a God who is present in the world has the power to have created it.
  - However, many religious believers do accept all these conflicting ideas. Hindus, for example, see Brahman as impersonal, but believe that Brahman can be approached through the many different personal gods worshipped by Hindus.
  - Christians believe in the Trinity — God as three in one. God is seen as the transcendent creator of the world. However, Jesus Christ might be seen as the immanent, personal aspect of God and the Holy Spirit as the impersonal power of God, active in the world today.
  Conclusion: Although many of these ideas about God seem to contradict each other, many believers find them a helpful way of describing their different experiences of God. The words help to explain their belief in a God who is the all-powerful creator of the world, but who also continues to be actively involved in the world and who cares for the people in it.

Page 6

Q1 Omniscient = All-knowing. Omnipresent = everywhere in the Universe at the same time.
Omnipotent = All-powerful.
Q2 Christians believe in the Trinity — God as three people in one. Jews believe that God is one person.
Q3 The Shema says that God is one.
Q4 a) Jesus Christ
b) God the Father
c) The Holy Spirit
Q5 The Devil brings evil and suffering to humankind.
Q6 There is no Devil in modern Judaism.
Q7 *Points that could be included:*
- There is only one God, but He is present in three forms - the Father, the Son and the Holy Spirit.
- God the Father is described as all-powerful and the creator of heaven and earth.
- God the Father does not act directly in the world but exists outside the world.
- God the Son is Jesus Christ — the incarnation of God on earth. Jesus Christ was born of a virgin.
- Jesus Christ came down to earth to sacrifice Himself for mankind — to save them from sin.
- Jesus Christ was crucified by the order of Pontius Pilate but rose from the dead three days later. The resurrection of Jesus means that all humans will have the chance to be resurrected.
- When Jesus went to heaven, the Holy Spirit remained.
- Jesus sits at the right hand of God in heaven.
- Jesus Christ will come back to earth in glory one day and will judge all people.
- The Holy Spirit is God's presence on earth.
- The Holy Spirit guides, comforts, and inspires humans.
Conclusion: The Creed explains the Trinity as the three aspects of God. Christians believe in only one God that has shown Himself in three different ways: as the Father - God that created heaven and earth, the Son - God that came down to live, suffer and die as a human to save mankind and the Holy Spirit - God that is present and working in the world today.
Q8 *Points that could be included:*
- Christians believe the devil is evil and tempts humans to do evil things.
- In the Bible, Adam and Eve were tempted by the devil into committing sin.
- In the New Testament it is described how the devil tempted Jesus for forty days and nights in the desert - remembered by Christians today during the festival of Lent.
- Some Christians believe that the devil is a real presence of evil in the world and fights against God to gain possession of peoples' souls.
- Some Christians believe people can be controlled by the devil and be possessed by demons.
- Some Christians also believe that humans have the power to cast out these demons through exorcism.
- Some Christians believe that the devil causes all the evil and suffering in the world today.
- Those Christians who believe in the existence of hell believe that the devil is in control of hell.
- Some Christians believe that the devil is a symbol for the evil in the world, rather than an actual being.
Conclusion: Many stories in the bible refer to Satan, and different Christians have very different views about him. However, all agree that the devil represents evil. Many Christians believe that the devil is a name given to the force of evil in the world. Others claim the devil is a real presence, responsible for the evil and suffering in the world through natural disasters and his ability to tempt humans to do evil things.

Page 7

Q1 Islam is monotheistic.
Q2 The literal translation of Allah is God.
Q3 a) Allah has 99 names in the Qur'an.
b) Allah is (four answers from): All-powerful, Merciful, Just, Compassionate, The Truth, The Forgiver (or any four of the 99 names of Allah)
Q4 Muslims see Allah as both immanent and transcendent.
Q5 Allah has intervened in human history.
Q6 Muslims believe the Qur'an is the word of God.
Q7 25 prophets are mentioned in the Qur'an.
Q8 Muhammad is the last prophet of Allah.
Q9 *Points that could be included:*
- It is impossible to picture what Allah is like - he is the Supreme Being and he has no equal. It's certainly not possible to draw a picture of him.
- God is seen as omnipresent (everywhere) as well, so this causes a problem thinking how a personal God can also be everywhere.
- Allah is 'outside' and 'beyond' both his creation and time itself.

The Answers

- He is not drawn, and is not seen; but he is near to us.
- We can see his wrath, his creations, his miracles and his power, but not Allah himself.
- Allah is seen through his 'messengers', called Prophets.
- As with any religion, belief in the nature of Allah is a matter of faith.
  Conclusion: We cannot know for certain what Allah is like. Muslims have faith in his nature, but this is not the same as having proof. So you could argue that we cannot know for certain. But a believer will believe for certain that he/she does know the nature of Allah.

Q10 *Points that could be included:*
- Islam is a monotheistic religion, meaning there is one God, Allah is one.
- Allah is a supreme being without equal.
- Allah is the creator and judge of humans - he knows everything we do.
- Although we have free will, our lives are predestined by Allah.
- Allah is immanent - the Qur'an refers to us as 'nearer to him than his jugular vein'.
- Allah is the power behind the Universe, so he is transcendent - outside and beyond his creation.
- In the Qur'an he is given ninety-nine names, showing aspects of Allah and his power - these include 'The Just', 'The Hearer' and 'The Merciful.'
  Conclusion: Muslims believe Allah is the Supreme Being and creator, and that Allah has no equal. Islam teaches that Allah is in our lives and has an awareness of all our actions, and that one day he will be our judge.

Q11 *Points that could be included:*
- Muslims feel we can know Allah through the message given to mankind by the prophets.
- Twenty five prophets are mentioned in the Qur'an including Adam, John the Baptist and Jesus.
- The last prophet, Muhammad, brought the final message of Allah to mankind.
- This final message is contained in the Qur'an, which provides guidelines Muslims try to live by.
- We can get closer to Allah by following the five pillars of Islam, these being: Shahadah (belief), Salah (regular prayer), Zakah (making donations to charity), Sawm (fasting in Ramadan) and Hajj (pilgrimage to Makkah).
  Conclusion: Many Muslims will try to learn the Qur'an by heart, as this is the word of Allah, and what they feel will bring them close to him. Also, living life according to the Five Pillars of Islam is believed to help Muslims get to know Allah.

Page 8

Q1 Flood, drought, earthquake, hurricane.
Q2 Human-made evil.
Q3 Famine can be caused by war.
Floods can be caused by deforestation. (or similar answers)
Q4 a) Some people think an all-powerful God should be able to prevent evil.
b) Some people think that God should answer people's prayers to stop suffering and evil. Not all prayers are answered.
Q5 Suffering can test the belief that God does things for the best. To pass the test, a person would cope with the suffering and accept it as God's will. They might think the suffering has a purpose in the long run.
Q6 Christians and Jews believe that evil was not in the world from the start.
Q7 a) Original Sin
b) The Fall
c) It was up to them, they did it of their own free will.
Q8 Satan was an archangel, but was thrown out of heaven. He is the personification of evil (the Devil).

Q9 *Points that could be included:*
- Some Christians feel that if we abuse the power of free will which God gave us, then we deserve to suffer.
- Christianity teaches that Adam and Eve brought suffering and evil into the world by disobeying God. Evil and suffering are therefore a consequence of disobeying God.
- Some people feel that those who live unholy lives will be punished by God.
- Some Christians feel that it is often innocent people who suffer. They try to see this as a test of faith.
- Many people suffer because of things like floods, earthquakes and hurricanes. They can't all have deserved it.
- Christians believe that innocent people often suffer because other people abuse the free will which God gave us.
- Christianity teaches that we should accept suffering just as Jesus accepted his suffering. Christians feel that it is important to show compassion to those who are suffering.
  Conclusion: Difficult to explain why innocent children get killed in natural disasters. It seems unlikely that they deserve to suffer. On the whole, disagree with the statement. Christianity teaches that suffering is a test of our faith and that faith in God can help us through times of suffering.

Q10 *Points that could be included:*
- According to Christianity, evil entered the world when Adam and Eve gave in to temptation in the Garden of Eden.
- Christians believe that God created humans with free will. This means that we can choose whether to commit evil deeds or not.
- Some Christians feel that evil is caused by Satan (the Devil). In the past Christianity taught that someone who performed evil deeds was possessed by the Devil.
- Some Christians believe that evil is a supernatural force which causes people to perform evil deeds.
  Conclusion: Some Christians believe that evil is caused by people abusing free will, while other Christians feel that evil is caused by the Devil.

Q11 *Points that could be included:*
- Christianity teaches that suffering and evil came into the world because Adam and Eve gave into temptation in the Garden of Eden.
- The change from paradise to a world with evil and suffering is known as "The Fall". We all suffer because we all have Original Sin.
- Christianity teaches that suffering is a test of our faith in God.
- Christians feel that those who experience suffering can find strength and support in their belief in God.
- Christianity teaches that we should accept suffering just as Jesus accepted the suffering he experienced.
- Many Christians feel that although we might not know why God allows people to suffer, he does have his reasons.
  Conclusion: Christians feel that human weakness brought suffering into the world and that when we experience suffering our faith is being tested.

Page 9

Q1 Judaism says we have free will.
Q2 a) Job questions God, but he does not curse Him. He accepts his suffering.
b) Job eventually accepts his suffering as part of God's plan.
Q3 Two reasons from: Suffering can bring people closer together. Suffering brings people closer to God (and makes them pray more). Suffering gives people an opportunity to help each other.
Q4 a) Allah allows Shaytan to tempt us because temptation is a test of our faith.
b) People have free will to give in to Shaytan or to resist him.
Q5 a) Allah tests people by making bad things happen to them.
b) Accepting suffering and continuing to trust Allah is the right thing to do.

The Answers

Q6 Allah forgives Muslims if they are truly sorry and pray for forgiveness.
Q7 *Points that could be included:*
- The Jewish view of suffering includes the idea that good can come from suffering.
- Some Jewish people believe that suffering can help to bring people closer together.
- Some Jewish people feel that suffering gives people the chance to make sacrifices for others.
- According to some Jews suffering means that people have to draw on their inner strength and faith in God. This can bring them closer to God.
- However, Judaism does not teach that all suffering has good results.
- Jews believe that suffering is a test of faith - some people fail that test and turn away from God.
- Suffering can make people bitter and could lead to them losing their faith in God.
Conclusion: Judaism teaches that suffering can have good results although it depends on the way people respond to it.

Q8 *Points that could be included:*
- Muslims believe that humans should accept suffering.
- Islam teaches that even though we may suffer in this life there will be joy in the afterlife.
- Muslims feel that Allah uses suffering to test us and to see if we will remain faithful to him.
- However, Muslims believe that Allah gave humans free will so we are responsible for a lot of the suffering in the world.
- Islam teaches that humans cause a lot of suffering by going against Allah's will.
- It is hard for anyone, including Muslims, to accept that innocent people should suffer as part of God's plan.
Conclusion: Suffering is difficult for anyone to accept, Muslims try to see suffering as a test of their faith in Allah. Since Allah is all-powerful, suffering must be part of his plan.

Q9 *Points that could be included:*
- Muslims feel that suffering is a way in which Allah tests humans.
- The Qur'an teaches that it is important for humans to stay faithful to Allah even when we suffer.
- Muslims believe that even if we suffer in this life there will be joy in the next life because Allah is compassionate.
- Muslims believe that they should tolerate suffering and remember that the most important thing is to remain faithful to Allah.
- Muslims believe it is important to be sympathetic to those who are suffering. Many Muslims are involved in working to help those who are suffering. Muslims feel that prayer is a way of coping with suffering.
- Muslims feel that suffering is a part of life that we cannot avoid.
Conclusion: Muslims feel that suffering is a test of our faith in Allah, if we pass the test we will be rewarded in the next life.

Page 10

Q1 The Big Bang Theory — the theory that the Universe began in an explosion of matter and energy out of nothing.
Q2 The Theory of Evolution (or Darwinian Evolution) — the theory that all plants and animals evolved from single cells over millions of years.
Q3 a) Taken literally, this contradicts scientific theories.
b) The religious explanation can be interpreted symbolically.
c) Space, the Earth, the atmosphere, plants, animals, people.
d) Same as c)
Q4 Orthodox Jews see Genesis as literally true.
Q5 Liberal Jews see the creation story in Genesis as a symbolic way of helping us understand Creation — not literal truth.
Q6 The Qur'an creation story is the easiest to square with science.

Q7 *Points that could be included:*
- Some scientists argue that the Universe began with an explosion. This theory is known as the Big Bang theory.
- Scientists argue that matter produced by the Big Bang formed the stars, planets and everything else.
- Scientists say the fact that the Universe is still changing and growing proves the Big Bang theory is true.
- Many scientists agree with Charles Darwin's theory of evolution. He argued that all life on earth gradually developed from single cells.
- The theory of evolution argues that humans have evolved over millions of years. The theory also says that humans evolved from apes and not from Adam and Eve.
- However, although there is a lot of evidence for these scientific theories, they cannot be conclusively proved.
- Even if evolution and the Big Bang Theory are correct, it does not mean that they were not initiated by God.
Conclusion: Although science provides a different idea of how the world was created this does not necessarily mean God does not exist. Science may tell us how the world came to exist while religion tells us why. The scientific theories cannot be conclusively proved either.

Q8 *Points that could be included:*
- Christian belief about the origin of the world is based on the idea that God created everything.
- The Christian creation story is outlined in the book of Genesis.
- According to the Bible it took God six days to create the universe and everything in it. First God created the heavens and Earth, then the atmosphere, land and sea, and finally plants, animals and people.
- The Bible says that humans are descended from Adam and Eve, the first people, not evolved from apes as Charles Darwin argued.
- Some Christians take the Bible's description of the origin of the world literally.
- Others see it as a symbolic description of an evolution which took millions of years and not six days.
Conclusion: Different Christians have slightly different ideas about how the world began but they all share the common belief that God is the overall creator.

Q9 *Points that could be included:*
- Some religious believers like Orthodox Jews find it hard to accept scientific theories while others, for example Muslims, are less likely to disagree with scientists.
- Some Christians take the Bible literally and they believe that God created the universe and everything in it in six days.
- Some Christians believe the Bible gives a symbolic description of a gradual evolution so they are able to accept scientific theories of creation.
- Orthodox Jews believe the Torah is the word of God and literally true so they find it hard to accept scientific theories about creation which challenge their ideas.
- Liberal Jews would suggest that the Torah should be used to understand creation and not explain it so they would be more open to scientific ideas.
- Muslims believe that Allah created the world and everything in it.
- The Qur'an's account of creation is similar in many ways to the scientific theories so Muslim ideas don't have to compete with the Big Bang theory or Darwinism.
Conclusion: How religious believers react to scientific creation theories depends on how they interpret scripture. Those who are more flexible can normally accept scientific explanations as well as the ideas in the scripture.

Page 11

Q1 The soul
Q2 Not everyone believes in life after death.

The Answers

Q3 a) People who have near-death experiences may see a bright light, and see what they believe is a glimpse of heaven. They may see and hear long dead family members.
b) Not everyone agrees that NDEs are proof of an afterlife.
c) NDEs may be caused by a lack of oxygen in the brain.

Q4 Ghosts and the paranormal are considered to be evidence for an afterlife.

Q5 a) A person must live a good life and accept the teachings of Jesus.
b) All the people in Heaven.

Q6 Hell is seen as being cut off from God's love for eternity.

Q7 Purgatory is a place where people are cleansed of their sins before they can go to Heaven. Roman Catholics believe in Purgatory.

Q8 Answer should say that Christians believe people go to heaven if they repent of their sins before they die. Answer should also mention that some Christians believe that everyone can be saved by God's grace.

Q9 *Points that could be included:*
- Christians believe that when we die our souls live on after our physical bodies die.
- Christians believe the soul goes on to either Heaven or Hell, depending on how you lived your life on earth.
- Christians see Heaven as a paradise where those who have lived a good life according to Jesus' teaching will spend eternity with God.
- Hell is seen as the opposite to Heaven; a place of pain and suffering where the souls of non-believers and people who lived bad lives go.
- Some Christians believe Heaven and Hell are real places but others see them as states of mind.
- Some Christians believe those who don't live spiritual lives are destroyed completely and their soul does not survive death.
- Roman Catholics believe in Purgatory which is a place where people are cleansed of their sins before their soul enters Heaven.
- Protestants don't believe in Purgatory because it is not mentioned in the Bible.
- Some Christians believe that even those who live sinful lives can find salvation because of God's saving power.
  Conclusion: Christians believe that although our physical body dies our soul goes on living. Depending on how we live our lives we may spend eternity in the paradise of Heaven or the torment of Hell.

Q10 *Points that could be included:*
- Some people, for example Christians, believe that when we die our soul goes on living.
- Some people believe that when we die there is no life after death.
- Some people say they see dead people and that this proves there is life after death.
- People have reported seeing ghosts and experiencing other paranormal events for centuries.
- However, many scientists say that paranormal events can be explained scientifically and that even if we can't explain everything now, we will be able to explain it at some time in the future.
- Christians have faith in Jesus' teaching that our souls survive physical death. They don't need any further proof.
  Conclusion: There is no scientific proof of a life after death, however this does not stop many people, including Christians, believing in an afterlife.

Q11 *Points that could be included:*
- Roman Catholics have different ideas to other Christians about what happens to a sinful person's soul after death.
- Roman Catholics believe that if you admit your sins and ask for forgiveness you can find salvation, even if you have led a sinful life.
- When a sinful person dies Catholics believe that their soul may either go straight to Hell or to a place called Purgatory.

- Those who have committed serious or mortal sins go straight to Hell, other sinners go to Purgatory.
- Purgatory is a place where people are cleansed of their sins before the soul can move on to heaven.
- The idea of Purgatory isn't in the Bible so Protestants don't share the Roman Catholic view.
  Conclusion: Roman Catholics believe that the souls of sinful people do not necessarily go straight to Heaven or Hell and they may go to Purgatory where sinful souls can find salvation.

Page 12

Q1 Sheol is where early Jews believed that the dead went. Sheol is damp and dark.

Q2 Modern Jews believe that Heaven is an eternity with God, and Hell is a place of punishment. Those who have lived good lives go to Heaven.

Q3 Jews believe that non-Jews can go to heaven if they have lived good lives.

Q4 Jews believe that the body and the soul both go to heaven or hell.

Q5 This means that people could be punished by God for things their parents and grandparents had done.

Q6 a) At the end of the Messianic Age.
b) Orthodox Jews don't cremate the dead.
c) They believe that only the soul will be judged by God, and the body is just a vessel for the soul.

Q7 *Points that could be included:*
- All Jews believe that death does not signify the end, that we exist both before birth and after death.
- Some Orthodox Jews believe that the soul goes to a spirit world when we die.
- One of the Thirteen Principles of the Faith is the belief in the resurrection of the dead. Orthodox Jews believe that people will be resurrected in their body.
- Orthodox Jews believe that God will create a new world, rebuilding Jerusalem and the Temple — an idea of heaven. The good will go to heaven, the bad to hell.
- Hell is not seen as a place of eternal torment to Jews, it is regarded as a cleansing process — so people who have been sent to hell may yet earn a place in heaven.
- Some Orthodox Jews believe only good Jews will live eternally in Jerusalem, while others believe that all good people will receive this reward.
- Jews believe that God is merciful to those who repent and those who can are expected to make a deathbed confession.
  Conclusion: Orthodox Jews believe that our time on earth is just a small part of our existence, and that after we have died, certain people will go to heaven (which may or may not include non-Jews, depending on your beliefs).

Q8 *Points that could be included:*
- Many Jews believe that our time on earth is a small part of our existence and people are on earth to carry out specific tasks.
- Reform Jews argue that we should concentrate on fulfilling our purpose on earth whilst we are here because we cannot know or understand what comes next.
- The preservation of life is the most important principle of Judaism and many Jewish laws are based upon this precept. So you could argue that Jews are more concerned with this life than the next.
- Jews believe you cannot get to heaven by committing good deeds for the motive of reward, which would encourage people to concentrate on life on earth and not a future afterlife.
- However, the idea that earthly life is such a small part of our existence would encourage people to focus on the afterlife.
  Conclusion: Some Jews would agree with the comment because preservation of life is one of the most important teachings of Judaism. However, since life on earth is such a small part of our existence, Jews would encourage people to focus on what comes next. It is difficult to separate the two, as to achieve happiness in the next life, Jews must live correctly in this life.

The Answers

Page 13

Q1 Akhirah is life after death.
Q2 Yawm-ud-din is the day of judgement.
Q3 Islam says people are judged on their character, their reactions to good and bad events, and their way of life.
Q4 The Muslim Paradise has gardens and birdsong, and it's very beautiful and peaceful.
Q5 The Muslim Hell is called Jahannam. It's full of fire, hot winds and black smoke.
Q6 Islam says we have free will.
Q7 Muslims should accept bad things as the will of Allah.
Q8 Humans know that they will die one day, animals don't.
Q9 *Points that could be included:*
- Muslims call the soul the ruh and believe that this is the real person — not the body that the ruh lives in.
- Muslim beliefs state that when a person dies, their body will stay in the grave until the Day of Judgement, when the body will be restored and be reunited with the soul.
- The soul is then judged by Allah.
- Muslims believe that Allah will show mercy to those souls that have repented during their lifetime.
- He will judge them not only on their actions, but also their intentions.
- Those Muslims who have chosen to do good or repented of the evil they have done will go to Paradise - a state of joy, happiness and peace. Here the soul will exist for eternity.
- Those Muslims who have chosen to do evil and not repented will be sent to hell, called Jahannam in the Muslim tradition, and which is described as a place of torment.
- Muslims believe that after death the soul lives individually and eternally in Akhirah, not bound by earthly relationships.
Conclusion: Muslims believe that every person has a soul, which is judged on the Day of Judgement. Those souls that have lived good lives and repented of evil will spend eternity in paradise, whilst those who have chosen evil will be sent to Jahannam.

Q10 *Points that could be included:*
- All Muslims believe in Akhirah (life after death), and a Day of Judgement (when all people will be raised from the dead and have to account for what they have done in their life on earth).
- Muslims believe that life on earth is a test and everything that happens to them is Allah's will. This may provide comfort during difficult times in their life as they look forward to entering Paradise.
- Muslims feel there is a purpose to our lives on earth and will not aimlessly wander through life and waste it as they may fail the test.
- Muslims are aware of God in everyday life and this prevents many Muslims from doing things that would give them selfish pleasure.
- Muslims will ask Allah's forgiveness for wrongs they have done so they can get to Paradise.
- Muslims will keep the Five Pillars and read the Qur'an because that is what Allah has instructed them to do.
- Muslims will follow the Shari'ah — the code of behaviour for Muslims.
- Muslims believe that Allah takes life when He is ready and will not mourn too long over someone, as death is a part of life.
- Muslim funerals reflect beliefs about Akhirah, with bodies always buried facing Makkah, ready for the Day of Judgement.
Conclusion: The idea that they will be facing Allah on the Day of Judgement encourages Muslims to follow the rules of their religion. Muslims may also find hope and strength in times of despair at the idea that if they past the tests that Allah has put before them, then they will spend eternity in Paradise.

Q11 *Points that could be included:*
- Muslims believe that Allah is merciful and will forgive people who ask Him.
- Muslims believe that Allah can forgive a person for all the bad things they have done as long as they ask for forgiveness before they die.
- Most Muslims believe that all non-Muslims will go to hell, as well as bad Muslims.
- However, other Muslims believe that Allah is merciful and may allow these people into Paradise.
- Muslims beliefs state that if a person dies fighting for Islam, then they will go straight to Paradise. This could mean bad people getting to Paradise.
Conclusion: Muslims believe that Allah is merciful and will admit bad people to Paradise who have repented for the evil they have done, and some believe that anyone who has died fighting for Islam will go straight to Paradise (including some bad people).

Page 14

Q1 Up until the 24th week.
Q2 The quality of life of the unborn child.
Q3 The Roman Catholic Church says abortion is unacceptable. The Roman Catholic Church believes that life begins at conception, therefore abortion is murder. It also goes against humankind's obligation to 'be fruitful and increase in number'.
Q4 If the pregnancy is a result of rape, if the mother's health is at risk, if there is no way the mother could cope with a child.
Q5 The Roman Catholic Church says contraception is wrong.
Q6 The "sanctity of life" argument says that we do not have the right to prevent a new life beginning, or to take a life — it's all up to God.
Q7 Voluntary euthanasia, or assisted suicide.
Q8 Relieving suffering is a compassionate thing to do. Also, Jesus commanded his followers to love their neighbour.
Q9 Medical resources would go to people who could be cured, not on keeping people alive who don't want to be alive. But, old people could feel pressurised to die before they're ready to.
Q10 *Points that could be included:*
- Christians believe that life is precious and that people are valuable because they were created by God.
- All life is believed to be a gift from God, so human beings do not simply have the right to take it away. Most Christians would agree that the foetus deserves to be protected. They would not support abortion in all circumstances. In 1983 the Church of England said that it would like to see a reduction in the number of abortions.
- However, some Christian churches (but not the Roman Catholic Church) would say that in certain circumstances abortion may be allowed, and that this may sometimes be the most compassionate thing to do.
- These might include situations where to continue the pregnancy would endanger the mother's life, or where the woman has become pregnant as a result of rape.
- Some groups, like the Methodists, also believe that it is right to take into account the circumstances in which the mother is living, including her family responsibilities and her financial situation.
Conclusion: Christians basically all agree that abortion is undesirable and that the foetus has rights and needs to be specially protected. However, some Christians would allow abortion in certain circumstances — they argue that it is important to show compassion and support for the woman whatever she decides to do.

Q11 *Points that could be included:*
- The Roman Catholic Church teaches that life begins at conception. Therefore they would consider the embryo or foetus to be a separate human being. It cannot be seen as simply part of the mother's body.

The Answers

- To support this view they might quote the part of the Bible which says, "You created every part of me; you put me together in my mother's womb."
- Roman Catholics believe in the sanctity of life. This is the belief that life is holy because it is a gift from God, so human beings do not have the right to take it away. As far as Roman Catholics are concerned this applies to the unborn child as much as to any other human being.
- As a separate person, the unborn child has rights of its own. Therefore it is not simply the mother's choice whether or not she has an abortion.
- The RC Church would see abortion as the killing of another human being, going against the fifth commandment "You shall not kill."
  Conclusion: Roman Catholics would argue that abortion is not the woman's choice alone because they see the foetus as a separate person from the moment of conception. They also believe that life is sacred. God gave life and so only God can take it away.

Q12 *Points that could be included:*
- One of the main arguments that Christians would use against euthanasia is that no human being has the right to take another person's life (which would still be true in the case of voluntary euthanasia, where a person has asked someone else to help them to die).
- Christians believe that the commandments forbid the taking of a human life - they believe that God created life so that only God can take it away.
- Some people are also concerned that if voluntary euthanasia were made legal the elderly or the terminally ill might feel under pressure to die rather than to continue to be a burden to their families, even though really they want to go on living.
- It would also put extra pressure on doctors and nurses. They are trained to save life not to end it.
- A person may make the decision to die when they are not rational enough to make the decision (perhaps because they are in great pain). They might also change their minds but be unable to let their doctors or families know.
- Some people also use the 'slippery slope' argument. They say that euthanasia devalues human life. Once we accept that it is acceptable to end the life of a very sick or elderly person, where do we draw the line and who makes the decision?
- Euthanasia allows people to avoid the responsibility of finding new ways of caring for the dying. Euthanasia would not be needed if there were better resources.
- Many Christians would say that euthanasia is unnecessary because there are alternatives, like the care given by hospices. These try to help people who are dying to face death with dignity. Patients are given pain relief and encouraged to talk about their fears and feelings about death.
- Christians might also say that what is really needed is a change of attitude towards the sick and the dying. Jesus always showed compassion for the sick. For example, he healed the Roman officer's servant and the woman with the severe bleeding.
  Conclusion: For Christians life is God-given and precious. They believe that it is important to show compassion and care for the sick and dying, but many Christians believe that they do not have the right to deliberately end a person's life.

Page 15

- Q1 a) Bad
- b) Bad
- Q2 This is considered to be OK by most Jews.
- Q3 Not all rabbis agree on abortion.
- Q4 Suicide is a sin in Judaism.
- Q5 This is considered taking a life, and wrong.
- Q6 It would be acceptable to switch off a life-support machine etc., to speed the death of a suffering patient.

Q7 *Points that could be included:*
- Jewish people believe that life is a gift from God so life is seen as sacred.
- Jews believe that those who feel despair should turn to God for help and salvation.
- Jews believe that only God can give life and only God can take life away.
- Judaism teaches that suicide is a sin.
- Those who commit suicide are buried in a different part of the cemetery from other Jews.
- Jews feel that anyone who takes their own life is rejecting God's gift.
  Conclusion: Jewish people believe that taking your own life is wrong and that people who do so are playing God.

Q8 *Points that could be included:*
- Judaism traditionally teaches that a child is a gift from God.
- The Bible teaches that it is important to have children.
- Judaism is generally opposed to contraception and abortion.
- However, most Jews are happy with the use of contraception for family planning.
- Most Jews feel contraception is acceptable if a woman might be harmed mentally or physically by pregnancy.
- Most Jews would accept contraception or abortion when the child is likely to be severely disabled.
  Conclusion: Although Judaism teaches that having children is important most Jews would accept contraception or abortion if the child was at serious risk of being severely disabled.

Q9 *Points that could be included:*
- Jews believe that a new life is a gift from God.
- Contraception and abortion both prevent new life from entering the world.
- Judaism teaches that it is important to have children but abortion and contraception both prevent this.
- Judaism teaches that abortion and contraception interfere with God's plan for who should live and who should die.
- However, most Jews feel contraception is an acceptable way of family planning.
- Some forms of contraception are considered more acceptable than others.
- Jewish people generally feel that abortion is worse than contraception because abortion prevents a potential life coming into the world.
- Jews do not believe that abortion is an acceptable way of family planning.
  Conclusion: Jewish people would generally consider abortion to be less acceptable than contraception because abortion ends a potential life, whereas in the case of contraception, a potential life has not yet been created. However, neither are seen as ideal.

Page 16

- Q1 a) True b) False c) True
- Q2 Abortion is permissible if the mother's life is in danger.
- Q3 a) Faiza and her husband can use condoms or the pill. It's OK to use contraception to avoid having a child you can't afford. Contraception must be reversible, so you can change your mind.
  b) It's not OK to get a vasectomy. Permanent sterilisation is frowned upon.
- Q4 It would be acceptable for them to use contraception.
- Q5 Euthanasia is not acceptable
- Q6 They should accept it as Allah's will, pray and wait.

Q7 *Points that could be included:*
- Muslims believe that all life is a gift from Allah - life is sacred and He decides when it begins and ends.
- Many Muslims argue that conception is the will of Allah. There are passages in the Qur'an to back this up. For example, "He bestows male and female children…and He makes barren whom He wills."

The Answers

- Islam teaches that contraception is not a particularly welcome practice. However, there are occasions where it may be permissible.
- If contraception is used, only 'reversible' methods are acceptable to many Muslims. This means vasectomies and sterilisation are not permitted.
- Condoms and the Pill would be acceptable because they are not permanent. The rhythm method is often used. This is a natural method and therefore permissible in Islamic teaching.
- Contraception is allowed if the woman concerned already has children, or if pregnancy would threaten her health.
- Contraception is allowed if the child has a high chance of being born with a disability,
- Contraception may be allowed if the family is too poor to properly raise a child.
  Conclusion: Islam teaches that contraception is generally unwelcome. However, if the child or the mother may be at risk then some forms of contraception would be permissible.

Q8 *Points that could be included:*
- The practice of ending someone's life because they are having to endure terrible suffering and want life to end is called euthanasia or assisted suicide.
- Muslims believe that all life is created by Allah — only He can decide when it begins and when it ends.
- Islam teaches that euthanasia is therefore wrong, and most Muslims would probably agree with this point of view, meaning it is not our place to decide when a life should come to an end.
- Islam also teaches that the suffering we endure on Earth is a test — Allah knows why we suffer because he has a plan for everyone. One of the 99 names of Allah is Ar-Rahman — The Merciful. On Judgement Day the reasons for our suffering shall be revealed.
- Many Muslims argue that those who suffer should turn to Allah for help through prayer.
- Suicide is also viewed as wrong by many Muslims.
  Conclusion: Muslims do not believe that they have any right to decide when a life should end — only Allah has that power and those who are suffering should turn to him for guidance.

Page 17

Q1 Artificial Insemination by Husband — sperm from the husband is used to fertilise the wife's ovum.
Q2 Artificial Insemination by Donor — sperm from a donor (from a sperm bank) is used to fertilise the wife's ovum.
Q3 AID is seen as being too much like adultery — the child conceived is another man's biological child.
Q4 Spare embryos are used for research or thrown away.
Q5 The Roman Catholic Church believes life begins at fertilisation, and that all human life is sacred. They believe that the embryo has rights to life, and killing spare embryos would be a sin.
Q6 a) Jewish teaching emphasises the importance of having a family — being fruitful and multiplying.
   b) The rabbi might say that the egg would have to come from a Jewish woman, or the child might not be considered Jewish.
Q7 *Points that could be included:*
- Christian, Muslim and Jewish teaching on fertility treatment are quite similar, and could have a major influence on a couple's choice of treatment if they are having difficulty conceiving naturally.
- All three faiths teach that a child is a gift from God — this means they all allow some methods of fertility treatment.
- Many Christians believe that it is okay for science to assist a couple in conceiving — as long as the eggs and sperm of the couple are used.
- IVF (In Vitro Fertilisation) and AIH (Artificial Insemination by the Husband) are seen as permissible in all three faiths because no 'third party' is involved in the process.
- Islam and Judaism believe that using donated sperm is comparable with adultery, so if the couple are Muslim or Jewish they would probably not use that.
- In Judaism, if a donated egg is used the couple might request that it comes from a Jewish woman.
- Judaism places a great deal of emphasis on having a family — it would be left to the individual couple to decide whether they require treatment or not.
- The Roman Catholic Church has stricter teachings on fertility treatment because it believes that life begins at conception. For example, IVF can lead to the production of 'spare' embryos which, in Britain, can be experimented on for up to 14 days — this might make the couple less interested in this form of treatment if they are Catholic.
  Conclusion: Depending on the couple's religious beliefs, there are various treatments they could use if they are having difficulty conceiving. Christianity, Judaism and Islam have quite strong views on the use of fertility treatment and the couple will perhaps be guided by these.

Q8 *Points that could be included:*
- AID (Artificial Insemination by Donor) is a method of fertility treatment where sperm from an anonymous donor is used.
- Many Muslims believe that this method is a sin — it is seen as being similar to adultery.
- This is because the woman has become pregnant using the sperm of a man other than her husband.
- There is also a belief amongst some Muslims that using anonymous sperm may lead to disease.
- Other forms of fertility treatment are generally accepted by Muslims as long as the husband's sperm is used.
- Although Judaism teaches that other methods of fertility treatment are generally acceptable, it teaches that AID is not permissible.
- Again, this is because the sperm of another man is being used — it may be seen as a form of adultery.
  Conclusion: Jews and Muslims generally see AID as unacceptable because the sperm used to help the woman conceive is not that of the husband — it is seen as a form of adultery by many Jews and Muslims.

Q9 *Points that could be included:*
- Roman Catholics see children as a gift from God, and believe it is good to have children.
- However, the Roman Catholic church is opposed to IVF.
- Many Catholics believe that life begins at fertilisation. This means that an embryo is seen as having similar rights to an adult.
- IVF treatment usually involves the creation of surplus embryos. These can be used for experimentation, or thrown away.
- This is seen as similar to abortion or even murder, because the embryo is killed.
  Conclusion: The Catholic Church is opposed to infertility treatment because it results in the creation of surplus embryos which are killed.

Page 18

Q1 Fewer people are getting married.
Q2 More couples are living together without being married.
Q3 Marriage is for two people to support each other, and for having children.
Q4 a), c) and d) are genuine Bible teachings
Q5 Christianity says that sex before marriage is not ideal.
Q6 a) The couple and witnesses must confirm that there is no reason why they can't marry.
   b) The priest or minister declares the couple married.
   c) The priest or minister says what Christian marriage is all about.

The Answers

Q7 *Points that could be included:*
- All weddings have different parts — some are religious and some are for legal reasons.
- Hymns may be sung praising God (they may have some special significance to the couple getting married). Prayers are said to bless the marriage.
- The Vicar or the Priest will make an opening statement saying what marriage is all about and why it is so important.
- Everyone attending the wedding will be asked if they know of any good reason why the couple should not be married. This is called the Declaration.
- The couple make vows (or promises) to each other and to God.
- Rings are given to the bride by the groom and vice versa. This symbolises a circle that should not be broken.
- The Vicar or the Priest announces to everyone that the couple are now husband and wife. This is called the Proclamation.
- A register is signed by the bride, the groom and the witnesses to make the marriage legal.
- There will be a final piece of worship (called Closing Worship) including blessings and prayers for the couple and the rest of the congregation.
- If it is an Orthodox Christian wedding, crowns are placed on the heads of the bride and groom.
- In a Roman Catholic wedding, the service will include Nuptial Mass. This is where the bride, the groom and the rest of the congregation take the bread and wine, representing the body and the blood of Christ.

Conclusion: A Christian marriage ceremony has a number of different symbolic parts — some of these are religious, some are legal and some change depending on which Christian denomination the couple are.

Q8 *Points that could be included:*
- Committed Christians believe that sexual activity should only take place within marriage. (However, many modern Christians would argue that this idea is a little outdated nowadays).
- A Christian would try not to be promiscuous — this means they would see it as wrong to have many sexual partners (even if they did not want to wait until they were married to have sex).
- Christian teachings say that Christians should not have sex with (or even have lustful thoughts about) someone they are not married to. One of the 10 Commandments is 'Do not commit adultery' (Exodus 20:14). When Christians get married they promise to be faithful and should stick to that.
- However, many Christians would try to be tolerant and understanding towards someone who had 'given in to temptation'.
- Christians believe that a couple should wait to have sex until they are married. Marriage makes sex special.
- In the U.S.A. organisations using slogans like 'True Love Waits' and 'Chastity Before Marriage' try to encourage young Christians to remain virgins until they are married.
- Some Christians might believe that homosexuality is wrong. - Christianity doesn't see same-sex relationships as the ideal although many liberal Christians have campaigned for gay and straight people to be viewed equally by the Church.
- Being a Christian might affect the kinds of contraception a couple use. The Roman Catholic Church, for example, believes that all 'unnatural' methods of contraception are wrong.
- Some really committed Christians may just give up sex altogether. Monks, nuns and Catholic Priests should not have sexual relationships — this is known as celibacy.

Conclusion: A committed Christian would have quite strong views about the role of sex and would argue that the only suitable place for it is within the context of marriage — they would argue that it is a very special gift and, therefore, adultery and sex before marriage are wrong. Their beliefs would affect their life quite significantly.

Q9 *Points that could be included:*
- Many Christians believe that there are many positive reasons to keep sex within marriage.
- To have sex outside of marriage would be against the teachings of the Bible.
- However, some Christians would say that the Bible was written in a time when cultural values were different and that things have changed since then. Bible teachings should be adapted to modern society.
- Sex is seen by Christianity as the ultimate sign of love. It is, therefore, very special and should not be entered into lightly. Self-control is important.
- Once married, Christian couples are supposed to be faithful to each other and not have sexual relationships with anyone else.
- However, many progressive or liberal Christians would say that in this day and age, sex before marriage may be acceptable. They would not promote promiscuity (having many sexual partners).
- Sex within marriage is still the ideal though.
- In modern Western culture, many non-religious people argue that it is good to have sex before marriage and live with a partner.

Conclusion: Many Christians would say that sex outside of marriage is a sin because sex is only permissible within the confines of married life. However, in modern society, many people (including some Christians) argue that this is impractical and that sex outside of marriage is not a sin.

Page 19

Q1 A nuclear family is mum, dad and kids.
Q2 Reconstituted families are step-families — where a parent has a new partner.
Q3 One in three marriages end in divorce.
Q4 a) The Roman Catholic Church.
    b) Catholics believe that marriage makes husband and wife one flesh, and they are inseparable.
Q5 Annulment is a declaration that marriage never really happened in the first place.
Q6 Iris can get an annulment because the marriage was not consummated — the couple didn't have sex, so they aren't really one flesh.
Q7 Jesus said that remarrying after divorce was like adultery.
Q8 c) is true
Q9 *Points that could be included:*
- One in every three marriages now end in divorce in the U.K. The old idea of husband, wife and 2.4 children is now much less common — the structure of families is changing.
- There are now more single-parent families and reconstituted families (where people who have been divorced remarry) than there were in the past. Christians believe that the ideal family is one where a mother and a father are present (preferably the child's natural parents).
- Some Christians, however, would argue that if a couple are no longer in love, or the marriage is not providing a stable and safe environment for the children, then divorce may be the only reasonable solution.
- Different Christian denominations have different opinions. The Church of England believes divorce is acceptable but divorced people cannot necessarily remarry in Church.
- The Roman Catholic Church sees marriage as a sacrament (something made by God) — it is, therefore, not actually possible to get a divorce.
- There are passages in the Bible which say that divorce is wrong. (ie. Mark 10: 2-12).
- The Church of Scotland will allow divorced people to remarry if the minister believes the new marriage would be a committed one. Remarriage would then be seen as a new start and a sign of God's forgiveness.

The Answers

- Other Christian denominations (for example Baptist and Methodists) will remarry people, but again, it is up to the individual minister concerned.
  <u>Conclusion:</u> Christians differ in their attitudes to remarriage after a divorce. Some denominations believe it is acceptable whilst others do not believe it is even possible as marriage is something created by God's love.

Q10 <u>Points that could be included:</u>
- Christians generally agree that divorce is not ideal. People should not enter into marriage lightly in the first place.
- If couples do have problems when they are married, most Christians would argue that they should work at solving them instead of ending the marriage. With God's help and strength they may be able to sort out any difficulties.
- However, sometimes problems cannot be solved. If this is the case, many Christians would say that divorce is acceptable. People should not be together if they are really unhappy.
- If children are involved, some people might argue that parents should stay together. However, it might be more better that the child is brought up in a happy, safe and secure environment with one parent, than in an unstable and volatile environment with two.
- Families are changing. More people divorce nowadays and there are many single-parent and reconstituted families in modern western society.
- Some people believe that marriage is outdated and unnecessary. People can live together, have children and be happy without having to go through a ceremony first.
- The Roman Catholic Church believes that marriage is made by God (it is a sacrament) and therefore cannot be broken. Catholics cannot divorce, but they can choose to live apart.
  <u>Conclusion:</u> One in every three marriages ends in divorce. Christians generally agree that divorce is not ideal, but many do believe that it is acceptable if the couple are unable to solve their problems or if the marriage is not a happy and secure environment for children.

Page 20

Q1 i) is true
Q2 As an emotional, intellectual and spiritual union.
Q3 They worry that the kids won't be brought up to be religious Jews.
Q4 A matchmaker who helps to find husbands and wives for Jewish people.
Q5 The marriage contract.
Q6 A chuppah or huppah.
Q7 To remind everyone of the destruction of the Temple in Jerusalem.
Q8 A religious divorce.
Q9 In Reform Judaism, the Bet Din can grant women a divorce if their husbands refuse to give them one.
Q10 <u>Points that could be included:</u>
- There are differences between the various Jewish communities. However there are some common features of all Jewish weddings.
- The groom will give the bride a valuable object, such as a ring.
- The 'ketubah' or marriage contract, which sets out the woman's right to be looked after by her husband, is read out.
- At least two eligible witnesses must be there to observe the ceremony.
- The ceremony will take place under a huppah, or chuppah, which is a wedding canopy. This is a piece of cloth supported by four poles, the cloth representing privacy and the open sides hospitality.
- A rabbi conducts the service and says prayers over the couple.
- The groom will break a glass with his foot in memory of the destruction of the Temple in 70CE.

- After the service, a festive meal with dancing follows. People will shout 'mazel tov!' (good luck, best wishes). In an Orthodox Jewish ceremony, men and women will dance separately.
  <u>Conclusion:</u> Marriage is a time of celebration for Jews. The giving of a ring, blessings being said by a rabbi and the feast afterward are common elements to weddings in several religions. Other aspects such as the breaking of a glass by the groom, and holding the ceremony beneath a huppah, are special to the Jewish faith.

Q11 <u>Points that could be included:</u>
- Divorce is difficult within the Jewish Faith, but it is allowed. It is called 'get'.
- This is an absolute last resort, and all attempts at reconciliation must have failed.
- A woman cannot initiate a divorce, but her consent is required for one to take place.
- The Jewish Court (the 'Bet Din') connected to Reform synagogues can free a Jewish woman to remarry if her husband will not grant her a 'get'.
- Orthodox Synagogues do not allow this. A woman may be called an 'agunot' or chained woman. This means that she wishes to get a divorce but her husband will not grant her one.
  <u>Conclusion:</u> Although not easy, it is generally possible for a Jewish woman to obtain a divorce. She would have to show that reconciliation had been attempted. The role of the Jewish Court in the reform synagogues allows women to get a divorce even if their husband doesn't want one. But in Orthodox communities the woman would require the agreement of her husband for the 'get'.

Q12 <u>Points that could be included:</u>
- About 40% of UK Jews 'marry out' of their faith, in other words they marry non-Jews.
- The Jewish faith has relatively few followers compared to Christianity or Islam. Many Jews worry that children of 'mixed marriages' may not be brought up within the Jewish faith.
- Some may see 'mixed marriages' as a 'dilution' of Judaism. In the Orthodox Tradition conversion into Judaism is extremely difficult — you have to be born Jewish. This means a non-Jewish spouse cannot convert.
- Many may feel that non-Jewish partners would not take the faith and its traditions as seriously as their Jewish partner.
- On the other hand, new members coming into the faith can be positive. It broadens views and gives a healthy new 'membership'.
- In more multicultural societies such as the UK young Jews may also resent having to choose their partners only from within their faith. Unless allowed to marry who they choose they might leave their religion.
  <u>Conclusion:</u> Accepting non-Jewish partners can be seen as a possible threat to the ancient traditions of the Jewish faith. In some Jewish groups, such as the Parsees, the children of mixed marriages are not accepted as members of the religion, and you cannot convert into the faith. Marrying out, can therefore cause the children of a Jew to be brought up outside the Jewish faith. This is worrying as there are relatively few Jews.

Page 21

Q1 Muhammad was married.
Q2 The sexual instinct is strong and needs to be channelled.
Q3 To bring up children, and for companionship.
Q4 When young people have boyfriend/girlfriend relationships, they will be tempted to have sex, and Islam says sex before marriage is wrong.
Q5 Nikah = the marriage contract
    Mahr = Dowry.
    Khutbah = A speech given after the
    marriage vows.
    Hadith = A saying of Muhammad, read out after the marriage vows.

The Answers

Q6   A man can say "I divorce you" three times, and that's it.
Q7   a)   Three months.
       b)   Divorce by talaq.
       c)   No, it's not part of British law.
Q8   *Points that could be included:*
- Muslims are taught that marriage is very important.
- Divorce is permitted in Islam but only if it is impossible to save the marriage.
- If a couple are having marriage problems a member of each family is appointed as an arbiter to try and solve the problems.
- Muslim teaching says that if a man says "I divorce you" three times then the marriage is over. This is known as divorce by "talaq".
- There is normally a three month period after the husband's first declaration of "I divorce you". This is to give the couple time to think things over and also to make sure that the wife is not pregnant.
- A woman can divorce a man in the same way but only if it was a condition in the marriage contract.
- A woman can also apply for divorce by "kuhl" through a Shari'ah court.
  Conclusion: Islam teaches that divorce should be avoided if possible, however, if all attempts to save a marriage fail then divorce is permitted. Divorces are relatively quick and easy.

Q9   *Points that could be included:*
- Islam teaches that marriage is very important and Muhammad himself was married.
- Muslims generally want their children to marry other Muslims because marriage to a non-Muslim can cause problems.
- Muslims generally believe that young men and women should not mix freely so dating is often forbidden.
- Islam teaches that divorce should be avoided. Muslim parents try to pick a partner for their child who is well suited to them and will work to make the marriage last.
- In most Muslim communities it is traditionally the responsibility of the parents to find a suitable partner for their children.
- Muslims feel that it is important that the families of the bride and groom are as well suited as the bride and groom themselves. The families meet to get to know each other before a marriage is arranged.
- Some Muslim parents use marriage agencies or even newspaper advertisements to help find suitable partners.
- If things go wrong in the marriage, parents have a responsibility to try to solve the problems.
  Conclusion: Islam teaches that divorce should be avoided. Muslim parents chose their children's marriage partners to try to ensure that their children enter into stable and secure marriages.

Q10 *Points that could be included:*
- Islam teaches that marriage is recommended because it provides companionship.
- Muslims are taught that Allah intended people to find a partner so that they could share love and comfort.
- Islam teaches that the companionship of marriage provides security and stability.
- However, Islam also teaches that marriage is a way of channelling and controlling the sexual instinct.
- Marriage is also important in Islam because it provides a secure environment for raising children as good Muslims. Islam teaches that marriage is not only important for the married couple but also for any family that they may have.
- Muslims feel a good marriage demonstrates the importance of being kind, considerate and affectionate to each other.
  Conclusion: Islam teaches that marriage is important because it provides companionship but Muslims also feel that it serves other vital purposes.

Page 22

Q1   Sex outside of marriage is traditionally seen as wrong.
Q2   Having lots of sexual partners.
Q3   Polygamy is not permitted in Christianity and Judaism.
Q4   Four.
Q5   a)   No, he shouldn't take a second wife. He should only marry again if he can support two wives.
       b)   Absolutely not. A man must treat his wives equally according to the laws of Islam.
Q6   16 years old.
Q7   b) is the general view.
Q8   *Points that could be included:*
- Polygamy is the practice of a man being married to more than one woman.
- Islam allows polygamy but it doesn't encourage it.
- Islam permits a man to have as many as four wives.
- Before a man can take another wife he must have the permission of his first wife.
- Islam only allows a man to have more than one wife if he can support them and treat all of them equally.
- Today polygamy is not as common as it was in the past and some countries have actually banned it.
  Conclusion: Islam does allow polygamy although it is not recommended and men can only take more than one wife if they are able support them all and treat all their wives equally.

Q9   *Points that could be included:*
- Christian religious scripture seems to say that homosexuality is wrong.
- In the past Christianity taught that homosexuality was a sin and should not be allowed.
- Some Christians now interpret the Bible's references to homosexuality differently.
- Some Christians today say that the scriptures were written at a very different time so we cannot apply them to modern society.
- Most Christians don't condemn homosexuality now, but it is still not seen as the ideal.
- Same-sex marriages are now recognised in the United Kingdom, but they're called 'civil partnerships'. Churches can't marry homosexual couples, but registry offices can. Some churches will bless homosexual civil partnerships.
- Christian homosexuals may choose celibacy. This means they don't have sexual relationships at all.
- Homosexuals who remain celibate are generally more acceptable to most Christians.
  Conclusion: Although Christianity does not condemn homosexuality any more, most Christians would still advise against same-sex sexual relationships. Christian teachings may encourage a gay man to remain celibate.

Q10 *Points that could be included:*
- Most religions are based on scriptures which were written a long time ago.
- When the main religions of the world began people and society were very different from the way they are today.
- Some people argue that religions do not try hard enough to adapt to modern sexual attitudes and behaviour. Society has become far more accepting of different sexual orientations and the idea of sex before marriage. Religions are not as accepting.
- Many people feel that it is wrong that people should be excluded from religion because of their sexual orientation or sexual practices.
- However, many religious people have tried to adapt their views of sex to the modern world.
- Religions and religious beliefs are always changing and developing as society changes and develops. If religions didn't adapt then they would lose their relevance.
- Some religious people argue that it is the modern world which is out of touch with religious beliefs and common morality.

The Answers

- Some people argue that if people don't follow religious guidelines on sexuality then they are disobeying God. Religions should not change their teachings just to accommodate social change.
  Conclusion: Generally, religion does lag behind modern attitudes towards sex, although some religious groups are more progressive. Most religious beliefs developed a long time ago so some argue it is important that people try to adapt their beliefs to the modern world. However, others argue that religions should not necessarily alter their teachings just to fit in with modern trends.

Page 23

Q1 a) sums up the Jewish and Christian view.
Q2 Islam says that parents should be fair and just.
Q3 Grown up children should look after aged parents, according to all three religions.
Q4 a) Everyone is born a Muslim, in submission to Allah.
Q5 No one is born Christian.
Q6 The baby must be born to a Jewish mother.
Q7 *Points that could be included:*
- In Christian families, children might try to follow the commandment: "Honour your father and mother."
- Young children could do this by listening to their parents and trying to respect their wishes. They might also help out with some of the chores at home, rather than expecting their parents to do everything.
- Adults might interpret this commandment by trying to take care of their parents in their old age, by remembering to keep in touch and visiting them, or caring for them if they become ill.
- St Paul says that children should obey their parents, but he also warns parents not to provoke their children. This means that parents should not make unreasonable demands on their children.
- The importance of children is stressed in wedding ceremonies in the Roman Catholic Church and in the Church of England. Parents believe that they have a responsibility to nurture their children (to help them to grow), not just physically but mentally, emotionally, morally and spiritually.
- For example, they would try to teach their children right from wrong and set a good example of the kind of behaviour they expect.
- They would also teach their children about their beliefs, perhaps by introducing them to Bible stories, teaching them how to pray and taking them to church.
- Many Christian parents would say that the most important thing of all is to show their children that they love and accept them, no matter what they do.

Conclusion: Whether it is within a nuclear family (parents and children), or an extended family (including grandparents, aunts, uncles, cousins), Christians believe that they have a responsibility to help their children to grow and develop into mature adults. Christians also believe that they have the responsibility of sharing their beliefs with their children.

Q8 *Points that could be included:*
- Most parents who hold religious beliefs feel that one of their most important responsibilities is to pass on their beliefs to their children.
- However, children grow up in a society where people hold many different religious beliefs or none. There are lots of other influences on children outside the home. It is also natural for children to ask questions. This may cause them to challenge what they are taught at home.
- Sometimes children reject their parents' beliefs as they grow up and parents often find this very hurtful or difficult to cope with.
- Some parents think that they should not put pressure on their children to accept their beliefs. It is better to allow them to decide when they are older.
- Others might say that the child can only make an informed decision if they are taught to understand what their parents believe and why it is important to them.

Conclusion: It is natural for parents to want their children to share the beliefs that are important to them, but it is very hard to make someone believe anything. All parents can do is teach their children about what they believe and then let them make their own decisions.

Page 24

Q1 Justice.
Q2 Making judgements about someone without the facts, or with no good reason.
Q3 Societies can pass laws that restrict a group's freedom.
Q4 b) is the most usual cause of prejudice.
Q5 "Do to others as you'd like them to do to you" (or any sensible paraphrase).
Q6 Christians believe that everyone was created equal by God.
Q7 A Jewish man was beaten up, robbed and left for dead. A priest and a Levite (both supposedly good religious Jews) don't bother to help him. A Samaritan (supposedly an enemy to the Jews) picks the man up and gives him a ride on his donkey to an inn, where the Samaritan pays for the man to be looked after. (or any accurate retelling)
Q8 This suggests that Christianity says that all races are equal and that racism is wrong.
Q9 a) *Points that could be included:*
- Prejudice means pre-judgement. Those who are prejudiced make up their minds about someone without knowing what they are like. When people discriminate, they act on their prejudice and treat people differently because of it.
- Christianity teaches that all people are equally valuable because they are all made in the image of God. Therefore Christianity teaches that it is unacceptable to discriminate against someone just because they are different.
- Christianity also teaches that people should not judge people on their outward appearance and treat them differently. So it is not acceptable to look down on certain groups of people.
- St Paul tells Christians not to discriminate, and that all the members of the community are equally important. He says, "There is no longer Jew or Greek, there is no longer slave or free, there is no longer male or female; for all of you are one in Christ Jesus." This might influence people not to be racist or sexist.
- Christians might also try to follow the example of Jesus who did not discriminate against those who were looked down on and rejected by society. He healed lepers who no one else would touch, and he went to dinner with tax-collectors who were hated for working for the Romans.

b) *Points that could be included:*
- Christians would not be expected to make racist or sexist remarks. They might challenge other people who make prejudiced comments or jokes and try to explain why those remarks are offensive.
- A Christian who recognises that they have a prejudice against a particular group of people might try to overcome that prejudice by finding out more about that group. Often prejudice comes from ignorance.
- A Christian who runs a business might try to make sure that they offer equal job opportunities to people, regardless of gender, race or disability.
- Christian parents could teach their children to respect and value all cultures, races and religions.

The Answers

- Young Christians at school might make sure that no-one is excluded or bullied simply because they have a disability or come from a different race or culture. They could make the effort to get to know other pupils from different backgrounds.
  Conclusion: Christian teaching makes it clear that it is unacceptable to discriminate against people just because they are different, so Christians need to educate themselves and to try to lead by example — always treating everyone with respect.

Q10 *Points that could be included:*
- In the story of the Good Samaritan, a Jewish man was attacked and robbed. A priest and a Levite (both respectable Jews) walked past and ignored him. A Samaritan stopped to help.
- In the time of Jesus there was a lot of prejudice between Jews and Samaritans — the two groups did not get on well.
- The Jewish people listening to Jesus' parable would not, therefore, have expected the Samaritan to do any good. They would have been shocked when Jesus made the Samaritan the hero of his story.
- One thing Christians can learn from this story is that they should try to overcome their prejudices and should not make judgements about people based on their religion or race.
- Jesus is also telling his followers that they have a responsibility not just to help people from their own community, but those who are different from themselves.
  Conclusion: Jesus told this story because he was trying to point out that, if anyone is in need, then Christians are expected to help, no matter what the differences are in their background, culture or religion.

Page 25

Q1 Stereotypes are fixed, standard images of people. They're often inaccurate and offensive.
Q2 Segregation is when different races are kept apart, either by laws, or because they choose not to live together.
Q3 No, it's illegal.
Q4 Today's Anglican Church is against all racism.
Q5 The Dutch Reform Church of South Africa.
Q6 Trevor Huddleston.
Q7 *Points that could be included:*
- Christianity teaches that prejudice and discrimination are wrong. All people have the right to be treated equally and with respect. Jesus also set an example by associating with people from different racial backgrounds.
- In Britain the Race Relations Act of 1976 made it illegal to discriminate against anyone on the basis of race or skin colour. This applies to areas like housing, employment and education.
- There is also a Commission for Racial Equality which was set up to investigate and deal with cases of discrimination.
- Some people think that society today is more tolerant than it used to be. They might point to the example of individuals from different races who have been successful in the media, the arts or politics (for example, as Members of Parliament, journalists, actors).
- However, the fact that some individuals have been successful does not mean that everyone has equal opportunities.
- Many black and Asian people still find it difficult to find suitable employment or promotion, despite being highly qualified.
- Some people are suspicious of refugees. They do not want them to live in their streets and towns.
- Some landlords will not rent out rooms to black and Asian people (even those who are British).

- There are still many violent racist attacks. People may suffer from abuse in their place of work or on the streets. Their homes may be attacked. Many of those responsible are never caught.
  Conclusion: Britain is a multiracial society with laws that are designed to prevent discrimination. However, the fact that it is illegal does not mean that discrimination has disappeared, and although the situation may have improved in some areas, many people still do not have equal opportunities in practice.

Q8 *Points that could be included:*
- A Christian might argue that there are many teachings in the Old and the New Testament which show that it is unacceptable for people to be racist.
- One passage mentions the importance of welcoming foreigners and showing them hospitality. It says, "You must count him as one of your own countrymen and love him as yourself."
- There are also instructions about the treatment of foreigners. They should be treated with justice and paid a fair wage for the work they do. Those in need should be provided for.
- Christians might use this to show how people today should be more welcoming to refugees rather than treating them with suspicion.
- A Christian might use this to argue that people of all races should have equal job opportunities and fair pay.
- Jesus also taught people not to be prejudiced. He associated with Samaritans and Romans who were disliked by the Jews at the time. In Luke's Gospel he healed a Roman officer's servant.
- His parable of the Good Samaritan showed that people should not be judged on their race, but on their actions.
  Conclusion: Christian teaching is about welcoming the stranger and showing hospitality to those of other races or nationalities. Christianity teaches that people have the right not to be judged on their race or colour but to be treated as individuals and given equal opportunities.

Q9 *Points that could be included:*
- Many of the Christian Churches work in multiracial inner-city areas, especially where there is poverty or racial tension. (Religious) ministers hope that they will gain a greater understanding of the problems people face, so that they will be able to help more effectively.
- Some Churches, like the Church of England, have investigated and reported on the state of race relations in Britain. The aim was to raise awareness of the problems and to try to work out what still needs to be done and how Christians can contribute.
- Education is one of the most important ways to combat prejudice. Church schools have an important role in teaching young people the importance of respect for all.
- Prominent members of the Christian church have spoken out against racial prejudice, for example Dr George Carey.
- Individual Christians have fought racial prejudice, for example Trevor Huddleston, an English bishop, fought Apartheid in South Africa using non-violent protests and boycotts.
  Conclusion: Respect for all peoples of the world is central to Christian teaching, and Christian Churches have encouraged this by working in communities of mixed cultures, trying to recognise the value of all cultures in their worship, and promoting racial harmony through programmes of education and awareness-raising.

Page 26

Q1 No, it's illegal.
Q2 It was unusual for religious Jews to mix with the opposite sex in those days.
Q3 St Paul said that women should be quiet, and that they shouldn't preach to men. However, in another passage he said that there is no difference between men and women.
Q4 Bonhoeffer spoke out against the treatment of the Jews.
Q5 Archbishop Romero was assassinated.

The Answers

Q6 The Catholic Association for Racial Justice, The Church of England Race and Community Relations Committee. (Other answers are possible.)

Q7 People sent to prison for speaking out against their government.

Q8 Amnesty International

Q9 *Points that could be included:*
- Christianity teaches that men and women are equal. Both were created in the image of God and are seen as equal partners.
- In British society, it is against the law to discriminate against women. In theory men and women have equal rights.
- Christians believe that they should follow the example of Jesus who valued and respected women. He had women among his friends and followers, and it was women who were the first witnesses to the resurrection.
- However, in today's society, women sometimes find it more difficult to gain promotion to top-level jobs, and many women still work in lower paid jobs. They are also sometimes treated as sexual objects.
- One area where Christians disagree is over the ordination of women. Some Christian denominations have women ministers. The Church of England has ordained women priests since 1998.
- The Roman Catholic Church teaches that only men can be ordained as priests, arguing that Jesus chose men as his twelve apostles and that this tradition has been handed down ever since.
- Traditional Christian language about God has always been male, although Christians do not actually believe that God is male or female in the same way that a human person is.
- Some Christians have tried to address this by using neutral language about God in their Bibles, prayer books and in their worship.

Conclusion: Although Christianity teaches that men and women are equal and Jesus treated women with respect, this is not always reflected in society today. Christians are trying to deal with some areas of inequality, although there are still disagreements over the role of women within the Church.

Q10 *Points that could be included:*
- Some Christians belong to organisations which campaign for human rights, like Amnesty International. Others get involved in letter-writing and sending Christmas cards to prisoners of conscience (people who are imprisoned for their beliefs).
- Other Christians support Fair Trade organisations by buying 'fair trade' goods so that the people who produce them receive a fair wage. They might also refuse to buy goods from companies who exploit their workers, especially those that use child labour.
- Some Christian individuals have devoted their lives to fighting for justice. Desmond Tutu and Martin Luther King both believed that in order to follow the teachings of Jesus, they had to use peaceful methods of protest.
- In South Africa, Archbishop Desmond Tutu used non-violent methods like demonstrations and petitions to protest against apartheid (the system that separated different racial groups and gave black people no rights).
- Martin Luther King also used non-violence to fight for the rights of black people in the United States of America. He led marches and made powerful speeches. Eventually black people were given the vote.
- Sometimes local Christian parishes in this country try to support refugees living in their area, especially those who have suffered violence or torture in their own countries.

Conclusion: Many Christians feel that their faith demands that they should do something about human rights, perhaps inspired by people like Desmond Tutu or Martin Luther King, and they may get involved in either local schemes or international campaigns.

Q11 *Points that could be included:*
- To say that people are equal does not mean that they are all the same. People are clearly very different from each other, but that does not mean that they are not equally important.
- Christians believe that all people are equal. In Galatians 3:28 St Paul writes, "There is no difference between...men and women: you are all one in union with Jesus Christ".
- It is clear that in today's society people are not all treated with equal respect. They may be discriminated against on the basis of their gender, race, colour, age or disability.
- If people just accept that there are inequalities, the danger is that they might give up trying to put the situation right. They might start to think that there is nothing they can do.
- It might sometimes be right to treat people differently because they have different needs. It is important to treat each person as an individual.
- However, this should not be used as an excuse to treat people badly or to ignore their rights.

Conclusion: Looking at society today it is clear that people are not treated equally. However, this does not mean that people don't have equal worth in society. Recognising the differences between people may help us to appreciate that everyone is equally valuable.

Page 27

Q1 No, they just have more responsibilities.

Q2 Ruth wasn't Jewish, she was a Moabite.

Q3 Women are traditionally mothers and wives.

Q4 a) describes an Orthodox synagogue.

Q5 Reform Judaism is less strict.

Q6 a) a minyan
   b) Women can make up a minyan in Reform synagogues.

Q7 *Points that could be included:*
- In the book of Genesis it says: "Male and female, he created them." God created man and woman, yet he created them differently. It is believed that they are different but equal — with different roles and responsibilities.
- Within Judaism there is a belief that motherhood is a privilege given to women, and that they should devote some of their lives toward it.
- Orthodox Judaism is quite likely to see women remaining at home as mothers and wives.
- Within the Reform Tradition, however, women may well go out to work and follow careers with no difference between them and men in that sense.
- Judaism sees the union between men and women in the form of marriage as extremely important — Jews are expected to marry and have children.
- Marriage between a man and a woman is believed to be the best way to provide companionship, and emotional and sexual union. It is also the base for family life and the best way to pass on Jewish customs and religion.
- Within the synagogue there are set rules for men and women. Usually ten men (a minyan) are needed for a service, and it is men who read from the Torah. Often men and women pray in separate areas.
- However, these rules are not accepted by all — Reform Synagogues can have women rabbis.

Conclusion: Judaism values the family unit and what it provides. Within that family the woman's role is valued as mother and wife. There are of course very different interpretations of the roles of men and women within individual families and from the Orthodox or Reform traditions.

Q8 *Points that could be included:*
- Racism is disapproved of in Judaism and the Jewish people have suffered more than most through it.
- The book of Genesis suggests that all humanity comes from the same source (Adam and Eve) and is therefore equal before God.
- The story of Ruth also promotes racial harmony.

The Answers

- Famine in Judah leads Naomi and her husband Judah to Moab. Naomi and Judah were Jewish yet their sons marry Moab girls. Ruth, one of these new daughters-in-law was not a Hebrew. Naomi's husband and sons die, yet Ruth stays loyal to Naomi and becomes devoted to God.
- Ruth's line eventually produces King David and this shows what benefit can be brought from being good to those from other lands.
- You can also find Jewish teaching in the books of Deuteronomy and Leviticus that preach tolerance toward others: "Do not abhor an Edomite, for he is your brother. Do not abhor an Egyptian, because you lived as an alien in his country."
- The book of Leviticus says: "When an alien lives with you in your land, do not ill treat him… Love him as yourself."
  Conclusion: Within the Hebrew Bible there is teaching against racism that forms an important part of Jewish belief. And since Jews have themselves suffered persecution as a result of racist beliefs held by others, they must know the unfairness and damage that such beliefs can bring.

Q9 Points that could be included:
- Jews have often lived in countries where they are the minority faith — they have lived among other faiths and worked alongside them.
- The preservation of a 'Jewish' identity and faith is vital. Too much mixing with non Jews can lead to risks, say some — such as a dilution of the faith by accepting traditions, festivals and partners of non Jewish origin.
- 'Ghettos', however, where Jewish communities live to the virtual exclusion of the majority community, can be seen as dangerous. In this sort of situation misunderstandings can occur and this leads to racism and suspicion.
- Many Jews in Britain participate in 'The Council for Christians and Jews' to help with mutual understanding.
  Conclusion: Although some worry about mixed faith marriages diluting the faith, many Jews favour positive interaction between faiths leading to better understanding and less racism in society.

Page 28

Q1 People of any race can be Muslim.
Q2 The Ummah.
Q3 Racial discrimination is wrong in Islamic law.
Q4 Everyone goes on the Hajj. Everyone wears the same kind of clothes. It proves that wealth and race are unimportant.
Q5 Islam says women and men are created equal.
Q6 Women are traditionally mothers.
Q7 No, one of Muhammad's wives was a successful businesswoman.
Q8 They say wearing a veil and modest clothing stops men looking at them as sex objects, and makes men treat them as people.
Q9 Points that could be included:
- Islam says that Allah created all people equal, although not the same.
- Allowing humanity these differences makes us individuals.
- All Muslims throughout the world are united through the 'ummah', this is the community of Islam.
- The 'ummah' includes all Islamic groups and sects, and is regardless of race or colour.
- On the pilgrimage to Makkah, the Hajj, there is a demonstration of equality and unity.
- All Muslims on Hajj have to wear white simple garments, so regardless of whether they are a king or a pauper all appear equal.
- All Muslims have to pray five times a day at set times, facing Makkah whilst doing so — this demonstrates unity.
  Conclusion: In the Hadith (the sayings of Muhammad) it says: "Everyone must respect the rights and properties of their neighbours. There must be no rivalry or enmity among you."

Q10 Points that could be included:
- Muslims may look toward the Hadith for the Prophet's words on equality contained in there: "All people are equal… as the teeth of a comb. No Arab can claim merit over a non-Arab, nor a white over a black person, nor male over female."
- Muhammad in his last sermon gave a message of tolerance and equality — he urged Muslims to respect the rights of others.
- In the Hadith Muhammad also warns against overt Nationalism.
- Islam promotes the 'ummah' or community as more important than national identities.
- During the Hajj a Muslim, all races and peoples are dressed the same in simple white garments. There is an equality between the people — no race or class is considered superior.
  Conclusion: Islam clearly takes a lead in placing the equality of Muslims worldwide as extremely important, no matter what someone's race is.

Q11 Points that could be included:
- The Qur'an says: "Men are the protectors and maintainers of women."
- Traditionally within Islam, men and women have different roles.
- Men have responsibility for providing for family, women are responsible for the home.
- However there is a tradition for Muslim women to be involved with business, one of the prophet's wives was a successful businesswoman.
- In the 21st Century Muslims are as successful in business as any other group and in all manner of jobs Muslim women are working and sometimes earning more than their husbands.
  Conclusion: There is no absolute answer to the question of the role of men and women within a Muslim family as each family may be living under very different circumstances. Although there are traditional roles, within a more modern family there may be a financial need for women to be out working and perhaps earning more than their husbands.

Page 29

Q1 Christianity is tolerant of other religions today.
Q2 In the Middle Ages (the 11th, 12th and 13th centuries especially).
Q3 c) best sums up the Christian view.
Q4 Spreading the Christian message to try to get people to become Christian.
Q5 The Roman Catholic Church says that it can and should try to convert everyone. (There are other possible answers.)
Q6 Missionaries travel the world spreading the Christian message.
Q7 Pluralism means living alongside other religions in harmony.
Q8 The Inter-Faith Network for the UK encourages dialogue and understanding between different religions.
Q9 a) Points that could be included:
- This describes a situation where only one religion is considered to be the right or true religion. It might be seen as the only path to God.
- Other religions are not respected or tolerated. In extreme cases followers of other religions may even be persecuted.
- Sometimes followers of this religion might try to convert others to their beliefs.
- Christianity in particular seeks to convert people. Some Christians believe that you cannot go to heaven if you do not believe in Christ, so it's vital to convert as many people as possible.

b) Points that could be included:
- This describes a situation where many religions exist side by side.
- It is recognised that there is value and truth to be found in all faiths.
- Whichever faith community people belong to they respect the right of others to practise a different religion from their own.

The Answers

- The Inter Faith Network for the UK is an example of people from different faiths communicating and cooperating.
  Conclusion: Many communities would now describe themselves as multi-faith communities, where people from many different world faiths live alongside each other and all are free to practise their own religion - this is one idea of religious pluralism.

Q10 *Points that could be included:*
- Christians recognise that they have much in common with other faiths, especially Judaism and Islam. All three religions worship one God and accept the teachings of key figures like Abraham and Moses.
- Today most Christians are happy to live in a multi-faith society. They would see it as unacceptable to discriminate against people from other faith communities.
- Most Christians believe that it is important to respect other people's religious beliefs and to get involved in dialogue with them so that they can learn about each other.
- This does not mean that Christians think that they can follow any religion. They believe that Jesus Christ came to teach them the truth about God. (Other religions would, of course, also say that their path to God is the right one).
- Most Christians believe that it is their responsibility to evangelise. In other words, they believe that they should try to spread the message of Jesus to others.
- They would say that this is what Jesus told his followers to do in the Commission when he said, "Go therefore and make disciples of all nations, baptising them in the name of the Father and of the Son and of the Holy Spirit, and teaching them to obey everything I have commanded you".
- In the past Christians have not always been tolerant of other faiths. Sadly, there are still some individuals and groups who remain intolerant. However, today, the Christian Churches do not think that you can force someone to convert to Christianity.
  Conclusion: Christians believe that Jesus Christ came to reveal the truth about God and that they are expected to tell others about what they see as the truth. However, most Christians would also say that it is important to respect other people's beliefs and to learn from them.

Q11 *Points that could be included:*
- Many schools teach about Christianity, but most schools, including Christian schools, believe that in a multi-faith society, it is important for children to learn about other faiths as well.
- Two of the main causes of prejudice are fear and ignorance. People are often afraid of things or people they do not understand.
- Learning about other religions in school might help children to understand the meaning of different religious customs and practices.
- However, families may have a much bigger influence on children than school. Unless children learn to respect other religions and cultures at home, learning about other religions at school may not be enough.
- Some people might think that the best way to combat prejudice is for children to actually meet and mix with people from all sorts of different backgrounds, rather than just learning about them in the classroom.
- However this is not always possible — some schools may see it as their duty to spread their particular faith and teach their pupils only about one religion.
  Conclusion: Although overcoming prejudice can take a long time, learning about different beliefs and lifestyles is a good way of helping children not to be afraid of people whose lives are different from their own.

Page 30

Q1 It's not considered OK.
Q2 Religious Jews don't try to convert non-Jews.
Q3 The seven Noahide laws (the ones given to Noah after the Flood).
Q4 Islam says that good Jews and Christians go to heaven.
Q5 Muslims try to convert non-Muslims to Islam.
Q6 Islam says that Jesus was one of the prophets of Allah, but he was just a man, not an incarnation of God.
Q7 Four from: Adam, Nuh (Noah), Ibrahim (Abraham), Musa (Moses), Isa (Jesus).
Q8 *Points that could be included:*
- Judaism teaches that it is the only true faith for Jews to follow, although there is an acceptance of other faiths.
- There is no real desire in Judaism to convert people to the faith, as any religion following the Noahide Code is considered righteous. (The Noahide Code is the seven moral codes given to Noah after the flood.)
- Islam and Judaism have very similar beliefs in the one God and share a heritage of prophet tradition.
- Also, both Islam and Judaism are pure monotheistic religions.
- Judaism does not consider Jesus Christ the incarnation of God, and so there are some differences of opinion between the two religions.
- Some Jews consider Jesus a Jewish Rabbi of the time, a teacher in the mould of John the Baptist, but no more.
- The 'Jewishness' of Jesus and the Jewish message that exists within Christianity are explored in interfaith groups such as 'The Council for Christians and Jews'.
- In recent years tension in the Middle East has placed difficulties in the relationship between Islam and Judaism.
  Conclusion: The Jewish faith lives alongside the Christian and Islamic world, and Judaism teaches tolerance and acceptance toward other faiths and sees all righteous people as having a share in a world where humanity will be united under God.

Q9 *Points that could be included:*
- Some see Judaism, Islam and Christianity as growing from the same Judaic seed — their belief in the prophets Adam, Noah, Abraham and Moses is shared.
- Because of this similarity of core belief, in one God and the prophets, some see pluralism of belief as a sensible standpoint.
- However, very significant differences between the faiths exist. Judaism does not recognise Jesus as the 'Son of God', Judaism does not recognise the Qur'an as the word of God.
- Islam recognises Jesus (Isa) as a prophet, but no more. It does accept the virgin birth, but does not accept that Jesus died on the cross. Islam recognises the Torah and the Bible as Holy Scripture but feels they are edited from their original form.
- Christianity places Jewish scripture in the 'Old Testament'. It does not recognise the Qur'an as the word of Allah.
- Each faith has its own set of festivals and practices connected to centuries of observance (which are often very different from each other).
- At times of national grief different faith groups have joined together with success to offer prayers to God — after all, the faith groups offer worship to the One God. This shows that people of different faiths can cooperate to achieve the same ends.
  Conclusion: Our society is increasingly pluralist, with different faiths meeting in joint faith groups. However, within these groups there may be much agreement but the faiths are always distinctly different. They may not differ on many points, but religious people see these differences as very important.

Page 31

Q1 Two valid answers, e.g. war, population growth, unfair trading practices (ie people in the Third World getting paid very low wages).
Q2 Two valid answers, e.g. homelessness, unemployment, drug addiction (including alcoholism), gambling addiction.
Q3 It's OK to have money, but not for it to be the most important thing.

The Answers

Q4 The sex industry (prostitution, pornography), the arms trade, gambling.
Q5 Yes, Christians should try to redistribute wealth and share it out fairly.
Q6 Possible answers: CAFOD, Christian Aid, Church of England Children's Society.
Q7 This saying means that doing good things for people is a way of doing them for Jesus — and showing love to Jesus.
Q8 *Points that could be included:*
- Some Christians might feel that it is irresponsible to gamble and to buy Lottery tickets when there is very little chance of winning. It is a waste of money which could be used for something else.
- Some might feel that if they have money to spare then it would be better to give it to people in need. Jesus told his followers to help the poor. (The rich man who refuses to help Lazarus ends up in hell.)
- They may feel that it just encourages people to be greedy and to want more and more material things. This goes against the teaching of Jesus who said, "Do not store up treasures for yourself on earth".
- Some people do not agree with the way the Lottery money is spent. They feel that more of it should go to charity.
Conclusion: Christians feel that they have a responsibility to use their money wisely, so they may feel that there are better ways of using it than gambling — it might be better to use the money to help those who really need it.

Q9 *Points that could be included:*
- When Christians give money to charity they are putting into practice the teaching of Jesus who told his followers, "Love your neighbour as yourself."
- Jesus often spoke about the importance of helping those in need and even said that God would judge those who did not do this.
- For most Christians, giving money to charity is the best way of helping the poor. In Matthew's Gospel Jesus tells the rich young man, "Go, sell all your possessions and give the money to the poor." The young man can't do this because his wealth is more important than the reward of eternal life. The message for Christians is that they should not be too attached to their money, but use it for the good of others.
- The parable of the Sheep and the Goats teaches that Christ is present in the poor and the needy. Christians believe that when they give to those in need, they are also showing their love for God.
- Christians believe that they have a responsibility to share what they have, especially if they have more than enough. It is not right that some people do not even have the basic things they need to survive, like food and clean water and shelter.
- Christians might also say that because they see God as their Father, all people are their brothers and sisters. Like any family they have to look after those who need help.
Conclusion: Giving money to charity is one of the ways that Christians can show their love for God and their love for others in a practical way. It is a way of recognising and respecting the rights of other people, and showing that they believe that they have a responsibility to help others.

Q10 *Points that could be included:*
- When people talk of helping the poor, they often think of those in developing countries who are living in absolute poverty — they might argue that the poverty Christians might see in their own towns is not as serious.
- However, there are situations of real need close to home. For example, there are homeless people or unemployed people who cannot afford to provide for their families. Christians should first try to help people at home before they help people overseas.
- The problem is that this might mean that some people in developing countries did not receive any help at all.
- When Jesus talked about 'loving your neighbour', he did not just mean the people in your own local area — a neighbour is anyone who needs their help.
- This can be seen in the parable of the Good Samaritan (Luke 10:30-37) where the Samaritan (a foreigner) helps the man who has been attacked even though his own people have ignored him.
Conclusion: For many Christians everyone is their neighbour — people overseas and those in their own towns are equally important.

Page 32

Q1 To help them to help themselves.
Q2 Collecting boxes for charity that many Jewish families have in their homes.
Q3 Tzedeka means giving money to the needy.
Q4 10%
Q5 A good thing (it means kind and compassionate actions towards the needy).
Q6 Gambling, alcohol, the sex industry (or anything sexually suggestive).
Q7 Islam says that lending money and charging interest on it is immoral.
Q8 Zakah
Q9 Additional charity on top of zakah — either money or acts of kindness.
Q10 *Points that could be included:*
- Islam sees greed and waste as wrong as all possessions ultimately are Allah's. The capitalist system of striving for profit is sometimes seen as wrong.
- The Islamic Shari'ah (rules for Islamic life) disallows any financial dealings that involve interest. The purpose of this is to forbid the rich making money at the expense of the poor, and to spread wealth fairly.
- Because the Western banking system functions on lending of money and then charging interest Muslims require a different form of banking system.
- Western Society also sees gambling shops, alcoholic sales and more sexually suggestive material than would be allowed within the Islamic World. In the West, this can give problems for parents trying to bring their children up to adhere to an Islamic way of life.
Conclusion: Adhering to Islam in the capitalist world may present problems when trying to get a loan, or a mortgage for a new home. However, many such difficulties are overcome by Muslims in the West.

Q11 *Points that could be included:*
- Judaism does not teach that everyone should try to be wealthy, although it is felt that extreme poverty may make you reliant on others.
- According to Maimonides, aid is "to help a person help themselves so that they may become self-supporting".
- As you become independent you too can begin to help others in need.
- Jewish teaching in Deuteronomy says "do not be hardhearted or tight fisted...." and Judaism encourages giving to charity.
- 'The love of wealth" may turn you away from God, and greed is looked down upon. But poverty is something to be avoided for the good of all the community.
Conclusion: Although it can be seen that Judaism looks toward making the poor able to fend for themselves, they are supported wherever possible by Jewish contributions to charity. It is seen as their duty to support those in need. However, Judaism does teach that poverty should be avoided if possible.

Q12 *Points that could be included:*
- Charitable work is an essential part of Judaism and Islam.
- In Islam one of the five pillars of the faith (Zakah) says 2.5% of your yearly savings should be given to those in need, no matter how rich or poor you are.
- Sadaqah is the giving of additional aid, which may include acts of compassion.

The Answers

- Judaism also has a requirement to give to charity: Tzedaka is financial aid and even the poorest are expected to contribute 10% of their wealth. (Wealth belongs to God and not giving to the poor deprives them of what they are owed.)
- Gemilut Hasadim is a kind and compassionate action toward those in need.
- Both Islam and Judaism have large scale organisations committed to charity, e.g. 'Jewish Care' looks at debt relief, refugees and the environment on a global scale.
- 'The Red Crescent' is the Islamic equivalent of the Red Cross and brings aid to countries suffering after war and famine.
  Conclusion: Charitable work is seen as essential in leading a righteous life within both Islam and Judaism, and collecting money for the poor is encouraged from a very young age.

Page 33

Q1 Three valid answers, e.g. three from: Global warming, the greenhouse effect, deforestation, plants and animals becoming extinct, pollution (and acid rain), natural resources running out.
Q2 Possible answer: The polluting way might be cheaper.
Q3 It's the job of humans.
Q4 Christianity and Judaism teach that all species are interdependent — so if something becomes extinct, the effects will hurt us eventually.
Q5 Jews believe that humankind's job is to look after the natural world.
Q6 At the day of Judgement / yawm-ud-din.
Q7 Interdependence is the idea that everything depends on everything else — each species depends on all the others.
Q8 Points that could be included:
- Christians believe that God gave mankind the Earth, and placed animals here for our use. However we have no right to abuse God's creation.
- This care for the planet is called 'stewardship.'
- Christians believe that everything on Earth is interdependent, everything depending on everything else.
- This means that if we abuse our stewardship of the planet then there will be problems for us in the longer term. For example destruction of the rain forests could lead to the extinction of species of plant which could have provided us with drugs to cure illnesses.
- God has put us in charge of the Earth and we must do our duty responsibly, even if it is difficult to balance care for the environment with the needs of business and government.
- There are a variety of Christian organisations devoted to caring for the planet, these include CAFOD, Christian Aid and Tearfund.
  Conclusion: Although Christianity sees mankind as at the head of the planet by design, with animals below, Christians try to encourage proper stewardship of the planet.
Q9 Points that could be included:
- Judaism sees mankind as 'custodians' of the planet, who must look after the natural world.
- Jewish teachings say that all creatures and aspects of nature are interdependent.
- Trees are seen as especially important, the State of Israel has attempted to reclaim the desert by planting millions of trees.
- As 'custodians' of the planet, Judaism would therefore encourage people to use 'green' products and help to conserve our planet's resources.
- Genesis (2:15) says "The Lord God took the man and put him in the Garden of Eden, to work it and take care of it."
  Conclusion: Judaism encourages people to care for the planet as an aspect of their faith — we are still to work the Earth and take care of it.

Q10 Points that could be included:
- In Islam the Earth is seen as a product of God's love, in return we should treat our planet with love.
- Religious leaders from all standpoints have told people that they have a huge responsibility to make sure we do not destroy our world, and action on a global scale is required to tackle problems such as the hole in the Ozone layer.
- Pope John Paul II in 1988 said "We have a responsibility to create a balanced policy between consumption and conservation."
- It is possible to argue that as creator of the world it is up to God to look after it.
- But the damage being done by mankind to our planet is ultimately our responsibility. If we do nothing there is a danger that the environment will suffer beyond our ability to repair it.
- The Muslim view of the position of mankind as 'trustees' of the Earth was outlined by Dr Abdullah Omar Nasseef at the 1996 World Wide Fund for Nature Conference, he said we: "are responsible for maintaining the unity of his creation, the integrity of the Earth, its flora and fauna, its wildlife and natural environment."
  Conclusion: We could say that God is all powerful and looks after mankind, so He ultimately is responsible for looking after the world. However, all major religions agree that God created the world and entrusted mankind with looking after his creation. It is our responsibility to look after the planet.

Page 34

Q1 Humans are seen as superior to animals.
Q2 Humans are superior to animals — animals are here for our use, but not to be abused.
Q3 Christianity is against cruelty to animals.
Q4 A Christian can be a vegetarian, it's their own personal choice.
Q5 Quakers.
Q6 Roman Catholics.
Q7 Jews accept medical experiments on animals as long as there's a real benefit to humans, and only as a last resort.
Q8 The animal's throat must be cut with a sharp blade for a quick, relatively painless death.
Q9 Islam strongly disapproves of cruelty to animals.
Q10 Points which could be included:
- In Islam cruelty to animals is forbidden, it is also forbidden to use them simply for pleasure.
- In the Hadith it says: "If someone kills a sparrow for sport, the sparrow will call out on the day of Judgement, 'Oh Lord, that person killed me for nothing. He did not kill me for any useful purpose.'"
- Islam teaches that animals must be slaughtered humanely. Animals used for meat must be killed according to Muslim law — by slitting the neck and allowing all blood to drain out.
- Although Christianity teaches that we must treat animals with kindness, animals can be used as long as they benefit mankind.
- The book of Genesis says: "They (human beings) will have power over the fish, the birds and all of the animals, domestic and wild, large and small." (Genesis 1:26)
- God may have created us as superior, but Christian teaching says that things are interdependent; so if we force an animal species into extinction, we will suffer for it. Our treatment of animals is a reflection on our character.
  Conclusion: Both Islam and Christianity allows the eating of meat, although Islam has strict laws about permitted meats. In Christianity we are seen as stewards of the Earth and that means treating animals with kindness, Islam also sees mankind as Khalifa or trustee of the planet.

The Answers

Q11 *Points that could be included:*
- Many religious people (and non-religious people) are very concerned about the use of animals in testing because it involves causing pain to animals.
- In Christianity some groups such as the Quakers are totally opposed to all animal testing. Other groups such as the Catholics will only see testing on animals as acceptable if it is to develop life saving medicine.
- Similar views can be found in Judaism where any experiment on an animal is only tolerated if it is to the benefit of mankind and even then, only as a last resort.
- Testing on animals for cosmetic purposes is not seen as vital for the health of humans. Religious teaching might cause a person not to use cosmetics tested on animals.
- Islam strictly prohibits any cruelty to animals. Muslims are not allowed to use an animal for pleasure; and cosmetics are for pleasure.
- With these issues in mind some groups such as The Church of England, teach that the medical and technological use of animals should be monitored 'in light of ethical principles.'
  Conclusion: Religious teachings say that causing pain to animals is wrong. Animal testing is seen by most religions as acceptable only if it is to develop a product of vital importance to mankind. Cosmetics are non-essential and considered by many as not a good enough reason to harm animals.

Q12 *Points that could be included:*
- Christianity teaches that God created us as superior to animals, and therefore they are there for our use.
- Therefore, if human beings are suffering in the world, excessive amounts of time and money should not be spent on looking after animals.
- However, Christianity also teaches that the way we look after animals reflects upon us as human beings. Humans have a responsibility for looking after God's creation.
- Christianity tells us that the interdependency of everything in the planet means that we must treat animals as well as we can, if we don't then it may reflect badly on us.
- Both Judaism and Islam see us as 'custodians' and 'stewards' of the planet, the welfare of the animal kingdom is our responsibility and will reflect upon us at the final judgement. However, both see humans as being more important than animals.
  Conclusion: The main religions agree that humans are more important than animals. However, they also teach that animals are not there for us to abuse, and that we should treat them well and look after the world we all share.

Page 35

Q1 The State, the police and the judiciary (court system).
Q2 Sins are when God's law is broken. Crimes are when the law of the land is broken.
Q3 Islamic religious law based on the Qur'an.
Q4 Jewish religious court.
Q5 b) is true.
Q6 Any three from: To protect society from the criminal, to make the criminal pay a debt to society for their crime, to reform the offender, to get revenge on the criminal, to display the authority of the law.
Q7 Punishment can't deter crimes that aren't premeditated. The person isn't planning to do the crime, and isn't likely to think of what the consequences might be.
Q8 Murder
Q9 a) *Points that could be included:*
- Generally, Christians are against capital punishment because it does not allow for reform.
- However, some Christians believe it protects the innocent and deters others from committing crime.
- Jewish people allow execution in certain circumstances. There must be witnesses to the crime. "If anyone takes the life of a human being, he must be put to death." Levit. 24:17.
- Muslims have a similar attitude. Execution is sometimes used for murders or for people who speak out against Islam.
- Some strict religious regimes favour capital punishment and take a hard line over all offenders.
  Conclusion: Some religions take a very hard line and support the use of capital punishment, particularly for murder. Others favour reform and do not feel it has a place in the modern world.

b) *Points that could be included:*
- Christianity teaches that killing people is wrong.
- Many Christians oppose capital punishment as it does not allow reform and repentance of the offender. For example, the 'Howard League for Penal Reform' was set up by Christians to campaign for punishments that allow offenders to reform.
- Capital punishment does not allow for 'forgiveness of sins'.
- There have been cases of people being found to be innocent of a crime after the punishment has been carried out. There is a chance that an innocent person could be killed unjustly.
  Conclusion: The weight of opinion in many religions is towards less severe punishments than the death penalty for serious crimes like murder. Opportunities for the offender to reform and for the victims to demonstrate forgiveness are favoured.

Q10 *Points that could be included:*
- Many people cannot be locked up for long periods without it having a negative effect on them. They must be encouraged to take a more positive place in society when they are released.
- Society can be best protected by helping offenders to see the error of their ways.
- Reform of criminals shows some compassion and forgiveness.
- The offender will be more likely to offend again if the only motive behind the punishment is revenge.
- The offender should be encouraged to repent their crimes. If they are Christian, they must do this so that they can gain God's forgiveness.
- However, others argue that punishment should be a deterrent. Reform shows a soft line against the offender. Punishment should make the offender afraid of re-offending.
- Punishment should allow the victims to feel that they have taken revenge against those who did them harm.
- Punishment must reflect the power of authority and the law over those who do wrong.
  Conclusion: Most religious people accept that effort must be put into ensuring that released offenders repent their crime and go on to play a more positive role in society. Most religions emphasise the importance of compassion and forgiveness over revenge. However there are those that disagree.

Page 36

Q1 Christianity generally opposes war.
Q2 A proper authority would be an elected government, a king or queen or a president.
Q3 Self defence against a country attacking your country OR to reclaim land that another country has invaded. (Also allow to defend an ally who is being attacked unjustly.)
Q4 Soldiers should only fight soldiers and not attack civilians.
Q5 A pacifist is someone who thinks war and violence are always wrong, whatever the circumstances.
Q6 A martyr is someone who will die for their faith.
Q7 Any two from: Nuclear weapons, biological weapons, chemical weapons, terrorism (include suicide bombs, car bombs). Also accept Weapons of Mass Destruction.
Q8 Nuclear weapons don't discriminate between soldiers and civilians.
Q9 Unilateral disarmament is when one country gets rid of all its nuclear weapons without needing other countries to do the same.

The Answers

Q10 *Points that could be included:*
- Some Christians are against war because they believe it is never acceptable to use violence or to kill another human being (a belief called pacifism). The Society of Friends (Quakers) are pacifists.
- One of the Ten Commandments is "You shall not kill" (Exodus 20:13). So some Christians refuse to join the army and fight in a war — they are known as conscientious objectors.
- Pacifists would say that Jesus taught his followers to be peacemakers. He told Peter not to use violence when he tried to prevent him from being arrested. Jesus said, "Blessed are the peacemakers" (Matthew 5:9) and in Matthew 5: 43-44 he also taught his followers to love their enemies.
- All Christians think that war should be avoided, but some Christians believe that it is sometimes necessary to fight and that a war can sometimes be justified. For example, some people felt that it was acceptable to go to war to stop Hitler. But people must only go to war as a last resort and with the aim of bringing about peace.
- The Just War Theory also says that there must be a reasonable chance of success and that you should not use more force than is necessary. Innocent civilians must be protected as far as possible. For this reason, many Christians are against the use of nuclear weapons.
Conclusion: Christians do not all agree about the right approach to war. Some believe that the teaching of Jesus means that Christians should never use violence. However, others think that it may sometimes be necessary to go to war to overcome a greater evil.

Q11 *Points that could be included:*
- One of the most important teachings of the Christian faith is about respect for life.
- It is not right to spend money on weapons and the armed forces — the money would be better spent on education or more hospitals.
- Jesus taught that it is wrong to take revenge, saying, "Do not resist an evildoer."
- Some Christians have refused to pay taxes which are used to pay for weapons.
- It can be right to fight to overcome a greater evil or to protect innocent life.
- Governments need to protect their countries, and having no weapons would mean that they were more likely to be attacked or invaded.
- Even if governments have to have conventional weapons (like tanks and guns) they should get rid of nuclear weapons because they cause such enormous and long-lasting damage.
- Some Christians would say that this is wrong not to pay taxes as a protest against arms. St Paul says that Christians should have respect for government authorities and this includes paying taxes. There are other ways to protest, such as going on demonstrations, signing petitions against war, or voting to elect politicians who are against war.
Conclusion: Whether or not Christians have a duty to end all wars and work for disarmament is probably a matter of their individual conscience. Christians have a responsibility to work for peace but some feel that war is sometimes a necessary evil.

Page 37

Q1 Shalom means peace.
Q2 Milchemet mitzvah means a war commanded by God.
Q3 b) and c) are obligatory wars
Q4 Because your enemy may be your friend one day.
Q5 Greater Jihad is the fight a Muslim fights against his or her own bad thoughts and selfishness in order to be a better Muslim.
Q6 a) A war to make people free from oppression is a just war.
Q7 A religious leader must declare a military Jihad.
Q8 They become a martyr and go immediately to Paradise without having to wait for the Day of Judgement.

Q9 *Points that could be included:*
- Jihad means 'striving'.
- There are two kinds of Jihad. A Greater Jihad is when a muslim makes a special effort to be pure and to fight against their own selfish desires.
- A Lesser Jihad may involve war. It should only be fought as a last resort.
- Such wars are often known as 'holy wars'. They are in the name of Allah and according to his will.
- A Jihad can only be declared by a religious leader and not a politician or military leader.
- A military Jihad has strict rules. It is similar to the Christian idea of a 'just war'.
- A Jihad is justified when it leads to freedom from tyranny, when it restores peace, when it combats oppression or when it puts right an injustice.
- The sick, the elderly, women and children should not be harmed in a Jihad.
- A Jihad should not damage the natural world and not involve indiscriminate killing.
- Dying in such a holy war turns a Muslim into a martyr and he or she goes straight to paradise. Martyrs do not have to wait for the day of judgement.
Conclusion: A Jihad is a 'struggle' that can be within an individual's conscience, affecting his or her thoughts or behaviour, or it may involve nations fighting a holy war. The conduct is governed by religious rules and the ultimate aim is to bring about peace or to end oppression.

Q10 *Points that could be included:*
- War is hated in the Jewish religion but it is recognised as sometimes necessary to bring about peace.
- The Jews divide war into two categories — an obligatory war (milchemet mitzvah) or an optional war (milchemet reshut).
- The threat of invasion could be seen as reason for an obligatory war. Obligatory wars allow a war in self-defence or a pre-emptive strike to avoid being attacked.
- The aggression of the other nation would be seen as an attack on 'God's chosen people' or on 'the promised land'. Both terms originate from the covenant between God and the Jewish people. The war would be 'holy' and 'just'.
Conclusion: A Jewish government would not wish for war. It would wish to do everything to secure peace. However, if there is no other option, war is justified under Jewish law as a means to secure peace. This includes making a pre-emptive attack to prevent invasion.

Q11 *Points that could be included:*
- Neither Jews nor Muslims believe in complete pacifism. Both acknowledge that sometimes peace must be fought for.
- A universal Jewish greeting is 'shalom' or 'peace'. However the people have sometimes had to defend themselves or have attacked first when they felt under threat.
- The Six-Day War of 1967 is an example of this.
- Muslim people believe that the Lesser Jihad or 'holy war' is a justifiable way of bringing about peace.
- However, war is hated in Jewish teaching. Jews believe that finding a peaceful solution is the priority and that war is a last resort.
- War is not permitted purely as an act of revenge. War is unacceptable if the aim is 'colonising' an area.
- Muslims believe that the sick, the elderly, women and children should not be harmed by a war. This may be an unavoidable result of conflict.
Conclusion: War is not desirable and both religions believe in this. Everything should be done to ensure peace. However, sometimes there has to be a struggle first to bring about peace. Both religions have rules that govern any conflict to minimise its effect on the weak and innocent.

The Answers

Page 38

Q1 Heroin and cocaine (including crack cocaine).
Q2 Any from: cannabis, amphetamines, ecstasy
Q3 Either tobacco or alcohol. Caffeine, at a pinch.
Q4 The body is a gift from God and we shouldn't abuse it. Drugs create a fantasy world which stop people dealing with the real world. Drug taking leads to neglecting responsibilities, and to crime.
Q5 a) Permitted. b) Permitted.
    c) Forbidden.
Q6 They are not approved of — they create a false world and don't allow people to show their true skills.
Q7 *Points that could be included:*
- Alcohol is forbidden in Islam, mainly because it causes people to lose control.
- It is seen as a weapon of Shaytan (the devil).
- A muslim should have a clear mind when praying and the effects of alcohol would not allow this. He or she would be unable to obey Allah.
- Alcohol can cause stupid and irresponsible behaviour. People could be harmed.
- Christians allow the consumption of alcohol. Wine was consumed at the Last Supper.
- This symbol is used today in the Holy Communion service.
- Drunkenness is frowned upon. Some denominations such as the Salvation Army are more disapproving than others.
- Judaism adopts a similar line, permitting alcohol but frowning on drinking to excess.
- The Midrash (a collection of moral stories) says "Wine enters, sense goes out."
Conclusion: Alcohol is acceptable and even symbolic in some religions. However, when consumed to excess, it is seen as a bad thing, being anti-social and even harmful to the individual. The Islamic faith feels that any alcohol can impair thought and make a Muslim unfit to pray.

Q8 *Points that could be included:*
- Christians see the mind and body as gifts from God.
- We do not have the right to abuse these gifts.
- Drugs are seen as bad in the view of the Christian faith as they damage the mind and body that God has given us.
- Continued and/or excessive use can lead to poverty and even death.
- Illegal drugs are completely disapproved of by Christians as they are a way of escaping the realities of life and to live in an artificial fantasy world.
- On a more practical level, drug taking can lead to irresponsible behaviour such as neglecting your family and friends. Drug taking is illegal and can lead to further Criminal activity to pay for the habit.
Conclusion: Christians take a strong line against drug abuse which is a very real problem today. The mind and body, which God gave us, can be seriously damaged and other problems like addiction, poverty and resorting to crime soon follow without help.

Q9 *Points that could be included:*
- This would acknowledge that cannabis is a 'soft drug' and even a 'social drug'.
- It would make its controlled use in medicine more acceptable and less shocking. This would allow the relief of suffering.
- However, there would be strong objections from those who see cannabis as a 'gateway drug' leading to the use of harder drugs.
- Cannabis still has the effect of changing moods and behaviour. Problems can result from this. In some people, cannabis can trigger mental health problems.
- Like drink and cigarettes, cannabis would become a 'problem influence' on society, particularly among young people. We should not introduce another mind-altering drug into society.
- Making alcohol illegal would acknowledge that it is harmful to the body. Religious teaching says that any drugs that harm the body are an abuse of God's creation.
- Alcohol can effect behaviour and lead to social-problems when taken to excess. All religions already condemn excessive consumption of alcohol. Alcoholism is a very damaging.
- Alcohol can be used to escape from the reality of problems and pressures as much as cannabis and other drugs can.
- However, there is evidence that if made illegal, the consumption of alcohol would 'go underground' as it did in the Prohibition era in the United States. Problems of high 'black market' prices would result. This would exploit the poor.
- The banning of alcohol would lead to problems due to the symbolic status of wine in Christianity.
Conclusion: This issue is far from simple as alcohol is not illegal but cannabis is at the current time. There seem to be arguments favouring moderate, even controlled use in the case of cannabis. Even medicine has pointed out benefits in both. With excessive consumption, problems result and the call for a ban is stronger.

Page 39

Q1 It's gone down — fewer people go to church.
Q2 More people watch TV.
Q3 Most broadcasting is not about religion and does not discuss issues from a religious standpoint.
Q4 There aren't any specifically Jewish TV programmes, and Jewish people are sometimes represented as stereotypes.
Q5 East (the BBC Asian issues magazine programme) and Black Britain (the BBC black and Asian magazine programme) — religious issues are also covered on the Heaven and Earth Show, and on other ethics documentaries, eg Heart of the Matter.
Q6 Soap opera and comedy characters are often stereotypes.
Q7 Newspapers can be biased.
Q8 Possible answer: The Satanic Verses, by Salman Rushdie
Q9 Pornography is available on the Internet, and people are worried about children seeing it. People are worried that children will be approached by paedophiles in Internet chatrooms.
Q10 *Points that could be included:*
- There is a tradition of broadcasting religious programmes on Sundays during the 'God slot'. Religious programmes rarely appear at other times.
- These programmes are nearly all Christian. This does not meet the needs of other religious believers.
- There are only a few programmes dedicated to other religions. There are no Jewish programmes at all. This leaves communities feeling frustrated and excluded.
- The media is important in educating people about different faiths and issues. Misrepresentation and bias are serious concerns for followers of all faiths. The opportunity to educate is not really being taken by the programme providers.
Conclusion: Religion only gets a small proportion of broadcasting time and even then this time is dominated by Christian programmes. The situation is slowly changing. There is concern that religious references in programmes are stereotypical and misleading.

Q11 *Points that could be included:*
- Television has a powerful influence on people especially the young. Scenes showing sex, violence, bad language and drug taking may have bad effects.
- A 'watershed' exists — for the BBC this is 9pm. After this time, programmes are aimed at adults. Children watch at their parents' discretion. Even so, the content of mainstream programmes before the watershed is often criticised for being too graphic.
- Strict guidelines exist on sex, bad language and the treatment of racial and religious issues. These are being reached and even crossed more and more frequently.

The Answers

- Excessive watching of television can have the effect of 'brainwashing' or 'indoctrinating' people with a 'fashionable' moral code. People should make up their own minds about right and wrong.
- The increasing influence of television may be a factor in the decline in church attendances.
- However, television can also inform and educate.
- Information on programmes is widely available and responsible decisions can be made as to what to watch, by whom and when.
- Some groups in the community may need the television to 'stay in touch' with news and issues. The elderly and those with mobility problems would suffer if it was banned.
- Television does a lot of good that is never publicised. We only hear about the controversial and the bad.
  Conclusion: At its worst, television can be seen as immoral and degrading. Guidelines are in place to responsibly manage the media. These are often challenged by programme makers. Television has many advantages and can make a valuable contribution if its content and viewing is 'managed'.

Q12 *Points that could be included:*
- The media can have a bad influence on people, particularly children, even with current controls and restrictions.
- Some content of TV programmes, films, newspapers and books is considered blasphemous. This causes great offence to followers of certain faiths.
- Films are officially classified to warn people about their content. Some people think that this does not go far enough and that certain scenes should be censored and cut out all together.
- Advertisements have been criticised for using sexual images to sell products to children. Some people believe advertisements should be censored to protect the young from 'materialism' and prevent them from making unrealistic demands of their parents.
- There is grave concern about the internet and how easily it can be used to access various material like pornography. Some systems filter out material but this is not consistently done and tighter control is needed.
- Some religious groups often say that violence is increasing because of the violence shown on TV.
  Conclusion: Some religious believers say that the media exerts an undesirable effect on society because the controls that exist do not go far enough. The only answer is to censor damaging content completely.

Section 2 — Christianity

Page 40

Q1 b) Apostles' Creed
Q2 Christ means the same as Messiah — literally "Anointed One of God".
Q3 c) "Jesus was 100% human and 100% God at the same time."
Q4 Through the influence of the Holy Spirit.
Q5 It is the name given by Christians to Jesus' return to life after having died on the cross.
Q6 Any two from: as a dove, as fire, as the wind.
Q7 By the death of Jesus on the cross.
Q8 The souls of the dead will be judged by God. Those God judges well will go to Heaven.
Q9 *Points that could be included:*
- The incarnation is the act by which God became a human being.
- Jesus was not 'half God' or 'half man', he was fully both.
- Christians believe in one God, existing in three forms — God the Father, God the Son and God the Holy Spirit.
- The second part of the Trinity (The Eternal son of God) became man in the person of Jesus.
- Jesus was born of a virgin. Mary become pregnant through the influence of the Holy Spirit.
  Conclusion: The nature of Christ incarnate is outlined in the 'Apostles Creed'. Christians believe Jesus was 100% human and 100% God at the same time. He was born of a Virgin who was made pregnant by the Holy Spirit.

Q10 *Points that could be included:*
- Christians do not see Jesus' death as a failure, but as the climax of his ministry.
- In his death on the cross Jesus paid for all the sin of mankind.
- Jesus himself was sinless. He died to redeem mankind because he was God incarnate as well as man.
- God is both merciful and just, but sin does have to be paid for. The sacrifice that Jesus made paid that price.
- Christ demonstrated the truth of his claims by rising from the dead. This is called the 'Resurrection'.
- In rising from the dead, he showed that the debt of man's sin had been paid, and that there is life after death.
- Because of the Resurrection, Christians believe that everyone who has died will be resurrected at the Last Judgement. This is a personal day of Judgement to see if you are to enter Heaven.
  Conclusion: In death, Christ showed his willingness to suffer and die for mankind. By dying, Christ paid for mankind's sins, and offered people the hope of eternal salvation. The Christian festival of Easter is bound up with the 'Passion, the death and Resurrection of Christ'.

Page 41

Q1 a) Old Testament
    b) New Testament
    c) New Testament
    d) Old Testament
Q2 The example of Jesus.
Q3 One of: Holy Communion (from the Last Supper), baptism (from the baptism of Jesus by John the Baptist).
Q4 The Roman Catholic Church
Q5 a) The belief that everything in the Bible is literally true.
    b) The belief that everything in the Bible is the Word of God, and shouldn't be questioned or open to interpretation.
Q6 a) (Biblical) Conservatism
    b) Brian's view is common in Christianity.
Q7 Possible answer: For moral guidance, and as an act of devotion to God.
Q8 *Points that could be included:*
- The New Testament is the specifically Christian part of the Bible.
- The Acts of the Apostles describe the early years of Christianity, how it has grown and spread and the stories of the early Christian martyrs.
- The 13 letters of St. Paul give advice about Christian life and its challenges, as faced by different communities.
- Eight further letters were written by early Christian leaders. These spoke of issues in Christianity and gave advice and shared experiences.
- The Revelation of St. John is an apocalyptic vision. It was written to give inspiration to Christians facing persecution from the Roman emperor Nero.
  Conclusion: These books contain much to inform, guide and inspire Christians today.

Q9 *Points that can be included:*
- Christians accept the Bible as authoritative in forming their beliefs and guiding their actions.
- The Bible gives direction on living a moral life. Jesus is the most important model for godly living and loving God by loving one another.
- Groups of Christians interpret the Bible differently. This influences how closely the teachings in it are followed.
- Literalists believe that virtually everything in the Bible is literally true, eg. Jesus really did walk on water.

The Answers

- Fundamentalists have a lot in common with literalists. They say that Bible teachings should not be questioned as it is dictated by God.
- The conservative view is perhaps the most commonly held. The teachings in the Bible were inspired by God and not dictated. Readers should seek to understand the writers' intentions.
- The Liberal view believes the Bible should be interpreted symbolically and not factually. It is open to interpretation as to the degree you accept or follow the teachings. For example, many liberal Christians may not follow the Bible teaching that homosexuality is a sin.
  Conclusion: The Bible is a complex book. Some take every word literally, but other Christians view the Bible as open to interpretation. You do not have to follow all the teachings of the Bible to be considered a good Christian by most people.

Page 42

Q1 The Ten Commandments (also known as the Decalogue).
Q2 Jews were not supposed to do any work on the Sabbath.
Q3 What your intentions were.
Q4 "Love the Lord your God with all your heart, soul, mind and strength."
Q5 Eros=sexual love. Philia=friendship with give and take. Storge=family affection. Agape=Christian love, like God's love.
Q6 Christian love does not keep score.
Q7 God
Q8 c) Love
Q9 *Points that could be included:*
- Christians believe that they will be judged on whether they have tried to love and serve God and whether they have tried to love their neighbour. The parable of the Last Judgement (Sheep and Goats) explains how Christians are expected to do this.
- The righteous (good) people are those who have shown the signs of love by caring for those they saw in need. They have shown love for their neighbour by feeding the hungry, giving drink to the thirsty, welcoming strangers, clothing the naked, caring for the sick and visiting those in prison.
- Those who have shown love and care for others are rewarded by God and welcomed into God's kingdom.
- Jesus tells them that when they failed to love the people around them, they also failed to love God.
- Christians also believe that they must not judge others and must learn to forgive if they also want to be forgiven. Jesus says, "Do not judge, so that you may not be judged". He also teaches, "Blessed are the merciful, for they will be shown mercy."
- He also says that his followers have to love everyone, including their enemies. They should not expect to be rewarded just for loving those who love them in return.
- In order to be welcomed into God's kingdom at the Last Judgement, it is important for Christians to show their love for God in action, not just in words.
  Conclusion: The type of judgement Christians will face depends on whether they have tried to do as God wants and to love others. The key point is that it is not enough to talk about love. Love has to be shown in action and this means caring for others in practical ways.
Q10 *Points that could be included:*
- Most Christians feel that it is important to keep the laws that God gave them. These might include the Ten Commandments and the teaching of Jesus in the Sermon on the Mount.
- Jesus thought the laws were important. He told his followers, "Do not think that I have come to abolish the law."
- However, Jesus was also criticised for breaking religious laws. He sometimes did this when he thought that people had forgotten the real reason why the law was there in the first place.
- For example, in Mark's Gospel he healed a man on the Sabbath because he believed that healing someone was more important than breaking the law about working on the Sabbath. The Sabbath laws were meant to make life better for people, not more difficult. Here Jesus is keeping to the spirit, rather than the letter of the law.
- In the same way, a Christian doctor or nurse today might believe that it is more important to go to work on a Sunday and care for the sick, rather than refuse to work because the Sabbath is supposed to be a day of rest and worship.
  Conclusion: The laws in the Bible are there as guidelines, so that Christians can work out what God expects them to do. It would not be acceptable to change or break the laws simply because they are inconvenient or too difficult to keep. However, as Jesus showed, sometimes it is even more important to think about the reason why the law was made in the first place.

Page 43

Q1 We need to repent of our sins.
Q2 Smoothing out the differences between people — getting back on good terms.
Q3 Some people think it makes the poor dependent on help, and stops them sorting things out for themselves.
Q4 b) Sort out the problem, and then forgive the person and move on.
Q5 Any three from: Scripture (the Bible), their own conscience, advice from others, Church tradition.
Q6 Christians must forgive each other. Forgiveness is not just God's job.
Q7 a) Christian compassion might suggest that you should turn the other cheek and forgive. Jesus said, "Let he who is without sin cast the first stone."
    b) Christian justice would suggest that criminals shouldn't be allowed to get away with crime. Letting the offender go free might create more victims and cause more harm.
Q8 *Points that could be included:*
- The idea of forgiveness is a central theme of Christianity.
- Jesus taught that God gives forgiveness to those that turn to Him.
- Christianity teaches that the sinner who repents is as welcome to God as the person who has kept all the rules.
- Jesus spent much of his time with sinners and outcasts - it was the wrongdoer and the outsider who needed his help. By forgiving their sins, he helped them get back into normal society.
- A Christian demonstrates his or her compassion by forgiving people's sins.
- Because Jesus was the Messiah, he could pass on his authority to forgive sin and so he instructed the disciples to continue forgiving others when they did wrong.
- Christians teach that Jesus died a painful and humiliating death in order to achieve the forgiveness of humankind's sins. Forgiveness is therefore very important.
- It is only by forgiving sin that enemies can be reconciled and Jesus taught that reconciliation must always be attempted.
- Sin has to be eliminated by forgiveness in order to establish God's New World.
  Conclusion: Forgiveness is a basic Christian idea. We all get things wrong — forgiveness not only shows a generosity of spirit but also acknowledges a common weakness. To be able to forgive someone is not a self-serving act but a condition of behaving as Jesus required. The Christian Church welcomes all sorts of people — it forgives past mistakes.
Q9 *Points that could be included:*
- To show repentance is to be sorry for previous acts or behaviour. It also implies a change of heart about the way one has acted.
- John the Baptist, who prepared the way for Jesus, taught that only by admitting and recognising wrongdoing could God's forgiveness be obtained.

The Answers

- In the Christian church, baptism, the symbolic washing away of sin by water, shows repentance.
- This sign indicates not only that people have turned away from their former lifestyle but also that they will now live according to God's rules.
- True repentance is demonstrated by acts of humbleness and penitence, virtues that were shown by Jesus. Repentance is important to Christians because it allows them to act in the same way as Jesus.
- Confession is an important part of repentance for Catholics. They tell their sins to a priest and ask for forgiveness.
- Repentance indicates an opening up to Jesus by renouncing previous bad practice.
  Conclusion: To repent is to say you are sorry for your behaviour and your actions and that you are going to change your ways and act in a more Christian way. Without repentance, Christians cannot get God's forgiveness for their sins and therefore cannot achieve eternal salvation.

Page 44

Q1 The meek — i.e. humble people who live simple lives.
Q2 He did not dig it. Jesus said that good things must be done out of love for God, not to make people think you're nice.
Q3 Christians should not pass judgement on others. It's hypocrisy because we all have faults.
Q4 "Do to others what you would have them do to you."
Q5 The salt and light of the world means the goodness of the world. Jesus meant that people should be a source of godliness and goodness.
Q6 Any from: serving others (e.g. nurse, doctor, teacher, etc.), showing compassion (volunteering at a hospice, etc.), seeking justice (campaigning for oppressed groups or political prisoners) or any other strongly Christian works.
Q7 He tried to get equal rights for black and white people in the USA.
Q8 She tried to help, clothe and feed desperately poor and dying people in Calcutta.
Q9 *Points that could be included:*
- Jesus refers to 'displaying religion' in Matt 6:1-18. He says that prayers and good deeds should not be done for show, but for God.
- Praying should be done in secret. Jesus teaches us that hypocrites say their prayers standing up for all to see.
- God sees and hears what is said and thought in secret. He will reward you.
  Conclusion: Jesus showed he had strong views about 'displaying religion' in the Sermon on the Mount. Prayer was what you thought and said in private to God. Things should not be done for show, but for God.

Q10 *Points that could be included:*
- The Sermon on the Mount contains many values that are at the heart of Christianity. These are reflected in the Beatitudes in Matt 5:3-12 and the teaching on 'Salt and Light' in Matt 5:13-16.
- Jesus' followers are meant to be 'Salt and Light', exerting a godly influence in the world.
- Christians have found various ways of doing this through action. Vocations include service to others in health work or education.
- Christians can also exert a godly influence by showing compassion, for example visiting hospices, and seeking justice for the oppressed such as political prisoners.
- Dr. Martin Luther King and Mother Theresa of Calcutta are two good examples of people who have tried to be 'salt and light'.
- In serving others, Christians have the opportunity to express many Christian values such as compassion, generosity and charity.
  Conclusion: The teaching on 'salt and light' shows the importance of exerting a godly influence in the world. Many of the 'caring professions' allow people to do this in every day life.

Page 45

Q1 Telling people the message of Jesus (and trying to get them to become Christians).
Q2 Challenging people's beliefs, and challenging their behaviour.
Q3 Laying out reasoned arguments in support of Christianity.
Q4 They believe that if someone doesn't accept Jesus as their personal saviour ("come to know Christ") then they can't get to Heaven.
Q5 Absolute morality is the belief that some things are *always* right, whatever the circumstance, and some things are *always* wrong.
Q6 Relative morality is the belief that something can be right or wrong depending on the circumstances.
Q7 They feel it's wrong and irresponsible to let things that they think are wrong carry on happening.
Q8 They think it's better to respect people's opinions, than to tell them what they can or can't do.
Q9 *Points that could be included:*
- Gospel means 'good news'. The good news is Jesus' message of hope and eternal salvation.
- Jesus instructed his disciples to spread the gospels.
- Christians are followers of Jesus — to be able to live like Jesus, Christians need to hear his message.
- It is an important part of Christian activity to bring the good news to others, so that they have the opportunity to share in Jesus' way of life.
- Many Christians believe that people who have never heard the message of the gospels cannot go to heaven.
  Conclusion: It is important to spread the word of the Gospels because the message they carry is so important. For Christians, the Gospel is the word of Jesus and of God. Unless people hear the word of Jesus from some source they cannot act upon it, and have eternal salvation. Spreading the gospels can also be considered as an act of devotion.

Q10 *Points that could be included:*
- The Christian Church is a large, highly organised social structure and all such structures have some political impact.
- The Christian message is concerned with issues such as poverty and how people should behave towards one another. These are political issues too.
- Christian beliefs may prompt people to become involved in politics, for example over issues such as the environment, marriage, or the justification of war.
- Christians may have a beneficial influence on politics, making it more concerned with ethical and moral questions, and focusing it on ideas such as compassion and charity.
- The bishops of the Church of England (a Christian church) sit in Parliament, in the House of Lords and therefore have some political influence. Many politicians are also Christian, and their religious beliefs may have some influence on their decisions.
- The Christian focus, however, is on the spiritual aspect of any question, whereas politics focuses on the practical and material.
- We live in a multicultural society so it is a bad thing for politics to be influenced too much by any one religion.
  Conclusion: Certain aspects of religion are connected to politics. This is difficult to avoid. They share some common themes and topics. Where they differ is in their approach to these common ideas. The Christian focus is on concern and caring and perhaps lacks the pragmatism needed to make effective political decisions.

Page 46

Q1 Evangelical Christians try to convert people to Christianity.
Q2 Alpha courses are an introduction to Christianity for non-Christians.
Q3 Non-Christians don't always want to listen to people talk about religion.

The Answers

The Answers

Q4 Any one from: through marriage, through family life, through work, through free time and hobbies.

Q5 Through vocation.

Q6 Vow of Poverty — promise to hold no personal possessions, but share everything in common with the other monks or nuns.
Vow of Chastity — promise to have no sexual relationships, but channel that side of their life into closeness and intimacy with God.
Vow of Obedience — promise to follow completely the rules of the community and to be completely obedient to God.

Q7 a) Contemplative congregations stay in their monasteries and pray for the rest of the world, and study Scripture. Examples: Benedictines (including Cistercians and Trappists), Carthusians, Carmelite nuns (but not Carmelite friars), Poor Clares.
b) Apostolic congregations get out in the world and serve the poor and sick, or teach. Examples: Franciscans, Dominicans, Little Sisters of the Poor, Missionaries of Charity.

Q8 *Points that could be included:* (For example...)
How they live
- Women who belong to Roman Catholic religious orders such as the Society of the Sacred Heart or the Sisters of Charity live an apostolic life (like that of the Apostles — devoted to religion and the service of others).
- They often live in small communities in ordinary houses.
- They try to meet together to pray at least once a day.
- They work, often in teaching, nursing or social work. Some also work as parish workers and catechists (catechists teach others about Christianity).
- The money they earn goes to their community. They don't own their own home or car, but have an agreed allowance for personal spending.
- They remain celibate. They do not marry and do not have sexual relationships.

Why they live this way
- They choose to live this kind of life because they feel that this is what God has called them to do. This is known as a religious vocation.
- They want to be free of family commitments so they can be available to help anyone who needs them.
- They can focus on developing their relationship with Christ.
- Not owning too many possessions means they are free to go wherever their order asks them to go and work. It also shows humbleness.
- Jesus said that his followers should not have too many possessions. In Matthew 6:19-21, he tells them not to store up treasures. In Matthew 19:16-30, he tells the rich young man to sell all he has and give the money to the poor.
- Jesus asked his first followers to "fish for people" (Mark 1: 17). In other words, he wanted them to spread his message and get more people to follow him. This is part of what religious sisters are trying to do in their life and work.
- They believe that they are trying to build the kingdom of God — trying to make the world the kind of place God wanted it to be.

Conclusion: Roman Catholic religious sisters live a life in the community centred on prayer and work. They choose to give up family life and many possessions. This leaves them free to help and care for anyone who needs it and to develop their relationship with God.

Q9 *Points that could be included:*
- Someone who chooses to live locked away in an enclosed community is wasting the opportunity to bring up and care for a family.
- They may have had a good education or a great talent that they are not putting to good use.
- They are not contributing to society because they do not have a job. They might do more good by being involved in the community and interacting with other people.
- However, members of enclosed religious orders do work within their community. They may grow some of their own food. Sometimes, they make vestments or altar cloths for parishes.
- Cutting yourself off from the rest of the world means that you are not doing anything positive to help others, which Christians are supposed to do.
- However, enclosed orders sometimes run retreat houses in their grounds where anyone can stay and have time to rest and reflect
- People in enclosed orders feel that their prayer is very important and can be powerful. They pray for the needs of people all around the world.
- Jesus pointed out the importance of prayer on many occasions. In Matthew 6:5-6, he tells his followers to shut themselves in their private room to pray. In Mark 1:35, he goes off to a lonely place to pray.
- In Luke 10:38-42, he says that Mary, who is sitting just listening to him, is doing a better thing than Martha who is busy doing all the work. He does not think this is a waste.

Conclusion: Although people in enclosed orders are cut off from the outside world, this does not necessarily mean that they are wasting their lives. Maybe it is important to have people who focus on praying for others, as well as those who are involved working in everyday life. Whether or not you see their lives as a waste depends on whether you see prayer as powerful and necessary.

Page 47

Q1 a) To teach that Jesus Christ is our Saviour, and to make people disciples of Jesus.
b) The Holy Spirit
c) Jesus Christ

Q2 The Communion of Saints

Q3 Ecumenism

Q4 The Pope's teaching

Q5 People who aren't ordained, but do the Church's work in helping the needy.

Q6 Two valid examples, e.g. individual church elders are respected and listened to; the Church guides people who may be called to the ministry; the Church is involved in international peace and justice movements.

Q7 Three valid examples, e.g. provides rites of passage; gives Christian teaching; helps the sick and needy; provides opportunities for regular worship; supports peace and justice.

Q8 *Points that could be included:*
- The mission of the church is to teach that Jesus Christ is our saviour and to make people disciples for him.
- It seeks to achieve this by teaching the things that Christ commanded.
- The teachings of the Church on moral issues such as abortion, sexuality and social responsibility continue to exert a strong influence on the way Christian believers think about issues.
- The Church also offers guidance to those who believe they may be called by God into a particular vocation such as the ordained ministry or the lay ministry.
- The Church's involvement in peace and justice movements makes Christians aware of such issues and encourages them to become involved in supporting these good causes.
- Church leaders are held in respect and their pronouncements are obeyed by faithful followers. They can provide important guidance in moral and spiritual matters.
- Catholics especially pay great attention to the guidance of their leader — the Pope.

Conclusion: The church has an important role to play in society today. Religious leaders can offer advice and guidance on a wide range of matters, which helps faithful followers and others who come for guidance.

The Answers

Q9 *Points that could be included:*
- The role and function of the local church is to put the Christian faith into action. It can do this in a number of ways.
- It can provide a regular pattern of worship so people can gather together in fellowship to practise their religion.
- It can provide 'Rites of Passage'. These include baptism, confirmation, weddings and funerals.
- It can provide Christian teaching at Sunday School, confirmation classes, Bible study groups, as well as the services themselves.
- It can minister to the sick and needy in hospitals and hospices as well as individuals with specific conditions and needs.
- It can support causes for justice and peace during troubled times.
Conclusion: The local church has a very varied role to play within its community. Aside from the religious ceremonial functions, a great deal of other work is undertaken that contributes to the spiritual and social well-being of the community.

Page 48

Q1 The Bible's
Q2 1054 — the Great Schism
Q3 The Orthodox and Roman Catholic branches (plus some Anglican churches)
Q4 Quakers
Q5 Pentecostals
Q6 The Magisterium is the teaching authority of the Pope and Bishops of the Roman Catholic Church.
Dogma is a firm belief of the Catholic Church, set out in the Catechism.
Q7 They are believed to be infallible — i.e. the Pope does not make mistakes in them.
Q8 Immaculate Conception
Q9 The belief that the bread and wine of Communion actually become the real body and real blood of Christ.
Q10 Fighting oppression and injustice.
Q11 *Points that could be included:*
- When looking for help and guidance, Roman Catholics accept the tradition of their Church (the official teaching that has been handed down) as well as the Bible. Protestants see the Bible as their main source of authority.
- Roman Catholics all over the world see the Pope as their leader. Protestants do not accept his authority.
- Catholics have seven sacraments — Baptism, Confirmation, Eucharist, Reconciliation, Matrimony, Holy Orders and Anointing the Sick. Many Protestants recognise only two — Baptism and Eucharist.
- The main form of Catholic worship is the Eucharist. They call this the Mass. Although most Protestants do celebrate the Eucharist sometimes, their worship is often focused on the Bible and preaching rather than the sharing of bread and wine in Holy Communion.
- Catholics believe that when the bread and wine are consecrated at Mass they become the body and blood of Christ. This is called transubstantiation. Protestants see the bread and wine only as symbols or reminders of the Last Supper.
- Roman Catholics give special honour to Mary (although they do not worship her). They believe she was born without sin. Protestants respect her as the mother of Jesus, but see her as an ordinary human being.
- All Roman Catholic priests are male and must remain celibate (they can't have a sexual relationship or get married). Most Protestant ministers can marry and there are many female ministers.
Conclusion: The main differences between Catholics and Protestants are their attitudes to authority and their different forms of worship and sacraments. There are major differences in their beliefs about the Eucharist and some differences in their view of the importance of Mary.

Q12 *Points that could be included:*
- You could argue that the beliefs that Christians share in common are the most important beliefs. They all accept that Jesus is the Son of God. They all believe that he died to save them from sin and rose from the dead on the third day.
- However, Christians do not always agree about how they should live their lives. They have different ways of interpreting the Bible. This can be very confusing when they have to make important decisions.
- It also means that Christians often have very different attitudes to personal and moral issues such as marriage, contraception, abortion or war. This is important because Jesus asked his followers to go and spread his message and sometimes Christians all seem to be saying different things.
- They also worship in many different ways, so that it is not always possible for them even to pray together. This lack of unity is not a very good example to other people.
- However, you could argue that, in spite of the differences, all Christians are trying to put into practice the teaching of Jesus that they should love God and love their neighbour (Mark 12: 29-31) and that this is more important than any differences between them.
Conclusion: It is impossible to ignore the many differences in the ways Christians interpret the teaching of Jesus and in the way they live their everyday life. However, it is also important that they all share the same basic beliefs and they are all trying to do what Jesus taught. The differences might be important, but they don't have to be a bad thing as long as Christians are prepared to listen and learn from each other. In this way, they can still love one another as Jesus taught.

Q13 *Points that could be included:*
- Many Catholics believe that Mary is a good example of trust and faith in God.
- When God asked her to be the mother of Jesus, she agreed to co-operate with God's plan. She said, 'nothing will be impossible with God' (Luke 1: 37), even though it must have been difficult to believe God's message.
- Mary is a good example of someone who was open to God and willing to do what God wanted, even though it must have been difficult for her. (Being an unmarried mother could get you stoned to death.)
- Because she agreed to do what God wanted, she helped to bring other people closer to God. This is something Jesus asked all his followers to do.
- Mary also sets a good example of how to pray. In Luke 1:38, she offers her whole life to God, saying 'I am the servant of the Lord'.
- At the wedding in Cana (John 2: 1-12), she gives an example of prayer of intercession (asking on behalf of others) when she asks Jesus to help the couple who have run out of wine. In the Magnificat (Luke 1: 46-55), she praises and thanks God.
- Catholics also see Mary as a mother figure. Catholic families might look to her as an example of how to live their family life.
- They believe that, as a mother, she is caring and compassionate. They might turn to her if they are in need, or see her as an example of the way they should care for others.
Conclusion: For Roman Catholics, Mary is an example of the way they should try to live their lives. This involves listening to God and being willing to co-operate with God. In order to do this they need to pray, as Mary did, so that they can discern (discover, or work out) what it is that God wants. They also see Mary as a good example of a mother who cared for others.

Page 49

Q1 St Peter
Q2 Cardinal
Q3 c) The Pope
Q4 Priests can celebrate Holy Communion.

The Answers

Q5 The ordinary, unordained members of the Church.
Q6 In a cathedral
Q7 The Archbishop of Canterbury
Q8 a) Anglican priests can marry.
    b) Catholic priests can't marry.
    c) Greek Orthodox priests can marry.
Q9 The congregation
Q10 The heads of the national churches in the Orthodox Church
Q11 *Points that could be included:*
- The Roman Catholic Church is a hierarchy. This is like a pyramid structure of power, with the Pope at the very top.
- Popes are the spiritual descendants of St. Peter whom Jesus is believed to have chosen as the first Pope.
- On matters of faith and morality, the pope is regarded as infallible and his word binding on all Roman Catholics.
- The Cardinals are just below the Pope. They are the highest rank of Bishop and act as the Pope's advisors. They appoint the Pope's successor. There's a Cardinal for every country where there are Roman Catholics.
- Bishops are below Cardinals. They are appointed by the Pope and serve an area called a Diocese.
- Priests are the heads of the local churches in each of the Catholic parishes. They are answerable to the Bishop. They are in charge of worship and education within the parishes.
- Deacons are candidates for the priesthood and are ordained. They may preach and lead worship but may not celebrate Holy Communion.
- The Laity are ordinary non-ordained Roman Catholics.
- Bishops, Priests and Deacons must be ordained (officially admitted into the priesthood) by the Catholic Church.
Conclusion: The Roman Catholic Church has a hierarchical structure like a pyramid. The Pope is the most senior member and is infallible in matters of faith. The Laity form a 'broad base' of non-ordained church members.

Q12 *Points that could be included:*
- Roman Catholic Priests and Deacons must remain unmarried. In effect they are 'married to the Church' and should give it their total attention
- This bond is set by the process of 'ordination'. This is seen as entering into a 'permanent state' in the same way that someone making marriage vows would.
- It is felt by the church that a Catholic priest cannot be married and has the special role of 'spiritual leader' in a community.
- St. Paul in his writings, encouraged 'fidelity, celibacy and chastity'. (1 Corinth 6:9-11)
- However, it can be argued that people wishing to become Deacons and enter the priesthood have such commitment that they would be capable of focussing on their special work in the parishes as well as on family life of their own.
- The experience of a matrimonial relationship could see a priest better able to advise on a range of matters with the benefit of personal experience. They would be better aware of the issues and the pressures.
Conclusion: The demands on a Roman Catholic Priest are significant in the modern world. They may be called to advise on a range of situations, some of which may be stressful and upsetting. Some feel that the best spiritual advice is given by someone who can focus on it wholly. Others feel that experience may be more supportive.

Page 50

Q1 To symbolise the Crucifixion.
Q2 To face the Holy Land, where Jesus lived and died.
Q3 a) To point towards Heaven/remind people of Heaven. To house the church bells. (In olden times) for defending the church and village.
    b) Transepts
    c) It is consecrated

Q4 Porch = Day-to-day entrance used by everyone.
    West Door = Large door used only for ceremonial occasions, e.g. when a bishop visits the church.
    Lych-gate = Where coffins are placed until the minister arrives to conduct the funeral service.
Q5 The nave
Q6 a) At the east end
    b) two from: Methodist, United Reformed and Baptist.
    c) They think that the word of God is the important part of Christianity.
Q7 *Points that could be included:*
- The tower draws people's eyes up to heaven to remind them of God.
- Transepts are the two wings of a cross-shaped church. They are set at right angles to the main nave.
- The churchyard is the consecrated ground surrounding the church. It is used for burials.
- The gravestones are stone memorials that mark where graves are.
- The weather-vane was very useful in medieval times when the weather was important to farmers. It was often in the shape of a cock to remind people of the story of Saint Peter.
- The churchyard cross represents the most important symbol in Christianity.
- The porch is the day-to-day entrance to the church.
- The west door is mainly used during ceremonies.
- The lych-gate is where coffins were placed to await the arrival of the minister to conduct the funeral service.
Conclusion: Christian churches often have very similar external features to each other. Smaller churches or chapels may have fewer features. Modern cathedrals such as Liverpool can have a very unusual layout.

Q8 *Points that could be included:*
- The altar is the most important place in church. It is a table that holds the items for the Communion service. It can be found at the east end of the church.
- The east window is often made of stained glass. It's right behind the altar and draws attention to it.
- The pulpit is a raised box from which the minister gives the sermon or talks to the congregation.
- The reredos is a decorated screen behind the altar. It often has pictures of Jesus, Mary or the saints on it. It draws further attention to the altar.
- The sanctuary is a raised platform where the most important part of the service takes place.
- The lectern is the stand for the church bible. It can be made of brass, and is often in the shape of an eagle.
- The covered font is used to hold holy water for baptisms.
- The nave is the main body of the church where the congregation stands or sits on pews or chairs.
- The aisles are the main walkways in the church. They are used for processions.
Conclusion: Christian churches often have similar internal features. The main focal point is usually the altar but there will be a pulpit and a lectern as well. In Methodist, Baptist and United Reformed churches, there will be no altar, but a very large pulpit instead. Chairs may be used instead of pews.

Page 51

Q1 To show their importance and give people a feeling of awe at the power of God (and the power of the Church).
Q2 The dome symbolises Christ's presence, eternity and the nearness of Heaven.
Q3 The word of God and the Bible are the most important thing in a Baptist church.

The Answers

Q4 a) Greek and Russian Orthodox
b) They kiss the icons
c) Icons represent the presence of the saints in the Church, and give focus for prayers.

Q5 Charismatic churches

Q6 To praise God, to give a focus to worship.

Q7 *Points that could be included:*
- Orthodox churches are based on a symmetrical pattern, either a square or a cross shape. They also have a dome on the top. The square or symmetrical cross represents order and equality. The cross is also a very important Christian symbol.
- The floor of the nave represents the earth and the four main corners represent the evangelists.
- Seats are provided only for the old and weak. People can move around freely during the service if they wish but they usually stand still to worship. The lack of barriers is symbolic, as is the respectful standing. People are free to worship as they wish.
- The churches are richly decorated to reflect the importance and power of God.
- The circular dome is located above the apex of the cross formed by the transepts. It represents eternity, Jesus' presence and the nearness of heaven.
- The walls are decorated with pictures of the saints, to represent their presence in the church.
- On the altar is a seven-branched candlestick which represents the seven sacraments and the seven gifts of the spirit.
- At the entrance to the church is the narthex. This is the stage that has to be crossed by new followers of the Christian faith and people who think they may wish to become followers.
Conclusion: The layout and features of the Orthodox churches are somewhat different from other branches of Christianity. The symbolism is plentiful with virtually all the major features representing some aspect of the Christian faith.

Q8 *Points that could be included:*
- Cathedrals are normally enormous and very imposing. This shows the importance attached to them. They were built historically at the very centre of a settlement to add to its status and reflect the wonder of God's kingdom on earth.
- Inside, the focus of attention is always towards the altar where the main acts of worship, like Holy Communion, take place.
- Many cathedrals are richly decorated with friezes, carvings, tapestries and stained-glass windows. These often show leading figures in Christianity and their deeds. These are often portrayed very grandly.
- For many centuries, the finest works of art were made, or composed for churches. They were designed to offer to God the highest expression of worship and to help create a sense of awe.
- The combined effect of the grand building and its decoration served to create the greatest possible impact.
- Awe can be further heightened by the music, the acts of worship and the ceremonies that occur in the Cathedral, both everyday and on special occasions.
Conclusion: It is very much part of a religion to create a sense of awe and wonder over the meaning of what it stands for in people's lives. A cathedral is the ultimate expression of the glory of the Christian religion. It combines great architecture, artwork and symbolism to the glory of God.

Page 52

Q1 On Saturday.

Q2 Two reasons from: Jesus rose from the dead on a Sunday. The Holy Spirit came down on the disciples (Pentecost) on a Sunday. Early Christians wanted to distinguish themselves from Jewish traditions.

Q3 It means that the service follows a set pattern which is written down. There will be set prayers and set Bible readings.

Q4 He said they represented his body and his blood.

Q5 Roman Catholics believe that the bread and wine of Communion become the real body and real blood of Christ, and so Mass is a literal re-enactment of Christ's sacrifice.

Q6 Leftover consecrated bread and wine must be eaten or drunk by the priest, or put in a ciborium and locked in a tabernacle.

Q7 Penitential Rite, Readings, Eucharistic Prayers, Rite of Communion.

Q8 a) The congregation confess their (general) sins and get absolution (forgiveness) for them.
b) The priest consecrates the bread and wine.

Q9 *Points that could be included:*
- Holy Communion is a very important part of worship because it contains many key statements of the Christian faith.
- Everyone asks for forgiveness for their sins so the Priest sprinkles holy water on them to show they are forgiven.
- There are always readings from the Bible.
- The Nicene Creed is recited, which is a statement of fundamental Christian beliefs. Other prayers are also said.
- The Priest makes the bread and the wine holy — this is called Consecration. The bread and wine representing the body and the blood of Christ are offered to God. Roman Catholics believe in transubstantiation — that it actually becomes the body and the blood of Christ. This bread is then shared by everybody.
- The 'Our Father' (also called the Lord's Prayer) is said by everybody.
- The congregation offer each other a sign of peace — usually by shaking hands or kissing one another.
- The service ends with a blessing from the Priest.
Conclusion: Holy Communion contains many of the most important acts of worship in Christianity.

Q10 *Points that could be included:*
- Holy Communion is a sacrament — a way in which God can directly communicate His grace or blessings to Christians.
- It is one of only two sacraments that date back to the time of Jesus so it is a very important Christian tradition.
- Holy Communion (often called the Eucharist by Anglicans and Mass by Roman Catholics) means 'Holy sharing'.
- Holy Communion involves eating bread and drinking wine — Christians believe that these items represent the body and the blood of Christ.
- This is because, at the Last Supper, Jesus told the disciples to remember him whenever they did this — Christians all over the world have continued this tradition.
- Christians, therefore, believe that they are 'sharing' in Christ by taking part in Holy Communion.
- During Holy Communion, Christians recite the Nicene Creed — this is one of the most important parts of Christianity and explains the idea of the Trinity.
- Some Christians would argue that, although Holy Communion is very important, there are other ways to worship such as the way in which they carry out the work and teaching of Christ.
Conclusion: Holy Communion is one of the key sacraments of Christianity and represents sharing in Christ. That is why it might be argued that it is the most important way for Christians to worship.

Page 53

Q1 Four Sundays before Christmas.

Q2 b) Ash Wednesday is the first day of Lent.

Q3 a) Epiphany commemorates the Wise Men seeing the baby Jesus. It's also the time of his baptism, and the time of his first miracle at the wedding in Cana.
b) Palm Sunday commemorates Jesus' entry into Jerusalem.
c) Pentecost commemorates the time when the Holy Spirit came down upon the disciples, giving them the strength to go and spread the word of God's Kingdom.

The Answers

Q4 The Transfiguration is the time when Jesus' clothes turned miraculously white, and he appeared to the disciples to be talking with Moses and Elijah.
Q5 To show they are sorry for their sins.
Q6 Ascension Day.
Q7 a) She was bodily taken up into Heaven.
    b) 15th August (Assumption).
Q8 *Points that could be included:*
- Lent is a period of 40 days and nights leading up to Easter which is important for helping Christians get ready for that festival. Lent helps Christians remember Jesus' fasting in the wilderness.
- The day before Lent begins is called Shrove Tuesday (we often call it Pancake Day) — some Christians use up all the rich food they have ready for Lent.
- Christians may give up certain luxuries during Lent and on Ash Wednesday (the first day of Lent) they may have ash put on their foreheads to show they are sorry for their sins.
- The last week of Lent is known as Holy Week — this lasts from 'Palm Sunday' until the day before Easter. During this week there are readings from the Gospels in Church because Holy Week commemorates Jesus' final week on Earth.
- The first day of Holy Week is called 'Palm Sunday' (or 'Passion Sunday') — Christians remember Jesus' entry into Jerusalem before his execution. They often do this by carrying palm branches to a special service where special hymns might be sung.
- On the Thursday of Holy Week (called 'Maundy Thursday') Christians remember the Last Supper — this is where Jesus told the disciples to remember Him when they drank wine and ate bread.
- On 'Good Friday' Christians remember Jesus' crucifixion — they have special services between midday and three o'clock when He was dying on the cross.
Conclusion: The period known as Lent and Holy Week all precede the festival of Easter and allow Christians to remember various important events leading up to Christ's crucifixion.

Q9 *Points that could be included:*
- Christmas is a celebration of one the most important parts of Christian faith — the time when God's son came to Earth as in human form.
- Advent (meaning 'coming') is the four weeks leading up to December 25th — it helps Christians remember the coming of Jesus.
- Christians may light candles on an Advent crown (or wreath) — this symbolises Jesus as 'the light of the world'.
- Although many shops begin the build up to Christmas as early as September, Christians do not believe that this really has anything to do with the birth of Christ.
- Many people would argue that the early start to the Christmas has got more to do with the secularisation of society — secularisation means that society is now less religious than it used to be.
- Even many Christians do not believe that Jesus was actually born on December 25th — however, this doesn't really matter as it is a traditional time to celebrate His coming into the world to save humanity from its sins.
Conclusion: Advent and Christmas is one of the most important times in the Christian calendar because it marks the coming to Earth of Jesus Christ. The early build up to Christmas in the shops has nothing to do with Christian belief.

Page 54

Q1 Deep prayer without words where the believer feels that God is very close.
Q2 a) Beads arranged in groups to help with prayer.
    b) Two from: Lord's Prayer (Our Father), Hail Mary, Gloria.
Q3 b) Marriage, c) Ordination and
    f) Reconciliation are Sacraments.

Q4 a) Extreme unction or viaticum
    b) Consecrated oil
Q5 The person must be sorry (contrition), must suffer/pay for the sin somehow (penance) and then the person is forgiven (absolution).
Q6 Baptism and Eucharist.
Q7 "Sacraments are so special because the grace of God enters into a person through the Sacrament."
Q8 *Points that could be included:*
- Rites of Passage mark special stages in life with religious ceremonies. Some rights of passage are known as sacraments and have a special religious status.
- The Roman Catholic and Orthodox Churches have seven sacraments whilst Protestant Churches only recognise two.
- A sacrament is a ritual that signifies that an internal spiritual change has happened, or is believed to be happening, to the person taking part.
- Baptism and Eucharist are the only two sacraments that are celebrated by all the Christian denominations.
- Baptism or Christening marks a person being officially accepted as a Christian.
- Eucharist is the taking of Holy Communion and the believer receives Christ into himself or herself afresh.
- The Roman Catholics and Orthodox Churches have five further sacraments. These may still occur in a form in the Protestant Church but they are not of sacramental status.
- Confirmation is when a Christian renews the vows made on his or her behalf at the ceremony of Baptism.
- Reconciliation involves confession of a sin followed by contrition, penance and absolution.
- Ordination is the rite in which ordinary people are made deacons before going on to the priesthood.
- Marriage is where a couple are joined in holy matrimony and they receive a special blessing.
- Anointing of the Sick may be for health or for preparing a dying person for his or her journey into the next life. This is also known as extreme unction or viaticum.
Conclusion: Although only two 'rites of passage' are celebrated as sacraments in the Protestant Churches, all are acknowledged or marked with ceremony of sorts. Roman Catholics and the Orthodox Churches see all as important enough to be sacraments.

Q9 *Points that could be included:*
- The whole point of prayer is for the believer to draw close to God, to communicate with him and hear what he's saying.
- Different Christians use very different ways of accomplishing this.
- Quiet Time — time spent alone with God. The believer could read from a bible or pray.
- Meditation is a form of prayer where the believer clears his or her mind of distracting thoughts and concentrates on God's nature and work. It may involve repeating a prayer over and over again.
- Contemplation — true Christian contemplation is not merely deep thinking but intimate wordless prayer in which the believer senses God's presence strongly.
- The Rosary is used by Catholics. It's a string of beads arranged in groups. As the beads are moved through the fingers, prayers are said. This may be the Lord's Prayer, Ave Maria (Hail Mary) or the Gloria.
- Icons — Orthodox Christians use icons, very often in the form of sacred pictures of saints. These help them to focus on God. Although they might light a candle in front of the icon or kiss it, they do not pray to it.
Conclusion: Private prayer is an opportunity to draw close to God and communicate with him. It is a deeply personal experience that may take on a number of forms in which the believer can feel at ease and express themselves.

The Answers

Page 55

Q1 John the Baptist.
Q2 After he was resurrected.
Q3 a) Because they believe that you shouldn't be baptised until you can understand Christianity and make up your own mind. (Also, Jesus was an adult when he was baptised.)
    b) Because they believe that baptism gives the baby a clean start, and makes the baby a member of God's family.
Q4 The parents and godparents.
Q5 The font.
Q6 To symbolise the light of Christ.
Q7 When they're 7.
Q8 The candidate for baptism answers questions about their faith and says why they decided to become a Christian. The minister dips them right under the water — it's baptism by total immersion.
Q9 *Points that could be included:*
- In early times, ritual bathing symbolised conversion to the Jewish faith. Christians also use it to mark someone becoming a Christian.
- Jesus himself was baptised by John the Baptist.
- Jesus told his followers to go and make disciples and then to baptise them in the name of the father. This is called the Great Commission, Matthew 28:19.
- Baptism represents a new life and the washing away of sin.
- A baptised person is sometimes said to be born again.
- It was traditionally thought that you could not go to heaven if you had not been baptised.
Conclusion: Baptism is a significant ceremony in the Christian faith. It represented joining the faith as well as the washing away of sins and a fresh start. Jesus instructed his followers to do it as they spread the word of early Christianity.

Q10 *Points that could be included:*
- Parents and Godparents make promises on the child's behalf. The child can later renew these if he or she wants to at their confirmation.
- A sign of the cross is made on the child and holy water is poured three times on the forehead in the name of the Father, the Son and the Holy Ghost. Orthodox Christians baptise babies by total immersion in water.
- The baptism is conducted over a font.
- The child is usually dressed in a white robe known as a Chrisom. The white represents purity.
- A lighted candle may be given to parents and godparents to remind them of their duty to bring the light of Christ into the child's life.
Conclusion: Baptism services can be varied in nature but normally involve parents & godparents making promises for the child. These may be renewed later on at the ceremony of confirmation when the child is old enough to understand them.

Q11 *Points that could be included:*
- Baptism shows that the child will be brought up in a Christian home under Christian principals. Parents and godparents make promises on behalf of the child.
- Parents want to show that their child is a member of the Christian faith.
- Parents want to name their child in a Christian ceremony.
- Committed Christians believe that baptism washes away the initial sin that we all have at birth.
- Traditionally it was thought that babies who were not baptised could not go to heaven if they died.
- However, some people may generally support the ideas surrounding baptism but feel that it is better for the child to decide for themselves when they are older whether they want to join the Christian church.
- They may feel that it is important for the child to understand what is happening to them and to take an active part in the ceremony.
Conclusion: Baptism is a very important step in the Christian faith. Promises are made, both about and for the child, by parents and godparents. Some people feel that children themselves should make these or at least know of them. They feel baptism should wait until the child is older. Some do not see the point of baptism in today's modern society and simply ignore the ceremony.

Page 56

Q1 Christians believe everyone can be resurrected.
Q2 God has perfect standards. Humans sin, so they don't meet God's standards. They aren't good enough to be allowed into Heaven.
Q3 The Christian Church believes that Jesus broke the link between sin and death by his own sacrifice.
Q4 Possible answer: "I am the Resurrection and the Life. He who believes in Me will live, even though he dies; and whoever lives and believes in me will never die" (John 11:25-26).
Q5 Christians believe that the body is just a container for the soul, and when the Resurrection happens they'll get brand new spiritual bodies.
Q6 A requiem Mass is to pray for the soul of the dead person.
Q7 A pall.
Q8 The bereaved person is told that the dead person is alive in Heaven with God, and that one day they will all be reunited.
Q9 They give counselling, or point the bereaved person towards someone who gives counselling.

Q10 *Points that could be included:*
- Christian burial or funeral services vary according to denomination.
- All Christian funerals contain a note of hope, which reflects the confident expectation based on God's promises (that followers of Jesus will live on after death).
- The coffin is carried into the Church and a bible reading (from John 11:25-26) is often given.
- There are hymns, further bible readings and prayers.
- The Priest or another nominated person often gives a short sermon or address. This will refer to the deceased, and mention is often made of 'life after death'.
- There are prayers for the bereaved and members of the congregation will express sympathy for the family and close friends of the deceased.
- Black clothes are often worn (although some now ask for this not to happen).
- The body might be buried or cremated.
- There's normally another short service at the graveside or cremation. Afterwards, there is a gathering with refreshments or even a meal for family and friends.
- A Roman Catholic funeral includes Holy Communion (The Requiem Mass). The priest wears white and the coffin is covered with a white cloth known as a Pall.
- The coffin is sprinkled with holy water and is also perfumed with incense.
Conclusion: Christian burial services can vary according to the denomination and the wishes of the deceased and the family. There is often an emphasis on 'hope' and a 'celebration' of life.

Q11 *Points that could be included:*
- Funeral customs offer help to support the bereaved.
- The Christian funeral services have a great deal to say about the hope of eternal life.
- The bereaved person is encouraged to believe that one day, he or she will be reunited with the deceased.
- It can help to talk to someone who does understand or who has even been through the experience of dealing with the loss of a close friend.

The Answers

- So in the days following the funeral, family and friends often try to contact those who were closest to the deceased and encourage them to talk through the grief.
- Usually the priest or vicar will also try to visit and may offer counselling him/herself, or perhaps suggest someone who can.
  Conclusion: Following a death, people may need some help to come to terms with what has happened. Christians often can and do give strong support to the friends of the deceased. The family can play their role in this too.

Page 57

Q1 Matthew, Mark and Luke.
Q2 Between 65 and 75 CE.
Q3 They think he didn't know Jesus personally.
Q4 At his baptism (a voice from Heaven), at the transfiguration (a voice from Heaven) and at the trial before the High Priest (Jesus says so himself in response to a direct question from the High Priest).
Q5 Daniel.
Q6 Christ.
Q7 She was actually anointing him. Messiah means "anointed one".
Q8 Bartimaeus, a blind man.
Q9 When he heals the daughter of a Syro-Phoenician woman.
Q10 Your answer should contain two titles from the list below.
(i) *Son of God — Points that could be included:*
- No person ever uses this title until after Jesus dies. It was blasphemous to Jews.
- At his baptism, and transfiguration, a voice came from heaven, referring to him as 'my dear son'.
- At his trial before the high priest (14: 53-65), Jesus is asked if he is 'the son of the blessed God'. He replies that he is.
- The significance of this title is clear — that Jesus is the Son of God.

(ii) *Son of Man — Points that could be included:*
- Jesus used this title when referring to himself. It symbolises the fact that Jesus felt ordinary human emotions.
- The prophet Daniel talks about a 'Son of Man' who would have authority from God, and so Jesus also uses this title to claim this authority.

(iii) *Christ, Messiah, Son of David — Points that could be included:*
- Christ and Messiah mean 'the anointed one', and Jesus was anointed with oil by a woman at Bethany.
- Jesus saw himself as the Messiah but most Jews were expecting someone rather different.
- 'Blind Bartimaeus' was the first person to call Jesus 'Son of David'. This was repeated by the crowd on Jesus' entry into Jerusalem. This indicated that Jesus was expected to be a king.
- Mark refers to Jesus as 'king' during the crucifixion.

(iii) *Saviour — Points that could be included:*
- 'The Calming of the Storm' and 'the Feeding of the 5000' show Jesus controlling nature and providing miraculous food to save the people from harm.
- In healing the Syro-Phoenician woman's daughter, Jesus demonstrates that his salvation can extend to Gentiles as well as the Jews.
  Conclusion: Jesus was known by a number of titles. Each of them gives us a clue as to who he is or was. The variety reflects the mixture of uncertainty against a background of danger from the temple officials and the occupying Romans.

Q11 *Points that could be included:*
- 'Messiah' and 'Christ' both mean 'the anointed one'.
- Jesus was anointed by the woman at Bethany, who poured a type of perfume over his body.
- The Jews had long been awaiting a Messiah, something that had been prophesied in the Old Testament.
- They had very different ideas as to what the Messiah would be like.
- Some expected a prophet like Moses.
- Some expected a warlike leader who would set them free from Roman occupation.
- Some expected a great king to rule over them.
- Jesus' immediate followers recognised him as the Christ at Caesarea Philippi.
- The Messianic Secret describes how Jesus doesn't reveal that he's the Messiah straight away.
  Conclusion: The term 'Messiah' is very significant in the Jewish religion. A messiah had been predicted but people did not really know what or who to expect, and so there were many ideas around at the time.

Page 58

Q1 He said, "The Kingdom of God is within you."
Q2 At the start of his ministry — He went into Galilee proclaiming the good news of God.
Q3 They should be trusting and grateful like a child, not cynical like an adult.
Q4 He said it was very difficult for a rich person to enter the Kingdom of God (it's easier to get a camel through the eye of a needle). Jesus also said it was not impossible for a rich person to enter heaven, because with God all things are possible.
Q5 They say that the Kingdom starts off small, grows gradually, and gets huge.
Q6 a) God.
    b) The Pharisees and the high priests.
Q7 It says that Jesus is a light. He makes things clear (and shouldn't be hidden).
Q8 *Points that could be included:*
- Jesus tells the story of a man who planted a vineyard, leased it to tenants and then went away to another country.
- He sent a servant to collect his share of the produce from the vineyard, but the tenants beat the servant and sent him away.
- The same thing happened to a second servant and the tenants killed the third servant. The man continued to send servants, but they were all beaten or killed.
- Eventually he decided to send his son, because he thought they would respect his son. However, the tenants also killed the man's son, because they thought that they would then inherit the vineyard.
- The owner then decided that he would have to get rid of the tenants and give the vineyard to new tenants instead.
- The religious leaders who heard this story were angry because they knew that it was aimed at them.
- The simple meaning of this story is that if religious people do not listen to God's message and do not want to be part of his kingdom, then it will be given to other people instead.
- The story can also be seen as an allegory (where each part of the story represents something else). The owner is God, the vineyard is Israel (God's people), the tenants are the religious leaders and the servants are the messengers or prophets sent by God to the people. The son is Jesus.
  Conclusion: The main message of the parable is about the importance of listening to the message about the kingdom of God, but the parable also criticises the religious leaders of Israel who refused to listen to the prophets when they came with messages from God. It warns them that if they will not even listen to God's Son (Jesus), the kingdom will be given to the Gentiles (non-Jews) instead.

Q9 *Points that could be included:*
- Many of the parables Jesus told were trying to teach people about the kingdom of God, trying to explain what the ideal world would be like if everyone accepted God as king. It would be a world where evil, injustice and hatred would be overcome.
- The kingdom of God is not somewhere you can find on a map — it exists wherever people accept God as their king and try to live their lives by doing what God wants.

The Answers

- In the parable of the Talents, Jesus talks about the importance of not wasting the gifts and abilities you have been given. In the parable of the Sheep and the Goats, he talks about the importance of caring for those in need.
- Jesus says that the kingdom has already arrived. By this he means that God is already working in people's lives and some people are trying to live by following his teachings. It can also be seen in the words and actions of Jesus, for example, when he heals the sick or casts out evil.
- Jesus also says that the kingdom of God is still growing because the message has not yet spread to everyone and not everyone will listen. However, it will succeed in the end.
- That is why many of the parables are about growth. For example, the parable of the Mustard Seed explains how the kingdom has small beginnings. In the parable of the Sower (Mark 4: 30-32), some seeds do not survive, but there is still a good harvest at the end.
- Some of the parables also talk about judgement, for example, the parable of the Weeds and the parable of the Net. Those who do as God wants will be welcomed into the kingdom, but those who choose to do evil will be turned away.
  Conclusion: The kingdom of God is Jesus' vision of a better world. It is present wherever people accept God as king and try to do as God wants. It is all about the way people live their lives and the way they treat others.

Q10 *Points that could be included:*
- Sometimes it might seem as though Jesus was deliberately trying to confuse people by speaking in parables. Even his disciples had to ask him to explain what some of the stories meant.
- Some Christians today also find the parables confusing and need to have the meaning explained before they can understand the message.
- However, in some ways parables were a very good way for Jesus to get his message across. They were simple stories, and people find it easier to listen to stories than to lectures.
- Jesus used everyday objects and situations to get his message across. Many of the people he was teaching were farmers or fishermen, so he used images like seeds, harvests, nets and fish.
- Jesus also used parables because sometimes people were not ready to hear his message. If he told a story, people might remember it later on and discover the meaning for themselves when they were ready.
  Conclusion: The parables sometimes seem confusing to modern Christians, but they were probably easier for people to understand at the time of Jesus because he used everyday situations to explain his ideas.

Page 59

Q1 Jesus calming the storm.
(Could also have Jesus walking on water.)
Q2 There were only 5 loaves and 2 fish to eat. Jesus said grace, broke the bread, and the disciples passed it around. There was enough for all 5000 people and enough left over to fill 12 baskets.
Q3 Jesus sent the spirits into a herd of pigs.
Q4 Four from: skin diseases, paralysis, haemorrhages (bleeding), deafness, blindness, mental illness.
Q5 The man with the skin disease, the blind man at Bethsaida.
Q6 c) Because he also forgave the man his sins, and the crowd said that only God can forgive sins.
Q7 *Points that could be included:*
- One example of a nature miracle is the Calming of the Storm in Mark 4:35-41.
- Jesus and his disciples were in a boat on the Sea of Galilee when a storm blew up. Jesus was asleep, but the disciples were so afraid that they woke him up.
- He said to the wind and the sea "Peace! Be still!" and they were calm again.
- He asked the disciples why they were afraid and why they had no faith.
- They were amazed and asked, "Who then is this, that even the sea and the wind obey him?"
- This miracle is important to Christians because it tells them something about the identity of Jesus. He is God's Son and has the power to bring order and calm out of chaos.
- It also teaches Christians the importance of having faith in Jesus, unlike the disciples who did not really understand who he was and what he could do.
  Conclusion: Nature miracles like this remind Christians of who Jesus is, the power and authority he has to overcome evil and chaos and the importance of having faith.

Q8 *Points that could be included:*
- Some say that if Jesus is God's Son then there is no reason why he could not heal the sick and cast out evil or overcome nature.
- If miracles are impossible then this puts limits on God. It's like saying that God is not all-powerful and can't get involved in the world.
- Some places like Lourdes are famous for healing miracles.
- Others say that it is nonsense to believe in miracles. And God doesn't get involved in the world nowadays, working miracles to help the poor and the sick.
- And the more important thing is the message of the miracle stories — they are there to show Christians that God is powerful and caring and to give them hope.
  Conclusion: There are several different ways of looking at miracles. Some Christians take the miracle stories literally, while others believe that the message of the gospel stories is more important than whether the miracles actually happened or not.

Page 60

Q1 By asking Jesus for help.
Q2 a) Jesus says He doesn't know who touched his cloak.
   b) He says her faith has cured her.
Q3 a) No.
   b) They must put their faith into action by doing something (e.g. asking for help).
Q4 The disciples failed to cure the boy possessed by an evil spirit. Jesus at first says that they did not have enough faith, then he says that only prayer works with this particular kind of evil spirit.
Q5 Jesus said, "Give to Caesar what is Caesar's and to God what is God's."
Q6 Jesus said that what a man does and says (what comes out of him) is what makes him clean or unclean, not what he eats (what goes into him).
Q7 The disciples picked corn on the Sabbath, and the Pharisees accused them of breaking the Sabbath laws.
Q8 *Points that could be included:*
- The Pharisees were a group of influential Jews that applied various religious rules very strictly.
- When Jesus' disciples picked corn on the Sabbath, they were accused of working on the holy day, which was against their religion's rules.
- Jesus reminded the Pharisees that David and his men ate bread that was destined for the High Priest on the Sabbath because they were hungry.
- Jesus said that the Sabbath was made for man and not man for the Sabbath.
- Jesus said the same when he healed the man with the withered hand. He emphasised that it is more important to do good on the Sabbath.
- Jesus challenged the Pharisees about their elaborate teachings on cleanliness and ritual washing.
- Jesus said that what a man does makes him unclean, not what he takes in.

The Answers

- He accused the Pharisees of being more concerned with their own traditions not God's word.
- Jesus was not afraid of directly challenging them. He did this through his parables, his teaching and by direct action. Jesus knew that it would be dangerous but it did not stop him in his work.
  Conclusion: Jesus challenged the Pharisees' interpretations of religious rituals when he felt it necessary, which very often was because he saw the rituals as being petty and outdated.

Q9 *Points that could be included:*
- Jesus exercised his own faith every time he performed a miracle.
- He showed that people could be cured miraculously of both physical and mental illness — as long as they had faith.
- In the story of Jairus' Daughter, a Jewish synagogue official shows his faith by coming to Jesus. He displays faith in the healing powers of Jesus on behalf of his daughter.
- In the story of the Boy with the Evil Spirit, the father admits to not having enough faith — he has doubts. Jesus says that he has used what faith he has, and his son is healed.
- While Jesus is on his way to Jairus' house a woman with severe bleeding (a haemorrhage) touched his cloak when he moved through a crowd. She is healed because of her faith, even though Jesus did not know who had touched him.
- These stories show that the faith that links Jesus with the healed (or their parents) must be an active one. The people are taking a 'step of faith' in the direction God is leading them and they expect God to intervene as a result.
  Conclusion: The relationship between Jesus and those he healed was one of faith. This faith had to be an active one, not just for convenience in word only. The healing extended to Gentiles and even to those who simply touched his cloak if faith was present.

Q10 *Points that could be included:*
- Jesus makes it clear that the law is to be obeyed.
- He made this clear when the trap about who to pay taxes to was set. (He replied, "Give to Caesar what is Caesar's, and to God what is God's."
- But he added that there are also God's laws to be obeyed as well.
- Jesus did challenge and even disobey some Jewish religious laws and rules which he saw as petty, outdated and even corrupt.
- This is shown with his attitude towards work on the Sabbath. Good works were justified, in his opinion.
- Also the rules on cleanliness were challenged when Jesus said that it was far more important to consider what a man does rather than what he consumes.
- This is why a lot of Christians will see it as a duty to confront authority when they feel it's morally right to do so.
- But as Jesus accepted the law of the land and focussed on petty rules that were inappropriate, many Christians believe they do not have a duty to challenge all authority.
- It could be said to be their duty, through their faith, to question anything that distorts or blocks the way to God.
  Conclusion: Jesus did challenge authority, but he did not challenge all authority. So I believe it would be right to challenge authority that was immoral. However, not all authority is immoral, and so authority should not be challenged at all times.

Page 61

Q1 a) Jesus gave the disciples authority over evil spirits.
   b) Any two from: bread, money, a bag, an extra coat.
   c) Jesus said they should shake the dust from their feet as a marker to others.
Q2 He meant that sinners were the ones who needed his ministry, not righteous people.
Q3 Jesus told Peter to keep it to himself.
Q4 b) Must love kids, c) Must be faithful to husband or wife, e) Must make financial sacrifices and f) Must preach the Gospel.

Q5 The story of the widow at the treasury.
Q6 The rewards are a hundred times bigger than the costs.
Q7 *Points that could be included:*
- Jesus taught his disciples that they must put themselves at the service of others if they wanted to follow him.
- To be a good disciple Jesus said that you must be willing to make personal sacrifices and put the needs of others first.
- Jesus taught the disciples that their mission was to bring the Gospel and salvation to as many people as possible. Jesus said that people could only be saved through believing in the Gospel.
- Jesus said that it was important for the disciples to love and care for children.
- Jesus said his disciples should serve all people whether they were rich and poor.
  Conclusion: Jesus taught his disciples that the best way to serve him was by serving and helping others.

Q8 *Points that could be included:*
- Jesus told his disciples that they were to give up all their possessions except for a staff and the clothes they wore.
- Jesus said that the disciples were not to carry with them any money, bread or extra clothing.
- The disciples were told to rely on other people to provide them with food and accommodation.
- However, Jesus did not expect everyone to give up their homes and possessions. He was talking particularly to the twelve disciples.
- It is still possible to be a disciple of Jesus if you follow the other guidelines which Jesus gave.
- It is acceptable to own possessions if you are generous and helpful to others.
  Conclusion: Although Jesus told the twelve disciples to give up their homes and possessions he did not expect everyone to do this, it is possible to have possessions and still be a good Christian.

Page 62

Q1 d) Passover.
Q2 a) He says that one of the disciples will betray him.
   b) He says that Peter will deny knowing him three times.
Q3 a) Sanhedrin, the Jewish religious court.
   b) The prosecution witnesses did not agree with each other.
Q4 They had been primed by the high priests to ask for Barabbas instead of Jesus.
Q5 Jesus of Nazareth, King of the Jews.
Q6 "My God, My God, why have you forsaken me?" (Bonus points for "Eloi, Eloi, lamma sabachthani".)
Q7 Mary Magdalene.
Q8 He told them to preach the Gospel and do miracles in his name.
Q9 *Points that could be included:*
- Christians don't believe that Jesus' crucifixion was a sign of his failure. Christianity teaches that Jesus' death was the climax of his ministry.
- Christians believe that Jesus sacrificed himself on the cross to pay for all humankind's sins. Christianity teaches that Jesus' death on the cross redeemed mankind because he was sinless and the son of God.
- The crucifix is a central symbol of Christianity.
- The crucifix reminds Christians of the sacrifices that Jesus made for humankind.
- Christians feel that Jesus' resurrection proved the truth of what he had taught people.
- By rising from the dead Christians feel that Jesus proved that there is life after death.
- Christianity teaches that at the Last Judgement everyone will be resurrected, as Jesus was.
  Conclusion: Christians believe that by suffering and dying for us Jesus gave us an example of how we should try and live.

The Answers

Q10 *Points that could be included:*
- Jesus and his disciples were eating the Passover meal together.
- Jesus tells the disciples that he knows one of them will betray him soon.
- All the disciples deny that they will betray Jesus.
- Jesus breaks a piece of bread and offers it to the disciples. He tells them that the bread is his body.
- Jesus offers a cup of wine to the disciples. He tells the disciples that the wine is his blood.
- Jesus tells Peter that very soon he will deny Jesus three times. Peter says that he cannot believe this.
Conclusion: Mark's Gospel tells us that at the Last Supper, Jesus showed the disciples that he knew what the future held and how the disciples would act.

Section 3 — Judaism

Page 63

Q1 Abraham believed in one god.
The people of Ur believed in many gods.
Q2 God told Abraham to go and live in Canaan.
Q3 There was a famine in Canaan.
Q4 The Jews were the slaves of the Egyptians for 400 years.
Q5 a) Moses
b) 40 years
Q6 On Mount Sinai.
Q7 They were enemies with the powerful Philistines and needed a strong leader.
Q8 Solomon built the first Temple in Jerusalem.
Q9 a) God promised Abraham many descendants, and said that God would always be there for them.
b) Abraham had to promise that all his male descendants would be circumcised.
Q10 When the Messiah comes.
Q11 *Points that could be included:*
- Abraham was the first of the Patriarchs who founded Judaism.
- God made a Covenant with Abraham - this forms the basis of Jewish law.
- God promised Abraham many descendants and that he would never abandon them.
- In return, the males should be circumcised. This was one of the terms of the Covenant.
- The Covenant was renewed with the giving of the Torah to Moses on Mount Sinai.
- 'Torah' means 'instructions' or 'laws' and it includes the Ten Commandments.
- Jews regard their history as the story of the Covenant.
Conclusion: The Jews regard the Covenant made between their people and God as the focal point of their religion - the story of this Covenant is Jewish history in itself.
Q12 *Points that could be included:*
- When Abraham was in the city of Ur, God told him to go to Canaan. This would be the Promised Land.
- God promised the land to Abraham's descendants.
- Abraham's descendants later had to leave Canaan because of famine, and they fled to Egypt.
- After 400 years in slavery there, Moses led his people to freedom. This is called the Exodus. They headed back to Canaan, their promised land.
- Moses' successor Joshua led the re-conquest of Canaan.
- David captured the city of Jerusalem back from the pagan Philistines and he made it his capital city. David's son Solomon built the first temple there.
- The Promised Land has also been known as the Holy Land and, later on, Israel.

- Jews look forward to the age of the Messiah when all of the land of Israel will belong to them and a new age of eternal peace will dawn.
Conclusion: Jewish people believe that God gave them the Promised Land, which they reclaimed after time as slaves in Egypt. This fact is at the root of modern land disputes with Palestinians and other Arab groups.

Page 64

Q1 There is only one God.
God's energy keeps the Universe going.
Q2 The Shema
Q3 Jews avoid referring to God by the name he calls himself in the Bible. Hashem means "the Name" and "Adonai" means "Lord.
Q4 To dedicate themselves to God, and to prepare the world for other people coming to know God.
Q5 Zionism is the belief that Jews should have a special Jewish homeland.
Q6 a) The 6th century BCE
b) The Romans
c) The diaspora
Q7 1948
Q8 Some Jews believed that they shouldn't try to make a Jewish homeland until the Messiah comes.
Q9 *Points that could be included:*
- Most Jews' beliefs about God have 11 things in common.
- …there is only one God.
- …God is not just a 'force' with no form, but a person (but he isn't an old man with a beard). He made humans in his own image but he doesn't necessarily look exactly like us.
- …he made the universe and everything in it.
- …it's obvious that he's there (there are no clever theories about his existence).
- …he did more than just create the universe, his energy keeps it going.
- …God is 'holy' — 'set apart' and 'completely pure'.
- …God is omnipotent or all-powerful (though he still allows each person 'free will').
- …God is 'omniscient' — he knows everything.
- …God is 'omnipresent' — he is present throughout the whole universe.
- …he is a 'lawgiver' — 'God wrote himself into the Torah'.
- …they will all face him one day, for death is not the end.
- …he is merciful — he will save his people from sin and suffering.
Conclusion: Jewish people don't all believe exactly the same things but most believe in certain features of their God.
Q10 *Points that could be included:*
- Because of the Covenant between God and Abraham, and its renewal with Moses, Jews believe they have a special role to play in history.
- They see themselves as 'God's chosen people'.
- However, they were chosen for responsibility not privilege.
- God wants a people who will dedicate themselves to him and prepare the world for when all human beings would know him.
- Zionism, named after Zion, one of the hills on which the holy city of Jerusalem was built, is a belief that God's chosen people would have a homeland of their own - a land God had given them.
- This belief is at the root of many disputes in the Middle East today as it clashes directly with the beliefs and ambitions of others.
Conclusion: Jews believe that they are God's chosen people and have a responsibility to prepare the world for all humans who would know him. They believe that they have a special place to live called the 'promised land'.

The Answers

Page 65

Q1 The Tenakh is the "Jewish Bible".
Q2 a) Nevi'im
    b) Torah
    c) Ketuvim
Q3 any two from: Isaiah, Jeremiah, Ezekiel (or any of the 12 minor prophets)
Q4 a) Rabbi Judah the Prince
    b) A commentary on the Mishnah
    c) The Talmud
Q5 Jewish Law — literally "going (with God)"
Q6 Panels of rabbis meet and discuss the questions, and give their response.
Q7 a) A Bet Din is a Jewish religious court.
    b) Business disputes, civil law, divorces. (Also certification of kashrut (what food's kosher and what's not), but that's not really a dispute.)
Q8 *Points that could be included:*
- The Tenakh is the holy book of the Jews.
- It is divided into three parts - the Torah (Teachings), the Nevi'im (the Prophets) and the Ketuvim (the writings).
- The Torah is the most important part of the Tenakh. It is the first five books of the Christian Old Testament. It was given to Moses by God on Mount Sinai.
- The Torah was a sign of the covenant (agreement) between God and the Jews. The agreement was that if the Jews kept Gods' mitzvot (commandments) then they would be his chosen people. The Torah contains 613 mitzvot.
- There are two types of books in the Nevi'im: history books with the stories of the prophets who explained about God to the Jews; books of the prophets that the Jews rejected.
- The Ketuvim are the least important books in the Tenakh. They do contain the Psalms that are used regularly in worship. Other readings are made from them - usually on festival days.
Conclusion: The Tenakh is the Hebrew holy Scriptures that is divided in three parts; no part of them is more valuable to Jews than the Torah.

Q9 *Points that could be included:*
- Teachings and explanation about the laws in the Torah were written down in the Talmud. It is the most important document in Judaism after the Torah.
- The Talmud tries to explain how the Torah should be applied as the world changes.
- It is made up of two parts: the Mishnah and the Gemara. The Mishnah was the collection of the spoken teachings into a written document. The Gemara comments on the teachings to help make them more understandable.
- It gives legal rulings on a wide range of issues in Jewish life.
- It gives guidance on moral and spiritual issues that can be related to modern life.
- It gives advice on how to live life at home, with the family and the outside world.
- It is still what is taught in seminaries (where rabbis are trained) and traditional Jewish schools.
Conclusion: Some Jews think that God gave the contents of the Talmud to Moses and that gives it very high status and authority.

Q10 *Point that could be included:*
- The Torah is central to the beliefs of Judaism. It is possible to be a Jew and not to follow the Torah. Such a person would not practice their religion. They are known as Secular Jews.
- Most Jews feel it is important to apply the Torah to modern life. There are three groups with different views on the Torah.
- The Ultra-Orthodox believe that everything in life is based on the Torah, the rules must be followed exactly.
- Orthodox Jews accept and live by the teachings in the Tenakh, the Talmud and the Midrash. These are God's words revealed to the world. This makes them binding on all Jews.
- Reform Jews follow the central beliefs and practices of Judaism but feel that some practices are outdated. They believe that God is still making himself known in the changing world of today.
- Using the Torah as a guide, panels of rabbis meet to formulate answers to new questions which are thrown up by modern life.
Conclusion: Jews today look upon the Torah as God's greatest gift to them and accept the need to live by its laws although Reform Jews say that some of the less important laws in the Torah no longer apply in modern times.

Page 66

Q1 Hatred of Jews and prejudice against Jews.
Q2 The Nazis blamed the Jews.
Q3 The Final Solution
Q4 Six million
Q5 "How can God allow such evil?"
    "How can Jews be the chosen people if God lets six million Jews be killed?"
Q6 Some Jews feel that if God existed, he'd have prevented the Holocaust. They feel that no God could have let it happen.
Q7 All people have some good and some evil in them, there aren't any 100% evil people.
Q8 They think that it would be like giving up and letting Hitler win if they stopped being religious Jews.
Q9 *Points that could be included:*
- The holocaust was an attempt to wipe out Jews in Europe, by the Nazis.
- All religions have a problem with the idea of evil. If God is all-powerful he can stop evil.
- If he loves people he should stop evil. So why does he allow evil to exist?
- For Jews the belief in their special relationship to God has been important in their survival as a people.
- For those who lived through the Holocaust many questions were raised. How could humankind behave in this way? Where was God? Was the suffering sent for a purpose?
- There were many responses to the Holocaust. Some Jews concluded that there is no God but many kept their faith. Some decided God was powerless. Others decided that it was a test of their faith.
- Some say that God could interfere but chooses not to. He has given people the right to choose good or evil (free will). He will not interfere even when it is abused. God is unable to destroy evil people, as no one is completely evil or completely good.
- Among survivors there have been many responses. Some have been unable to speak about it. Others have set up memorials and museums. Some survivor groups have visited schools. Their hope is that their experience will stop it happening again.
Conclusion: There is no single response to the holocaust, different people responded in different ways, but many of those ways were surprisingly positive.

Q10 *Points that could be included:*
- All religions have a problem with the idea of evil. If God is all-powerful he can stop evil. If he loves people he should stop evil. So why does he allow evil to exist?
- This can lead some people to question their faith or even reject it.
- Others say that we cannot know why suffering exists — only God can. Suffering therefore is a test of faith. God will have his reasons even if we do not know what they are.
- Judaism teaches that we all have free will. This can lead us to make mistakes and cause suffering.
Conclusion: Great good can come out of terrible suffering. It can bring people closer to each other and God. By allowing people to make sacrifices for others it helps them to develop their inner strength by testing their faith.

The Answers

Page 67

Q1 Secular Jews don't practise Judaism.
Q2 a) e.g. Spain, Portugal, North Africa
   b) Central and Eastern Europe
Q3 a) The moral commandments
   b) The ritual commandments
Q4 a) Orthodox Jews believe that people should see the Torah as important and relevant today and live by the rules within it.
   b) Progressive Jews believe that the Torah is open to interpretation in response to changes in society.
Q5 The Hasidic movement
Q6 b) Orthodox Judaism
Q7 Reform Judaism and Liberal Judaism
Q8 Orthodox Judaism
Q9 Obeying any mitzvot is a matter of choice.
Q10 *Points that could be included:*
- Orthodox and Reform Jews are two of the largest groups of Jews yet they have very different beliefs.
- Orthodox Judaism is the oldest and most conservative form of the religion. They have kept the religion as close to its original form as possible and believe that the traditional beliefs and practices are still important and relevant today.
- Orthodox Jews obey the 613 religious commandments (the mitzvot). An example of this is that they would never work on the Sabbath, will only ever eat kosher food and they celebrate all Jewish festivals.
- In Orthodox synagogues women are seated separately from men and do not lead any part of a service if there are men there.
- Reform Judaism began at the end of the eighteenth century in Germany. It began when Jews were accepted into society and some Jews felt that Judaism needed to change for Jews to fit into this society.
- Reform Jews still follow some of the original laws and traditions but have a more open-minded or liberal approach to them.
- Women were given a more equal role. In Reform synagogues men and women can sit together and women can also actively participate in public worship and can even become rabbis.
- In Reform services, modern languages such as English are used in worship and not just Hebrew.

Conclusion: Many of the Jews in Britain are Orthodox and their beliefs are founded strongly upon the sacred texts of the Torah. They believe that they must stick rigidly to these traditions and laws in order to serve God. Many think that Reform Jews or Progressive Jews have betrayed Judaism by changing it. Reform Judaism has arisen from a need for Jews to live and be accepted in a modern society and Reform Jews, whilst still believing many of the same things as Orthodox Jews, interpret and adapt the laws and beliefs within a more modern context.

Q11 *Points that could be included:*
- The Torah is part of the Jewish 'Bible', which is called the Tenakh. It contains instructions, laws and teachings. The Jews believe that God gave it to Moses and consider it to be the holiest part of the book.
- 'Torah' can also be used to describe all of the teachings, which grew over the centuries to explain how the Torah should be applied in a changing world. Within the Torah you will find the 613 commandments (mitzvot), which dictate how Jews should live their lives. Some of these are Ritual and some are Moral.
- Orthodox Jews believe that God gave them the Torah as a guide and that if they obey the commandments within it, they will live the obedient and holy life that God wanted them to live.
- The reason why upholding the laws of the Torah is so important to the Orthodox Jews dates back to the beginnings of Judaism where a covenant was made with God. Orthodox Jews believe that Jews were chosen as God's own special people and it is their responsibility to obey the mitzvot and be an example to all other human beings.
- Orthodox Jews believe so strongly in the sacred texts of the Torah that they resent the Progressive Jews who they feel have betrayed Judaism by adapting or changing the Torah for whatever reason.
- As Progressive Judaism came about because some Jews felt the need to bring the religion into the modern world they have had to adapt the Torah to fit in with this.
- Progressive Jews believe that the Torah is people's interpretation of the word of God and is therefore guidance rather than actual law.
- However, Progressive Jews still believe in the moral laws of the Torah although some of these are open to interpretation. They feel that the ritual laws need to be changed or abandoned to fit in with a more modern society.
- Liberal Jews go as far as to believe that each individual can choose whether or not to obey any mitzvot.
- Some of the mitzvot within the Torah are no longer relevant in modern society as they apply to particular people, places or rituals that no longer exist.

Conclusion: There is no doubt that the Torah is an important part of all types of Judaism and forms the basis of how Jews lead their lives. Different groups of Jews interpret the Torah in different ways according to what they believe. There are great benefits in trying to adapt the Torah to modern society, but in doing this, Jews may risk compromising its full meaning.

Page 68

Q1 613
Q2 Mitzvah, mitzvot
Q3 a) A commandment about how people deal with each other.
   b) A commandment about the relationship between the Jewish people and God.
Q4 Jews believe that the best way is to obey God.
Q5 Keeping the Torah (obeying the laws), and being considerate to other people.
Q6 The Torah, the Talmud, and then other Jewish teaching.
Q7 a) A ritual bath — a pool about 4 metres by 3 metres filled with rainwater.
   b) Women go to the mikveh before marriage, after menstruation and after childbirth.
   c) Men go to the mikveh before Yom Kippur.
Q8 *Points that could be included:*
- A mikveh is a ritual bath that contains rainwater.
- It is a bath for spiritual cleansing and purification. It is not a bath for getting rid of dirt - Jews have to be clean before entering it.
- Once they are in, all body parts have to be cleaned thoroughly.
- A woman would visit the mikveh after her menstrual cycle, before her wedding and after giving birth.
- A man would use the mikveh in preparation for Yom Kippur. A priest would also use it before a divine service.
- Anyone who is converting to Judaism must also visit the mikveh as part of the process.
- Finally, a separate mikveh is used for the preparation of a dead person before they are buried.

Conclusion: Spiritual cleanliness is an important part of Judaism. By visiting the mikveh, Jews make sure that they are clean and pure before or after any significant act or event that requires it.

Q9 *Points that could be included:*
- The mitzvot are the religious commandments that Jews believe that God gave to them in the Torah.
- The most famous mitzvot are the Ten Commandments but there are in fact 613 altogether. Each of the 613 Mitzvot tells Jews what they should and shouldn't do.
- An important part of Judaism is that Jews should live their lives in a way that is pleasing to God. All actions, however simple and ordinary, are turned into ways of serving God by obeying all of the mitzvot.

The Answers

- Many of the mitzvot are moral or ethical and tell the Jews how to deal with other people. They teach that Jews should have respect and concern for others.
- By observing the mitzvot, Jews believe that they will lead disciplined and ordered lives and behave in a way that is morally acceptable.
- Some of the mitzvot are no longer relevant as they apply to particular people, places or rituals that no longer exist.
- The word mitzvot can also mean a good deed, making it something that is always relevant to Jewish life.
- For an Orthodox Jew, the mitzvot are necessary. God gave them these commandments and it is their duty to obey them.
- However, Progressive or Reform Jews believe that the mitzvot and the Torah are not actually the words of God but words written by humans that were inspired by God. So they think that any mitzvot that outdated or irrelevant can be adapted or abandoned.
  Conclusion: The mitzvot are an essential part of Jewish life. For most, they dictate the way in which a Jew lives his life and ensures that they are moral and ethical human beings. However, these commandments were written a long time ago and for practical reasons some of these rules are no longer relevant. However, many of the mitzvot are still relevant in a modern society and this is why they are still adhered to both by Orthodox and Progressive Jews, if not always to the same extent.

Page 69

Q1 Shul, or Bet ha Knesset
Q2 Six-pointed star
Seven-branched candlestick
Shield (in the sense that a magen David is a shield of David)
Q3 Aron Hakodesh: Large cupboard or alcove, with doors or a screen, set on the wall facing Jerusalem. This is the most important item of furniture in a synagogue.
Ner tamid: A light which never goes out. It represents the menorah which was always kept alight in the Temple.
Sefer Torah: Parchment scrolls that must be handwritten by a sofer (scribe), and are usually decorated.
Bimah or Almemar: Raised platform with reading desk, normally in the centre of the hall.
Q4 Rabbis are not priests because the only place priests can officiate is the Temple in Jerusalem, and that doesn't exist any more. Also, Jews do not believe that rabbis should mediate between an individual Jew and God.
Q5 a) Cantor
b) The chazan leads the congregation in singing, and chants some Shabbat prayers. He also sings at receptions and parties.
Q6 a) *Points that could be included:*
- There are no rules as to what a synagogue should look like on the outside.
- The only indication could be signs like a seven-branched candlestick (a menorah) or a six-pointed star (the magen David).
- All synagogues share four features in common:
- All synagogues have an Ark or 'Aron Hakodesh.' It's a large cupboard or alcove with doors or a screen. It is set in the wall facing Jerusalem.
- They have a Perpetual Light or 'Ner Tamid', a light that never goes out. It is set above the Ark.
- They also have Scrolls of the Torah or 'Sefer Torah', made of parchment. There is a wooden pole at each end so the scrolls can be wound to the correct place for a reading. They are often decorated.
- And they have a raised platform with a reading desk, or Bimah, or Almemar.
b) *Points that could be included:*
- The Ark is the most important item of furniture.
- It contains the scrolls of the Torah.

- The scrolls were carried by Moses and his followers in a similar casket.
- The Perpetual Light represents the Menorah that was always kept alight in the Temple.
- The scrolls of the Torah are handwritten by a scribe, just as Moses wrote down the original laws on Mount Sinai.
- The raised platform and reading desk are in the centre of the building, reflecting the importance of the readings.
  Conclusion: The synagogue is the place of worship for the Jewish faith. Externally there may be little to indicate its presence but inside there are a number of features which are symbolic of the faith and its meaning.

Q7 *Points that could be included:*
- The Jewish place of worship is a synagogue but sometimes it is called 'Bet Ha Knesset' meaning 'house of meeting'.
- It is often like a community centre and in addition to a prayer hall, it will have a hall for wedding receptions and parties.
- It has classrooms for study groups.
- It can also have a Mikveh for ritual bathing.
- Rooms can be used for youth clubs, mother and toddler groups and senior citizens clubs.
- Jewish people can share their culture and traditions as well as their spiritual needs.
- The synagogue is therefore a focal point in the Jewish community.
- However, if Jewish people are to be fully accepted in a multicultural society they should make an effort to mix with other faiths and cultures.
- The more the synagogue meets social needs as well as spiritual ones, then the less the incentive for Jewish people to mix with the broader local community and its facilities.
- This could mean the local non-Jewish community is unlikely to get much of a chance to learn more of the faith and culture of Jewish people.
- Also, not every town has a synagogue so Jewish people could have to travel further if a synagogue is to be the centre of their life.
  Conclusion 1: The synagogue is a very significant building in the Jewish religion meeting a range of needs. As well as this, it can make a very effective social centre.
  Conclusion 2: The synagogue is a very significant building in the Jewish religion meeting a range of needs. However, the fact that the building provides so much may lead to an isolation in the local community.

Page 70

Q1 It is forbidden to make images of God.
Q2 a) A case containing a small scroll inscribed with Bible verses.
b) On every door in a Jewish house (except bathroom door and toilet door).
c) They are a reminder of the covenant.
d) Deuteronomy 6:4-9 and 11:13-21.
Q3 As a sign of respect to God.
Q4 a) Tefillin are small leather boxes containing scrolls.
b) They are worn on a man's head and on his upper arm.
c) During morning prayers (except on the Sabbath and festival days).
d) The first two paragraphs of the Shema (Deuteronomy 6:4-8), Exodus 13:1-10 and 13:11-16.
e) They remind the wearer to serve God with his head and his heart.
Q5 a) A Tallit
b) Tzitzit
Q6 *Points that could be included:*
- Ritual dress is important in Judaism.
- Many men and boys wear a small hat called a Kippah. It can also be called a yarmulka, a capel or a skullcap.

The Answers

- It is a sign of respect to God, and a reminder that God's intelligence is far higher than ours.
- There is no law for men to cover their heads when praying but it is almost universally done.
- The Tefillin or Phylacteries are two small leather boxes.
- One is worn on the upper arm close to the heart, the other on the head.
- Inside are tiny parchment scrolls containing four bible passages.
- They are worn for all morning prayers but not on the Sabbath or festival days.
- They remind Jews to serve God with head and heart.
- The Tallit is a prayer shawl worn by males during morning prayers.
- It is a square or triangle of silk or wool.
- Some Jews wear a 'Tallit Katan' or small tallit under their clothes.
- The Tzitzit are fringes attached to each corner of the tallit in obedience to two Bible readings.
  Conclusion: The wearing of ritual dress is particularly important for Jewish males at prayer. The items are symbolic of important aspects of the religion as a whole as well as of individual Bible readings.

Q7 *Points that could be included:*
- Some people choose to openly show their beliefs by wearing symbolic clothing or even by changing their personal appearance as with a hairstyle. Or they may speak and behave differently.
- People may openly react to this by behaving negatively for a number of reasons.
- They may disagree with your beliefs or they may simply react because you look different from them or from the 'norm'.
- This reaction may be because you represent a minority group that stands for different things within the society. People may feel threatened by this.
- If the visible difference is seen to represent a controversial cause, people may react as well.
- However, people should be able to express themselves in different ways within a free society.
- Many modern fashions are significantly different from what people might see as 'the norm'. Looking different is often not seen as unusual nowadays.
- Passover (or Pesach) and Hanukkah are two Jewish celebrations where other community members are invited to share. Other religious festivals also include people from other (or no) faiths, and this can help overcome any prejudice that is present.
  Conclusion: Being visibly different, whether it is in dress, behaviour, personal features or words always invites attention. Some people (but certainly not all) choose to show dissatisfaction and even prejudice as they can feel threatened. Multicultural societies are slowly creating increased openness and acceptance.

Page 71

Q1 a) Brit Milah
   b) 8 days old
   c) A mohel
Q2 30 days
Q3 Zeved habat
Q4 Two from Hebrew, Torah and Talmud.
Q5 Two from: At Pesach, it's the youngest child's job to ask questions about the festival.
   At Purim, children drown out the name of Haman with football rattles and other noisemakers.
   At Hanukkah, children play with dreidels (spinning tops).
Q6 a) 13 years old
   b) He can wear tefillin.
   c) There is a service at the shul (synagogue), a small reception, and sometimes a big party with entertainment.
   d) "Daughter of the Commandment" and "Daughter of Excellence" — coming of age ceremonies for girls, similar to Bar Mitzvah for boys.

Q7 *Points that could be included:*
- Judaism has three important birth ceremonies - one of them is Brit Milah or the 'Covenant of Circumcision'.
- This involves the removal of the foreskin from the penis and is therefore exclusively for boys.
- The baby boy is officially named in the Jewish faith and afterwards the family share a celebration meal.
- The circumcision is done when the baby boy is 8 days old and it is for religious reasons rather than any medical purpose.
- The operation is carried out in hospital, at home or at the synagogue by a specially trained 'Mohel'.
- The child is normally held by the 'sandek' while this is done, who is often the grandfather.
  Conclusion: The ceremony of Brit Milah is one of three important birth ceremonies in the Jewish religion - it is a symbol of the Covenant between God and his 'chosen people'. It is carried out on baby boys and accompanies the naming ceremony.

Q8 *Points that could be included:*
- Bar Mitzvah is the 'coming of age' ceremony for boys in the Jewish faith.
- At 13 a boy becomes Bar Mitzvah or a 'Son of the Commandment'.
- It reflects the beginning of a new chapter in a young believer's life, namely the move towards 'adulthood' and the full responsibilities of the faith.
- He becomes responsible for keeping the Mitzvot for himself, and begins to wear Tefillin for prayers.
- On the Sabbath after the 13th birthday, there is a special service followed by a small reception.
- Some families favour a lavish party but this is not always approved of as it is a deeply religious occasion whose meaning should not be lost in celebration.
  Conclusion: Bar Mitzvah represents an important stage in a person's life. It marks the beginning of adulthood (in a religious sense).

Page 72

Q1 Sheol, the underworld.
Q2 The dead will be resurrected and judged.
Q3 They should confess their sins and recite the Shema.
Q4 To symbolise shock and grief at the death.
Q5 It is put in the mikveh.
Q6 a) A white linen shroud.
   b) A plain coffin of unpolished wood.
Q7 A prayer is read, praising God for giving life and taking it away. Psalms are read, and the rabbi often makes a speech about the life of the dead person.
Q8 Kaddish
Q9 a) Shiva
   b) Cutting their hair, shaving, having sex, listening to music.
   c) Things gradually go back to normal. The men of the family say kaddish at the synagogue.
   d) One year

Q10 *Points that could be included:*
- There are many rituals in Judaism concerned with death, funerals and mourning.
- The Jewish family often wants to gather together to be near a loved one who is dying.
- The dying person should spend his or her last moments confessing sins and reciting the Shema, one of the most important prayers in Judaism.
- After the death, each member the family makes a tear in their clothing to reflect the grief and shock.

The Answers

- The dead person must not be left alone and must be buried, not cremated, within 24 hours of death or at the earliest possible time.
- The body is washed and put in a mikveh or ceremonial bath. It is then put in a plain linen shroud before being put in a plain, unpolished wooden coffin. Death sees both rich and poor as equal.
- At the funeral service Psalms and a short prayer are read, praising God for giving and taking life. The rabbi may give a short address.
- The first week after the funeral is called Shiva, meaning 'seven'. The family stay at home and relatives visit. They all pray together three times a day. They do not cut their hair, shave, listen to music or have sex during the first week after death.
- Men recite a prayer called the Kaddish.
- The month after the funeral is Sheloshim meaning 'thirty'. Life gradually returns to normal but the Kaddish is still recited.
- If you lose a parent, you must mourn for a year.
- On the first Yahrzeit or anniversary, a headstone will be erected by the grave.
- Each year a candle is lit for 24 hours and the men recite the Kaddish.
  Conclusion: Most Jews believe in 'life after death' but they also feel great loss at the death, and they know that family and friends need support. The rituals and customs reflect the importance of this 'rite of passage'.

Q11 *Points that could be included:*
- There are many rituals in Judaism concerning death.
- They are designed to help the bereaved accept what has happened, to help them give expression to their grief, receive comfort and come to terms with the loss.
- Just prior to the death, members of the family gather together in a supportive group.
- The dead person is not left alone by members of the family before the burial.
- In the first week after death, the immediate family are visited by other family and friends and they pray together.
- The men recite the Kaddish together. This is a famous prayer.
- People are encouraged to talk about the dead person and not keep feelings trapped inside.
- During the first month after death, male mourners continue to go to the synagogue for prayers.
- Anyone who has lost a parent must mourn for a year and appropriate support is given in the community around them.
- A headstone is erected after a year as a lasting memory and tribute to the deceased. Often a candle is lit for 24 hours on the anniversary.
  Conclusion: Many rituals surround a death in the Jewish faith and although some of them serve to prepare the deceased for the afterlife, others help and give comfort to the bereaved, allowing them to grieve and come to terms with what has happened.

Page 73

Q1 Morning, afternoon and evening.
Q2 A minyan
Q3 The 10 Commandments say they must. Sabbath commemorates the day of rest that God took after creating everything.
Q4 a) Friday at sunset.
   b) Saturday at dusk (when it's dark enough to see the first stars).
Q5 a) The cantor/chazan
   b) Musical instruments were used in the Temple. It's thought to be wrong to have instrumental music at worship while the Temple is still in ruins.
Q6 The rabbi gives readings from the Torah, and gives a sermon. Seven men from the congregation say a blessing. Another man from the congregation reads from the books of Prophets (Nevi'im).

Q7 Clean and tidy the house, get all food for Shabbat cooked and ready, take a bath or shower.
Q8 The mother of the family lights the Shabbat candles.
Q9 Kiddush
Q10 Blessings are said over a plaited candle, a cup of wine, and sweet spices.
Q11 *Points that could be included:*
- The Jewish holy day is called the Shabbat or Sabbath. Prayer is important on every day of the week but particularly so on the day of rest.
- The Sabbath commemorates the 7th day of the Creation when God rested after making the universe.
- It begins at sunset on Friday and ends on Saturday evening when the stars appear.
- The 4th commandment instructs Jews to remember the Sabbath and to keep it holy.
- There are three separate services in the synagogue on this day.
- The Sabbath is welcomed on the Friday evening as a queen or bride with singing by a chazan or 'cantor'. No instruments accompany this.
- The main service of the week is on Saturday morning. The rabbi reads from the Torah and gives a sermon. Seven men are called up to read or recite a blessing.
- An eighth reads a portion of the Nevi'im.
- In an Orthodox Jewish synagogue, women sit separately and play little part in proceedings.
- A Saturday afternoon service includes a reading from the Torah and three special prayers.
  Conclusion: Jewish believers remember the 7th day in the Creation Story as a day of rest. It is celebrated with due ceremony (especially by Orthodox Jews), but like all 'holy days' it is under increasing pressure from the distractions of everyday life.

Q12 *Points that could be included:*
- The Shabbat is celebrated with equal seriousness and attention to detail in both places.
- Indeed, many Jews will gather in the synagogue as well as celebrating at home.
- More liberal Jews may perhaps choose to just follow a simple observation at home. The home is important in that it is principally a family celebration.
- There is an emphasis on the sharing of food and wine together. It is specially prepared and sanctified.
- Some of the ceremony is repeated in the synagogue.
- The children are blessed by their father.
- However, the celebration in the synagogue is of a rather different emphasis, being for the Jewish community in general.
- The sharing of a meal is replaced by unaccompanied singing, readings and prayers.
- The ritual is rightly formalised (in the eyes of more Orthodox Jews) in the form of three services.
  Conclusion: Shabbat is an especially significant day and it is acknowledged in rather different ways between home and the synagogue. The former further emphasises a strong family unit whilst the latter is more formalised for the community, relying as it does on readings from the scriptures and unaccompanied singing.

Page 74

Q1 Pesach, Shavuot and Sukkot
Q2 a) In Jerusalem. It's what's left of one wall of the Temple.
   b) 1000 Jewish Zealots defended Masada against the Romans. They all committed suicide rather then being taken alive and made into slaves.
   c) Yad Vashem
Q3 Treifah ('torn')

The Answers

Q4 a) Kosher
    b) Treifah — doesn't chew the cud
    c) Kosher
    d) Kosher
    e) Treifah — no fins or scales
    f) Treifah — no scales

Q5 Meat and dairy mustn't be eaten together — or even mixed in the belly.

Q6 The throat must be slit with one cut of a very sharp knife.

Q7 Sorrow, grief and repentance

Q8 Jewish New Year.

Q9 The crying out of the soul longing to be reunited with God.

Q10 a) The Day of Atonement
     b) 10 days of repenting sins
     c) 25 hours

Q11 *Points that could be included:*
- Rosh Hashanah is the Jewish New Year.
- Judaism teaches that Rosh Hashanah is a time when God judges the way people have lived over the previous year.
- Jews believe that, after judging people, God then decides what their circumstances will be in the New Year.
- On Rosh Hashanah a shofar is blown to symbolise the soul crying out to be reunited with God.
- The tashlich ceremony involves a prayer asking God to take away the sins of his people.
- The ten day period between Rosh Hashanah and Yom Kippur is a time for people to repent for their sins.
- Yom Kippur is also known as the Day of Atonement when Jews make amends for the sins they have committed.
- Yom Kippur is a time to renew the bond between God and the Jewish people. It is also a time to prepare spiritually for the New Year.

Conclusion: Rosh Hashanah and Yom Kippur are two stages in a very important period of judgement and repentance for Jewish people.

Q12 *Points that could be included:*
- The Kashrut is the name given to the Jewish food laws.
- Orthodox Jews follow a special diet which is based on the Kashrut.
- Jews must make sure that any food they eat is Kosher which means they are allowed to eat it.
- Jews can only eat meat from a mammal which has split hooves and chews the cud.
- Jews must be careful not to eat meat and dairy products together.
- The only seafood that is Kosher is fish with fins and scales.
- For meat to be Kosher the animal must be killed in a special way. The animal should be cut once across the throat with a sharp blade.

Conclusion: In their everyday life Jews must be careful to only eat food which is allowed in the Kashrut.

Page 75

Q1 a) Early springtime
    b) The story of Queen Esther

Q2 The giving of the Torah to Moses

Q3 a) Sukkot (Tabernacles)
    b) A sukkah
    c) The journey through the desert from Egypt with Moses.

Q4 God sent plagues against the Egyptians, including an angel of death that would kill the first born sons of every family. The angel passed over the houses of the Jews.

Q5 Leavened bread is forbidden, and so is anything that might make bread rise, or any flour that makes a dough that rises.

Q6 Five from: matzah, wine, salt water, bitter herbs, karpas, burnt egg, bone.

Q7 Simchat Torah

Q8 a) Hanukkah
    b) Purim
    c) Shavuot
    d) Simchat Torah

Q9 a) *Points that could be included:*
- The Passover (Pesach) feast lasts for seven or eight days.
- Before the festival begins the house is carefully decorated and all traces of leaven are removed. Leaven is anything which is used to make bread rise, for example, yeast. Jews must not eat or use leaven at all during Passover.
- On the first two nights of Passover friends and family gather for Seder meals. Seder means order and the meals are arranged in a special order.
- The food served includes matzah (biscuit), wine, salt water, bitter herbs, karpas (a vegetable), burnt egg, bone.
- The Haggadah is read out telling the story of the Jews in fourteen steps.

    b) *Points that could be included:*
- Pesach celebrates the exodus from Egypt when Moses led the Jews from slavery to freedom.
- Pesach is also a time to remember when God sent an angel of death to kill the first born sons of Egypt. The angel passed over the Jewish first born.
- There are certain foods eaten during Pesach which remind Jews of important things. Not using leaven symbolises when the Jews had to leave Egypt in such a hurry that they did not have time to let their bread rise. Bitter herbs are used in the meal to remind Jews of the bitterness of slavery. Salt water is used to remind Jews of the tears which their ancestors cried when they were slaves.

Conclusion: Pesach is a very important time for Jews when they follow special customs to help them remember how the Jewish people were saved by God.

Q10 *Points that could be included:*
- The Book of Leviticus tells Jews that they must perform Sukkot.
- Sukkot is a time when Jews remember the trek through the desert with Moses and how God protected them.
- Sukkot is also known as the Feast of Tabernacles.
- The word Sukkot means hut and the main way Jews celebrate the festival is by building huts.
- By building the huts Jewish people are remembering the shelters that their ancestors camped in during their time in the desert.
- Jews also perform the Sukkot ritual using four special types of plant. The four types of plant that Jews celebrate with are etroy (citron), lulav (palm branch), aravot (willow) and haddassim (myrtle).

Conclusion: Sukkot is an important festival which helps remember the trials of their ancestors and also to focus their thoughts on God.

Section 4 — Islam

Page 76

Q1 The belief that God is one, supreme, almighty and holy.

Q2 Regarding anything as being equal to Allah.

Q3 Shahadah

Q4 "And Muhammad is the Prophet of Allah."

Q5 Five times a day

Q6 a) Any three exposed parts of the body (e.g. feet, hands, arms, mouth, nostrils).
    b) Wudu

Q7 Compulsory giving to the poor

Q8 Fasting during Ramadan

Q9 a) Makkah
    b) They are very basic and everyone wears exactly the same thing.

The Answers

Q10 *Points that could be included:*
- Muslims believe that Allah is the creator of everything.
- There are ninety nine names for Allah but Muslims believe that Allah is one. This belief is called Tawhid.
- Allah cannot be thought of as human.
- Allah is the Supreme Being and has no equal.
- Muslims believe Allah is immanent and transcendent.
- According to Islam, Allah is not like anything we know so we cannot compare him to anything.
- To deny that Allah is supreme is the worst possible sin in Islam. This sin is called Shirk and it is the opposite of Tawhid.
  Conclusion: Muslims feel Shirk is the worst sin because it denies everything which the Qur'an teaches about Allah.

Q11 *Points that could be included:*
- The five pillars of Islam are the Shahadah, Salah, Zakah, Sawm and Hajj.
- The Shahadah is the Muslim declaration of faith.
- Salah is the duty of prayer. Muslims must pray five times a day.
- Zakah is the duty of giving charity to help those in need.
- Sawm is the duty of fasting during Ramadan.
- Hajj is a pilgrimage to Makkah which Muslims should make at least once during their lifetime.
  Conclusion: The five pillars of faith are a guide to Muslim life which gives Muslims the chance to know and be close to Allah.

Page 77

Q1 a) Risalah
    b) Rasul
Q2 c) "Allah gives his message to angels. Angels pass on Allah's word to prophets, and the prophets pass it on to everyone else."
Q3 Three from: Angels need no food, angels need no drink, angels need no sleep, angels obey God's will perfectly and automatically.
Q4 25
Q5 a) Nuh (Noah), Ibrahim (Abraham), Musa (Moses), Isa (Jesus), Muhammad
    b) Adam
    c) Ibrahim (Abraham)
    d) Musa (Moses)
Q6 Yes — Muslims believe that humans have free will.
Q7 Khalifah
Q8 *Points that could be included:*
- Khalifah is the Muslim idea that we should take responsibility for the world in God's name.
- Khalifah means Vice-Regent or Trustee.
- Muslims believe that God expects us to look after the world He has created.
- Muslims believe that cruelty to animals is a sin against Allah.
- Islam teaches that we should treat all living creatures with mercy and compassion.
- Muslims are taught that animals which are used for meat must be killed humanely.
- Khalifah is the idea that we should try to make the world the place Allah wants it to be.
- Muslims believe that if we cannot look after the earth properly then Allah will send help. This shows his compassion and mercy.
  Conclusion: Khalifah is the idea that God has trusted us to look after his creation and treat the world with respect.

Q9 *Points that could be included:*
- Risalah is the idea that Allah uses messengers to communicate with humans.
- Muslims believe Allah is beyond our understanding so he must use messengers to communicate with us.
- Islam teaches that angels are the messengers which Allah uses to communicate with us.
- Muslims are taught that angels are created by Allah and obey him completely.
- Islam teaches that angels don't need food, drink or sleep.
- Muslims believe that angels communicate with human prophets who then bring Allah's message to his people.
- The Qur'an teaches that the first man, Adam, was also the first prophet.
- The five main prophets are Nuh (Noah), Ibrahim (Abraham), Musa (Moses), Isa (Jesus) and Muhammad.
- The Qur'an names twenty five prophets, but some Muslims believe that there have been 124,000 prophets.
  Conclusion: Muslims believe Allah shows his compassion and mercy by sending messages to help us.

Page 78

Q1 Yes — Muslims see the Qur'an as the literal word of God
Q2 Muhammad took care not to forget anything, and his followers wrote everything down and learned it by heart. (now there's a good idea...)
Q3 The Caliph Uthman
Q4 Muslims believe that Allah gave Muhammad the Qur'an in Arabic. Translations from Arabic lose some of the precise meaning of Allah's word.
Q5 Three from: They keep it wrapped up, they wash their hands before touching it, they keep it on a higher shelf than other books, they put it in a special stand to read it.
Q6 Ramadan (the 9th month of the Islamic Calendar)
Q7 a) One chapter of the Qur'an
    b) A verse of a surah
Q8 A phrase meaning "In the name of Allah, the Merciful, the Compassionate". It's at the beginning of most surah of the Qur'an (all except one).
Q9 a) The Hadith
    b) The Sunnah
Q10 *Points that could be included:*
- Muslims see the Qur'an as Allah's guide showing Muslim's how they should live.
- The Qur'an tells Muslims what they must believe and how they must live in order to reach paradise.
- Muslims feel that if the Qur'an tells them to do something then they must do it. If the Qur'an tells them not to do something then they must not do it.
- Many Muslims learn the Qur'an's every word and all try to live according to what it says. The Qur'an is read during private and public prayers so Muslims come to know it very well.
- Muslims also take lots of guidance from the Hadith. The Hadith are the sayings of Muhammad which were not part of the Qur'an.
- Muhammad was chosen by Allah so Muslims feel his example is a good one to follow.
- Islamic law, the Shari'ah, is based mainly on the Qur'an and also take guidance from the Hadith. The legal systems of many modern Muslim countries are based on Islamic law.
  Conclusion: The Qur'an and the Hadith have a big effect on the lives of modern Muslims from the way they live to the way they worship. It can also affect the state laws they must obey.

Q11 *Points that could be included:*
- Muslims believe the Qur'an is the most important book in the world.
- Islam teaches that the Qur'an is a record of the exact words of Allah as revealed to Muhammad.
- Muslims are taught that the Qur'an is totally accurate and unchanged. There is only one version of the Qur'an.
- Muslims are taught that it is important to read the Qur'an in Arabic because that was the language in which it was revealed to Muhammad.
- Muslims feel that the Qur'an gives them a complete guide to life.

The Answers

- Muslims believe that because the Qur'an is so important it must be treated with total respect. Muslims often keep their Qur'an wrapped up to protect it, wash their hands before touching it and keep it on a shelf higher than other books.
- During the month of Ramadan the Qur'an is read from start to finish during worship in the Mosque.
  Conclusion: The Qur'an is vital to Muslims and it is treated with total respect because Islam teaches that it records the exact words of Allah, by which every Muslim must live their life.

Q12 *Points that could be included:*
- Islam teaches that the Qur'an is a guide to how a Muslim should live so, without the Qur'an, Muslims would be unsure how to live, and would risk going to hell after judgement day.
- The Qur'an records the words of Allah so Muslims know exactly what God expects of them.
- Whenever Muslims have a problem or are unsure about how to act they can look to the Qur'an for help and advice.
- Muslim law, the Shari'ah, is based mainly on the Qur'an.
- However, Islam teaches that Allah gave us free will so it is up to us to decide how to behave.
- The Qur'an was written a long time ago so people need to decide for themselves how to apply its teachings to modern life.
- Muslims also rely on religious leaders like Imams to give them advice on how to behave.
  Conclusion: The Qur'an is important. It teaches people how to live as good Muslims. But Muslims must also decide for themselves what is right and wrong.

Page 79

Q1 Muhammad was born in Makkah in about 570 CE
Q2 Muhammad worked for her — she was a businesswoman.
Q3 Muhammad was meditating in a cave on Mount Nur.
Q4 a) Be honest in business, and look after the poor in society;
   c) Worship only one God, Allah;
   e) Listen to the words of Muhammad, prophet of Allah;
   f) Do God's will, or you'll end up in Hell.
Q5 The people of Makkah laughed at Muhammad and said he was mad. They also threatened him and his followers, and were violent to them. They stopped Muhammad from preaching in the city. A very small number of people listened to him.
Q6 Madinah (or Medina or Medina Nabi)
Q7 The Hijrah is the emigration from Makkah to Madinah. After the Hijrah, Muhammad was able to convert lots of people to Islam, and set up a Muslim community in Madinah with Muslim traditions.
Q8 a) Muhammad and the people of Madinah won.
   b) Muhammad won, just.
   c) In 630 CE
Q9 *Points that could be included:*
- Muhammad often went away to be on his own and meditate.
- In 610 CE Muhammad was meditating in a cave on Mount Nur when Allah called him.
- Allah sent the angel Jibrail (Gabriel) to call Muhammad.
- The angel Jibrail (Gabriel) gave Muhammad Allah's first command.
- At first Muhammad was very frightened by his experience.
- Muhammad's wife Khadijah helped him to realise that Allah was calling him to be a Prophet.
- Muhammad received many more revelations from Allah.
- The Qur'an records all the revelations that Muhammad received from Allah.
  Conclusion: Allah called Muhammad through the Angel Jibrail because Allah himself is beyond human understanding.

Q10 *Points that could be included:*
- In 622 Muhammad and his followers were forced to leave Makkah.
- Muhammad became the leader of a place called Yathrib. Yathrib was later named Madinah after Muhammad.
- In Madinah Muhammad built a strong Muslim community.
- After the Hijrah, Madinah and Makkah went to war with each other.
- Muhammad won three battles with the people of Makkah - the battle of Badr, the battle of Uhud and the battle of Trench.
- In 630 Muhammad and the Muslims took control of Makkah.
  Conclusion: When Muhammad died in 632 the Muslims had won control of Makkah and Islam was spreading quickly through Arabia.

Page 80

Q1 Sunni and Shi'ism (or Shi'a)
Q2 Abu Bakr, Umar, Uthman, Ali
Q3 The Sunnis
Q4 The Rightly Guided Caliphs
Q5 No — According to Sunnis, no one after Muhammad gets special revelation from Allah.
Q6 The Sunni tradition
Q7 Imams
Q8 Ali (the fourth caliph)
Q9 Ali and his sons, Hasan and Husayn
Q10 Shi'ite religious leaders, chosen by the Imam.
Q11 *Points that could be included:*
- After Muhammad died the Muslim community was divided by arguments over who should lead them and how their leaders should be chosen.
- Sunni Muslims believe leaders should be chosen because they are good Muslims and able to lead.
- Sunni Muslims believe that Muhammad was the last person to get special knowledge from Allah.
- Sunni Muslims believe that religious leaders should be elected by the community.
- Sunni Muslims feel it is wrong to pay special attention to Ali and his sons because it draws attention away from Allah and Muhammad.
- Shi'ite Muslims believe that Ali was the first true leader of Islam after Muhammad.
- Shi'ite Muslims believe that Ali and all the leaders descended from Muhammad are given special knowledge by Allah.
- Shi'ite Muslims believe the last Imam (religious leader) went into hiding. Shi'ite Muslims believe that since the last Imam went into hiding other leaders have been chosen by him.
- Shi'ite leaders take guidance from the Hadith of Ali as well as the Hadith of Muhammad.
  Conclusion: Sunni Muslims feel their leaders should be elected by the majority, Shi'ite Muslims believe their leaders should be descended from Muhammad.

Q12 *Points that could be included:*
- By arguing with each other Sunni and Shi'ite Muslims make Islam seem like a divided religion.
- Some people might say that if Muslims can't agree on their beliefs then who can know what is true and what is false?
- Sunni Muslims and Shi'ite Muslims are damaging the Islamic religion by arguing with each other.
- Islam would be a much stronger religion if all Muslims shared the same beliefs.
- But although Sunnis and Shi'ites disagree over leadership and authority they agree on a lot of the most important beliefs.
- Islam is changing and developing all the time so it is impossible for all Muslims to agree.
- There are so many Muslims that it would be very hard for them all to have exactly the same beliefs.
  Conclusion: Islam teaches that Allah gives people free will so individuals must decide on their own beliefs.

The Answers

Page 81

Q1 To be at one with God and reach mystical and spiritual truths which are beyond human understanding.
Q2 They try to purify their actions and their thoughts. They try to be constantly aware of the love of Allah.
Q3 a) Sacred poetry and chanting
    c) Trying to live like Muhammad
    d) Meditation
    e) Self-denial
Q4 The relationship between an individual Muslim and Allah.
Q5 Whirling Dervishes are a group of Sufis. They use fast spinning to lead to a kind of trance which is regarded as a form of prayer.
Q6 Rabi'a al-Adawiyya
Q7 Some Muslims feel that God is completely separate from human beings, so it's wrong to say that a person can merge with God.
Q8 *Points that could be included:*
- The main difference between Sufism and mainstream Islam is the way that they interpret the Qur'an.
- Sufis aim to be at one with God and try to reach truths beyond human understanding.
- Sufis don't believe that the way a Muslim practices their religion is the most important thing.
- Sufism teaches that the most important part of Islam is the bond between each person and God.
- Sufis feel that being Muslim is not just about obeying rules.
- Some Sufis feel people should try to join together with Allah.
- They try to achieve this by copying Muhammad's lifestyle of self-denial, and by using ritual dances and chanting.
- Many Muslims feel that the Sufi idea of joining together with Allah is unacceptable because Allah is beyond our understanding.
Conclusion: Although Sufism shares many important beliefs with mainstream Islam there are some big differences, the most obvious difference being the different views of an individual's relationship with God.

Q9 *Points that could be included:*
- Sufism teaches that the words of the Qur'an hide a mystical message.
- Sufis believe that to find the hidden meaning in the Qur'an you must purify your thoughts and actions.
- Sufism teaches that you must always be aware of the love of God so you can join together with Him.
- Sufis try to imitate Muhammad's way of life.
- Sufism teaches that it is important to live a humble life.
- Sufis try to live a life of asceticism (self-denial) and meditation.
- Sufis use ritual practices like sacred dances and chanting.
Conclusion: Sufism teaches that just obeying rules is not enough and that people must also look closely at their relationship with God.

Q10 *Points that could be included:*
- Sufis don't agree with some of the mainstream Islamic beliefs.
- Sufism teaches that people should join together with Allah but most Muslims would argue that this is not possible because Allah is so far above man and human understanding.
- Sufis feel that following rules is not the most important thing, but most Muslims feel that it is vital to live by Islamic rules.
- Sufis feel that there is a hidden meaning in the Qur'an.
- However, Sufis share many of the same beliefs with mainstream Islam.
- Like all Muslims, Sufis see the Qur'an as their guide to life.
- Sufism can be seen as just another type of Islam.
Conclusion: There are some big differences between Sufism and mainstream Islam, but they also share many important beliefs.

Page 82

Q1 Muslims please Allah by obeying him.
Q2 Muslims who do not please Allah are punished after they die / go to hell.
Q3 Submission to God/Obedience to God.
Q4 Islamic religious law
Q5 The Qur'an, the Hadith and Sunnah, traditional Muslim customs.
Q6 They discuss and try to reach an agreement based on their knowledge of Islam.
Q7 They trust that Allah will make sure they'll reach the right decision.
Q8 Possible answers include: The Qur'an forbids alcohol because it clouds the mind, but doesn't say anything about other drugs. Other drugs cloud the mind, so Islam should forbid them as well.
Q9 *Points that could be included:*
- The most important source for Islamic scholars and lawyers is the Qur'an.
- Any moral guidance in the Qur'an is included in the shari'ah.
- The shari'ah also looks to the Hadith (sayings) and Sunnah (lifestyle) of Muhammad for guidance.
- Muslim scholars and lawyers would also consider the custom and practice of the Muslim community.
- The shari'ah is influenced more by customs and practices that can be traced back to Muhammad's time than by more modern traditions.
- Using the Qur'an, the Hadith, the Sunnah and Islamic tradition, Muslim scholars try to reach agreement on how to act.
- Muslim scholars and lawyers trust that Allah's guidance will help them to make the right decision.
- When Islamic scholars can't find guidance on an issue they look for guidance on something similar. This is also known as finding an analogy.
- The Qur'an does not give guidance on modern issues like drugs. Islamic scholars say that drugs are forbidden because like alcohol, which the Qur'an forbids, they are bad for the user.
Conclusion: To decide if something is right or wrong Islamic scholars look for advice in Islamic holy books and tradition.

Q10 *Points that could be included:*
- The Qur'an is a vital guide to Islam and some people feel that without it Muslims cannot know what Allah expects of them.
- The Qur'an, the Hadith and the Sunnah provide the basis of Islamic law so without them people cannot know how to be good Muslims.
- The Qur'an records Allah's own words and to be a good Muslim it is important to know what Allah told us.
- Islam teaches that the Qur'an must be treated with respect and one way of doing this is to look to it for help and guidance on a regular basis.
- However, most Muslims would feel that just reading the Islamic holy books is not enough to make someone a good Muslim.
- Muslims feel that there is no point in having faith if you don't act on your beliefs.
- Muslims generally consider that those who follow the Five Pillars of Faith are living a good Muslim life.
- The Islamic holy books were written a long time ago so Muslims must sometimes find guidance elsewhere on living a good modern Muslim life.
Conclusion: Muslims believe the Qur'an is the most important book in the world but just reading the holy books is not enough to be considered a good Muslim. What is important is that you obey Islamic teachings. The Qur'an is very helpful in doing this.

Page 83

Q1 a) Allowed, clean
    b) Forbidden, unclean
Q2 Men and women must wear loose, modest clothes

The Answers

Q3 The veil — a head covering for women.
Q4 They must have their throat slit, and all the blood must be drained out.
Q5 a) vegetable oil (the others are all animal fat, which is forbidden)
Q6 Gambling harms others. Any money you win is money that someone else has lost.
Q7 Shari'ah law forbids charging interest on loans. Western banking charges interest.
Q8 The greater Jihad is the personal fight to be a better Muslim. It's a spiritual fight against a Muslim's own bad and selfish side.
Q9 Fighting poverty and injustice in the world is part of the lesser Jihad.
Q10 *Points that could be included:*
- The Qur'an says that Muslims should always consider modesty and cleanliness when they are dressing.
- The Qur'an teaches that all people should wear loose and modest clothing.
- The Qur'an forbids people from wearing close-fitting clothing because it may arouse desire.
- According to the Qur'an when women leave the home only their face, hands and feet should be seen.
- The Qur'an says that when outside the home a woman should wear the hijab. The hijab is a veil which covers the hair.
- In Western countries women often take a more relaxed attitude to dress laws.
- The Qur'an teaches that men should not wear expensive clothing.
Conclusion: The Qur'an basically teaches that clothing should not be worn to encourage desire in others or to show off wealth.

Q11 *Points that could be included:*
- To stop rich people making more money at the expense of poorer people, the Shari'ah forbids the charging of interest.
- Islam teaches that wealth should be spread fairly between people.
- Muslims won't use most Western banks because they use interest.
- Charging high rates of interest is called riza in Arabic.
- The Western economic system depends on money lending and charging interest so Muslims in these countries must run their businesses differently.
- Muslims normally need to use a separate banking system which does not involve interest.
Conclusion: Islam teaches that financial deals involving interest are forbidden so Muslims in non-Muslim countries must find a separate way of banking and investing.

Q12 *Points that could be included:*
- Some people would feel that it is unfair to expect a Muslim to eat only halal food in a non-Muslim country because it is very difficult to find halal food.
- In a non-Muslim country it can be very difficult to know whether food is halal or not.
- Even if a Muslim can find halal food it is often more expensive than other food because it is harder to prepare.
- However, even in non-Muslim countries it is possible to find halal food shops and restaurants.
- Some people would say that if Muslims can't find places which provide halal food then they should be vegetarian or prepare their own halal meals.
- Lots of Muslims in non-Muslim countries manage to follow a halal diet so it is possible.
Conclusion: Generally Muslims would feel that, if at all possible, a Muslim should follow a halal diet although in some circumstances it may not prove possible.

Page 84

Q1 Masjid (or Musjid)
Q2 a) The dome represents the Universe.
    b) The minaret is for calling Muslims to prayer.
Q3 The muezzin calls out the call to prayer (the adhan).
Q4 A mihrab is a niche in the wall that shows the direction of Makkah.
Q5 A minbar is a pulpit from where the imam leads the prayers.
Q6 The imam
Q7 c) Women can only lead other women and children in prayer.
Q8 Pictures of Allah and Muhammad are forbidden. The word of Allah in the Qur'an is what's most important, so calligraphy from the Qur'an decorates the mosque.
Q9 Two from: Muslim teachings, Muslim customs, how to read the Qur'an, how to recite the Qur'an from memory.
Q10 The Shi'ite tradition.
Q11 a) *Points that could be included:*
- All mosques have a minaret which is a tall tower from which the muezzin sounds the call to prayer.
- Mosques are often colourfully decorated by beautiful mosaic tiles or Arabic calligraphy but there are no pictures of Allah or Muhammad.
- A mosque should have a room or an area where Muslims can wash.
- Mosques have no seats but the floor is normally covered in thick carpet.
- All mosques, even simple ones, have a dome shaped roof.
- In one wall of the mosque is a niche or alcove called the mihrab.
b) *Points that could be included:*
- The minaret is a tall tower so that the adhan (call to prayer) can be heard from a long way off.
- There are no pictures of Muhammad or Allah because the Qur'an forbids them.
- It is important to have washing facilities because Muslims must be pure and clean when they pray to Allah.
- All Muslims should kneel when they pray as a sign of submission to Allah so there is no need for chairs.
- Mosques have a dome shaped roof to symbolise the universe and remind people that Allah is the creator of everything.
- The mihrab is important because it shows the direction of Makkah which Muslims must face when they pray.
Conclusion: All mosques share a number of features which honour Allah and help Muslims to fulfil the duty of Salah (prayer).

Q12 *Points that could be included:*
- Islam teaches that it is possible to pray in any clean place providing you follow the guidelines which are laid down.
- So long as a Muslim has a prayer mat it is possible to pray anywhere.
- Islam doesn't teach that you must attend a mosque to be a Muslim.
- However, mosques are important because they provide an ideal place for Muslims to fulfil the duty of Salah (prayer).
- A mosque is not only important as a place of worship, it is also an important centre for the Muslim community.
- Mosques provide Muslims with a chance to demonstrate their devotion to Allah.
- Mosques are also important as schools where people can learn about Islam and develop as Muslims.
Conclusion: It is possible for Muslims to pray in most places providing they have a prayer mat, but mosques are important centres for worship and provide a focus for the Muslim community.

Page 85

Q1 Shahadah — the belief that there is no God but Allah, and that Muhammad is the Prophet of Allah.
Q2 Muslims believe that they should be pure and clean before praying to Allah.
Q3 Qiblah is the direction of Makkah. Muslims must face Makkah when they pray.
Q4 Salat-al-Jum'ah (or just Jum'ah)

The Answers

Q5 Muslims would be at work or at school during prayer time, and it might be hard to get time off.
Q6 Sunrise and sunset (daylight hours).
Q7 All those things are definitely forbidden, except for toothpaste. It's OK to use toothpaste as long as you don't swallow any. Many Muslims prefer not to use toothpaste, just in case.
Q8 Children under 12 don't fast. Pregnant women and women on their period don't have to fast. Ill people can be excused from fasting. You can be excused if you are travelling, but you must make up the days you miss.
Q9 It helps Muslims understand hunger so they will want to help poor and hungry people. Fasting also shows that Muslims are willing to give things up for Allah.
Q10 Id-ul-Fitr
Q11 Hagar and Ismail's
Q12 *Points that could be included:*
- Islam teaches that you cannot be a Muslim unless you pray as Muhammad did.
- Muslims are expected to pray five times a day. They pray at sunrise, early afternoon, and late afternoon, after sunset and late at night.
- The muezzin makes the call to prayer from the minaret of a mosque.
- Before prayer Muslims must wash themselves to make sure they are pure and clean when they approach Allah. This process of washing before prayer is called wudu.
- Muslims should face Makkah when they are praying.
- Muslims must follow the rak'ah which is a set rituals for prayer. A rak'ah involves standing, then kneeling, then putting your forehead on the ground to show submission to Allah.
- When Muslims are praying together they perform rak'ah at the same time to show unity.
Conclusion: Salah is one of the Five Pillars of Faith and it is an essential part of a Muslim's life.

Q13 *Points that could be included:*
- The Hajj is a pilgrimage to Makkah and it is the Fifth Pillar of Faith.
- All Muslims on Hajj wear special clothing called Ihram. Ihram is very basic clothing and because everyone wears the same it demonstrates equality before Allah.
- When they arrive at Makkah Muslims walk around the Ka'ba seven times touching the stone if they can. Islam teaches that the Ka'ba was built by Adam, rebuilt by Ibrahim and then made pure by Muhammad.
- Muslims must also walk between the hills of Safa and Marwa seven times. This task is called the Sa'y.
- The pilgrims also draw water from the Zamzam well which Muslims believe Allah made for Hagar.
- Pilgrims also have to make their way to Mount Arafat where they stand and pray for Allah's forgiveness. Mount Arafat is the place where Muslims believe Adam was forgiven after he was thrown out of the Garden of Eden.
- When the pilgrims reach Mina they throw stones at three pillars to symbolise driving the Devil away.
- Towards the end of the Hajj there is a four-day festival called Id-ul-Adha. During Id-ul-Adha there is a prayer in the mosque followed by a family gathering and the sacrifice of an animal.
- Those who complete the Hajj are given the title Hajii.
Conclusion: By completing Hajj Muslims demonstrate their unity with other Muslims and their faith in Allah.

Page 86

Q1 Allah
Q2 7 days old
Q3 Aqiqa
Q4 They shave off the hair from the child's head, and give gold or silver that weighs the same or more than the hair.
Q5 Yes — circumcision is required for Muslim boys.
Q6 They should keep the dying person company, look after last-minute business, and pray with the dying person.
Q7 The body is washed and wrapped in a white shroud.
Q8 a) The dead are buried lying on their right side.
   b) The dead person's face must point towards Makkah.
Q9 3 days
Q10 *Points that could be included:*
- When a Muslim dies the body is washed as a mark of respect.
- The body is then wrapped in a clean, white shroud - this shows that everyone is equal in the eyes of Allah.
- Improper handling of a body can be distressing to Muslims families - it should really be carried out by family or members of the Muslim community.
- Special funeral prayers are said prior to the burial - these are called Janaza prayers and often take place in the mosque.
- They ask that Allah is merciful when judging the soul of the deceased and that a place in Paradise (al-Jannah) will be granted.
- The body is buried lying on its right side and facing towards Makkah - the centre of the Islamic faith.
- Some Muslims believe that burial should be in its simplest form without using a coffin - this was how the Prophet Muhammad was buried.
- A period of mourning is then kept for three days, finishing with Qur'an readings and prayers for the dead person.
- Muslims are generally opposed to the practice of cremation.
Conclusion: A Muslim funeral, like any funeral, is a very sacred occasion and must be carried out according to certain guidelines - if it is not carried out correctly it may be upsetting to the family of the deceased.

Q11 *Points that could be included:*
- Aqiqa is the Muslim naming ceremony. Aqiqa takes place when the baby is seven days old.
- When the baby is first born the adhan (the call to prayer) is whispered in its ear.
- The child's head is shaved - a donation of gold or silver, weighing the same as the shaven hair, is then made to the poor. The removal of the hair represents the removal of misfortune from the baby.
- It is traditional for an animal sacrifice to be made to Allah - this is to give thanks for the birth. Some of the meat is given away to the poor - the rest is shared amongst the family. If a girl is born one sheep or goat is sacrificed - two are killed following the birth of a boy.
- The child will then be given a name - this may be a name that shows obedience to Allah, or it could be named after one of the Prophet Muhammad's family or companions.
- Baby boys may be circumcised at aqiqa although this is often done later.
- Aqiqa usually involves a big party to give thanks for the gift of a new life.
Conclusion: During the ceremony of aqiqa many symbolic events take place, welcoming the new baby into the world and giving thanks to Allah.